COUPLE AND
FAMILY THERAPY
OF ADDICTION

LIBRARY OF SUBSTANCE ABUSE AND ADDICTION TREATMENT

A Series of Books Edited By
Jerome David Levin, Ph.D.

Substance abuse and addiction are the third most common cause of mortality in the United States. They are among the most prevalent mental illnesses, not only in the United States, but throughout the world. They are also notoriously difficult to treat. Mental health professionals see few patients whose lives or illnesses have not been profoundly affected by their own use or that of their families or peers. Addiction is not peripheral but central to the human condition and research into it is illuminating our understanding of self.

The *Library of Substance Abuse and Addiction Treatment* is dedicated to providing mental health professionals with the tools they need to treat these scourges—tools ranging from scientific knowledge to clinical technique. Non-ideological, it is equally open to behavioral, cognitive, disease model, psychodynamic, and least harm perspectives. An overdetermined disorder affecting millions of people requires multiple viewpoints if it is to be successfully treated. The *Library* provides those multiple perspectives for clinicians, students, and laypeople as articulated by the most insightful workers in the field. Practical, utilitarian, scholarly, and state-of-the-art, these books are addressed to all who wish to deepen their understanding of and increase their clinical efficacy in treating addiction.

COUPLE AND FAMILY THERAPY OF ADDICTION

JEROME DAVID LEVIN, PH.D.

JASON ARONSON INC.
Northvale, New Jersey
London

The author gratefully acknowledges permission to reprint material from the following source: Edward Kaufman and Pauline Kaufmann, "Common Features of the Addict," from *Family Therapy of Drug and Alcohol Abuse*, 2nd edition. Copyright © 1992 by Allyn & Bacon.

This book was set in 11 pt. Berling by Alpha Graphics in Pittsfield, NH and printed and bound by Book-mart Press, Inc. of North Bergen, NJ.

Library of Congress Cataloging-in-Publication Data

Levin, Jerome D. (Jerome David)
    Couple and family therapy of addiction / Jerome David Levin.
        p.   cm.
    Includes bibliographical references and index.
    ISBN 1-56821-641-6 (alk. paper)
        1. Substance abuse—Treatment.   2. Family psychotherapy.
    3. Marital psychotherapy.   I. Title.
    RC564.L48   1998
    616.86'0651—dc21   97-29588

Printed in the United States of America on acid-free paper. Jason Aronson offers books and cassettes. For information and catalog write to Jason Aronson Inc., 230 Livingston Street, Northvale, New Jersey 07647-1731. Or visit our website: http://www.aronson.com

For

Clementine, the Alpha

The spirit of liberty is the spirit which is not too sure that it is right.

Judge Learned Hand

❖ CONTENTS ❖

❖ PART II ❖
Clinical Practice

❖ PREFACE ❖

When I told an analytic friend that I was planning to write a book on couple and family therapy of the addictions, he said, "What do you want to do that for? It's always the same—he's a sullen lout, and she's 500 pounds." Having suffered through all too many couple therapies in which the drug/alcohol using husband sat silent and furious while the dragon-incarnating wife berated away, I couldn't help thinking that while my friend's attitudinal and countertransferential problems would make me hesitate before sending any referrals, at least of substance abusers, his way, I had to admit that his phenomenology wasn't bad. He drinks, she eats, the kids suffer; she drinks, he leaves, the kids suffer; and a thousand variations characterize work with substance abusers. Treatment can be at any level: molecular (e.g., the use of naltrexone, a narcotic antagonist, to block the high), personal (e.g., individual dynamic therapy), systemic (e.g., strategic couple therapy), or societal (e.g., the war on drugs). I am not suggesting that these approaches have equal value or make equal sense; I am merely stating that they exist. Thinking of my friend's reaction and of the all-too-common ignorance, misunderstanding, and fear of addiction and addicts, not only in the lay public but in the professional therapeutic community, as well as the resistance to systemic treatments in some members of the analytic community, I, a child-less only child, who doesn't particularly enjoy family counseling and finds much of its literature vacuous, decided to go ahead and write this book. It has been an adventure, one in which I have learned a great deal that I hope to share with the reader.

This is a book addressed to both students and mental health professionals who wish to treat addiction, whether such treatment be individual, couple, family, or group. (The insights of family therapy can be highly useful in doing individual work.) It is a book that provides the knowledge of addiction and its psychological, psychodynamic, biological, pharmacological, and systemic concomitants necessary to work with addicts. It provides a cognitive-informational base to enable the family therapist who has not worked with addiction to expand his or her practice to include substance abusers. But I do not wish to speak only to family therapists who want to learn more about addiction. I equally wish to address individual therapists—dynamic, cognitive, behavioral—who want to learn more about a systems approach to doing family and couple work. Therefore, I have tried to elucidate the theory and practice of each major school of family therapy as clearly and succinctly as possible. Having covered both the addiction side and the family therapy side in fairly theoretical ways, the remainder of the book is clinical, an attempt to show how theory, research, technique, and flying by the seat of your pants can integrate into a therapeutic style that helps substance abusers, their significant others, and their families. The reader is invited to ponder how he or she would treat the various cases presented in these pages. These cases are something of an imaginative reconstruction and, although drawn from clinical experience, have been altered both to conceal identities and for didactic purposes.

A word about language. I find a great deal of family therapy literature dreary at best, the pretentiousness and artificiality of the language being directly proportional to the vacuousness of the content. This is not to say that there are not family therapists such as Salvador Minuchin who can be masterful writers. The clarity of the work of the epigones, however, tends to fall off precipitously. Coming from the psychodynamic tradition, I am much more comfortable with such terms as *projective identification, metapsychology, intrapsychic conflict,* and *sublimation,* although I recognize that they too can denote nothing or obfuscate, as has been pointed out by such critics of psychoanalytic terminology as Roy Schafer (1976). Having expressed my distaste for much of the jargon of couple and family therapy, I have reluctantly concluded that we are stuck with it. It is too embedded in the literature and in the speech of practicing therapists to be discarded. Accordingly, I have used the characteristic language of the various schools, trying to define their concepts as clearly and simply as possible.

I have used two condensations. Since "couple and family therapy" is a cumbersome phrase, I generally simply use "family therapy" inclusively, reserving "couple therapy" for situations that are clearly reduced to couples. I use the terms *substance abuser* and *addict* interchangeably to vary the text, although I believe there is an important and valid distinction to be made between problem drinking/drugging and alcoholism/addiction. I have further telescoped alcoholism and drug addiction where drug choice is not a central issue. I have also used alcoholism as a model addiction, extrapolating to other drug abuse sometimes with tenuous warrant, simply because we know so much more about alcoholism than about other addictions, the research literature on alcoholism and alcohol abuse being far richer than the research literature on other drug use.

A word to students. Although my aims are to teach substance abuse treatment to professional therapists of various persuasions and to teach family therapy to psychodynamically oriented and other individual therapists, I assume very little and have conscientiously tried to make this book a suitable and useful text for alcoholism and chemical dependency counseling, psychology, and social work students. I believe that it fills a gap. To the best of my knowledge, the available texts on substance abuse therapy, including those with a family therapy orientation, either assume too much knowledge of the major schools of family therapy or are too specialized, while the family therapy texts do not treat substance abuse with significant depth. It is my hope that the first half of this book is constructed in such a way as to remedy these defects and to take the student up parallel paths of addiction research and dynamic and systems theory until they meet on the clinical bridges of the second half. In addition to trying to bring together our knowledge of addiction and our knowledge of how systems work, I am particularly interested in bridging the intrapsychic and systemic. Jill and David Scharff (1991) have created such a linkage in their work on object relations family therapy. I find their work of much value, as I do to a lesser extent that of Nathan Ackerman (1994), coming from a more traditional drive oriented psychodynamic model.

In Chapter 2, I have attempted an original contribution by modifying Heinz Kohut's self psychology, which was construed as an individual therapy, for use, theoretical and clinical, in work with families. Since I have argued in a series of works going back a decade (Levin 1987, 1991, 1993, 1995) that a self psychological approach is particularly useful in the treatment of the addictions and the elucidation of their dynamics, it is fitting that I struggle to adapt self psychology as an instrument for family therapy of addiction. I believe that the model offered in Chapter 2 both makes sense of the data and is clinically useful.

As noted above, this book is addressed to two audiences: mental health professionals and students. As such, it has some problems as to level and audience. For example, some of the psychodynamic and philosophical theorizing may be of scant interest to chemical dependency counseling students who are using this book as a text for a course on family therapy of the addictions. I suggest that they skim or skip these sections. On the other hand, some mental health professionals may not require a survey of the major schools of family therapy. They too can skip and skim. With these admonitions, I believe that this book can be of great value to both groups. Don't get bogged down in what is too arcane for you or allow yourself to be bored by what is old hat to you. Plenty of meat remains to be enjoyed.

I'd like to thank my publisher and friend, Jason Aronson, for pushing his reluctant author into writing yet another book. Once entered into it, it has been one of those painful pleasures I should not wish to have missed. Ginny Wray transformed dictation of my handwritten first version into a word processed manuscript with her usual skill. I am deeply appreciative of her efforts. I would also like to thank my students at the New School for Social Research and the Eastern Campus of Suffolk Community College for letting me try out some of the material that found its way into this volume and to especially thank my patients who are always my best supervisors and teachers.

Jerome David Levin, Ph.D.

PART I

❖

Understanding the Context of Addiction

❖ ❖ ❖

❖ C H A P T E R   1 ❖

Thinking about Family Diseases

Alcoholism and addiction are said to be "family diseases." Leaving aside for the moment the vexed issue of the validity of the "disease concept," what, if anything, is meant by conceptualizing addiction as a *family* disease? On the surface, such a way of looking at addiction seems both illogical and contrary to fact. Surely, addiction is an individual matter—somebody is hooked—and any account of addiction must be an account of the relationship between that person's emotional and psychological makeup and the pharmacology of the drug, an account couched in terms of the addict's genetically determined neurochemistry, or in terms of his or her intrapsychic world with perhaps a passing reference to environmental-cultural and social factors in determining the individual addictive behavior. Depending on which theorist one reads, any or all of the above factors are called into service to construct a phenomenological and etiological account of addiction. Such approaches, though they may take cognizance of environmental influences, are essentially framed in terms of the relationship between a person and a drug and they are powerful, explaining much, drawing on a considerable body of empirically confirmed evidence, having major heuristic potential, and serving as a theoretical base for effective therapies.

Why then twist the frame and reinterpret addiction as a family disease? Although many reasons—ideological, epistemological, and personal—could and have been cited, albeit not necessarily acknowledged as such, for me the best reason lies in the recognition that no single paradigm does justice to the complexities of reality, especially the reality of such a multifaceted phenomenon as addiction. Multiple perspectives have a better chance of "saving the phenomenon," that is, giving a veridical account of "what appears," which is Plato's (368 BC) criterion for a useful scientific theory. It is worth noting that in his dialogue, *Theaetetus*, on the epistemology of science and on how we can have scientific knowledge, Plato, who had his own belief in a nonempirical, purely rational realm of certainty, maintained that the most that we could expect from an empirical scientific theory was probable knowledge. I agree. We always see "through a glass darkly" and all of our theories, intrapsychic and familial, are but approximations and partial views. They are no less valuable for being limited, and to recognize that limitation is of the essence of sanity. Otherwise, theory becomes ideology and fanaticism, and schisms which seemingly are more characteristic of religious and political institutions come to characterize "scientific" movements. The best corrective for the limitation of any particular perspective is a multiplicity of perspectives.

When I can obtain (or afford) only a "limited view" seat at the symphony or opera or theater, I take it, but try to move to another limited location, if that is all that is available, at the next performance I attend. Of course all of the seats in the house have "limited views" in a sense of unique perspectives, although they are not labeled as "limited view" seats. I am arguing not that the intrapsychic approach to the understanding of addiction is invalid; quite the contrary, all experience is the experience of somebody and it is only by analogy that we speak of the experience of families, of cultures, of historical epochs, and of societies, although in some far from understood sense those experiences are real too. Rather, it is for the purpose of enrichment and doing justice to the complexity of the phenomenon, that I am suggesting that considering addiction a family disease is equally valid, and that it is a viewpoint that can cast light not emanating from intrapsychic theory on what is happening, why it is happening, and what we can do about it when we are confronted with a person who is addicted to drugs.

My choice of the quotation from Judge Learned Hand, "The spirit of liberty is the spirit which is not too sure that it is right" (1944, p. 3) as the epigraph for this book on the family therapy of addictions must seem odd. I chose it for three reasons: it speaks to the ill-advised war between schools of therapy and modes of psychological explanation, both within and without the addiction field; it offers one clue to what might characterize a "healthy" family (or person); and it reflects my personal values. The recognition that our "knowledge" is provisional and partial, and a commitment to a multiple perspective epistemology, in no way precludes conviction or passion in our theorizing or in our treatment. Nor does it imply that the clinician should stretch him- or herself beyond natural limits and talents to become a jack of all therapeutic trades and master of none. To truly master any therapeutic approach is work enough for a lifetime, yet we as therapists do need to be flexible and even if we, as is likely, work in one, or a select few, ways, that work will be enriched if we can understand that our way of making contact and of enabling change is but one way, and that our patient—individual, couple, family, or system—can and should be understood in a multiplicity of ways ideally integrated into a synoptic vision, a task to be understood as an ideal to be striven for, not as a demand to reach a destination. Passion and conviction need not imply dogmatism and rigidity. As Heinz Kohut (1977a, p. 206) so well put it, "All worthwhile theorizing is tentative, probing, and provisional—contains an element of playfulness."

In physics, the principle of complementarity conceptualizes electromagnetic phenomena, including light, sometimes as waves and sometimes as particles, with some electromagnetic phenomena being better understood as wave occurrences while others are best understood as the effect of particles. Physicists don't really know how light, for example, can be both a particle and a wave, yet the theory "works"—saves the phenomenon. Similarly, in giving an account of addiction, we sometimes have a clearer understanding and can give a better account of the phenomenology by viewing it as an individual disorder and sometimes by viewing it as a family disorder. Here I invoke, by analogy, the principle of complementarity.

There is another way to understand the relationship between the two modes of explanation, that is, to see them as hierarchical rather than complementary. In the hierarchical model, we attempt to understand addiction successively as a molecular, cellular, systemic (e.g., the nervous system), organismic, psychic, personal, familial, cultural, and societal event. All these levels of explanation are seen as having validity but as being of different logical types needing differing modes of explanation. This sort of hierarchical model is not reductive; each realm, molecular to societal, is seen as having its own reality emergent from but not reducible to "lower" levels of organization within the hierarchy. There are also those models that are reductive viewing "higher" level entities as epiphenomena of lesser ones; essentially this approach has as its goal the explanation of all levels of human behavior including addiction in terms of electrochemical events. I think that the relationship between intrapsychic and familial, individual and systemic, can be organized either in terms of complementarity or of hierarchy, making for a sort of metacomplementarity. As we will see, unlike the disjunction between wave and particle as the embodiment of electromagnetic force in quantum mechanics, there *is* a bridge between the intrapsychic and the familial. That bridge is the psychoanalytic notion of internalization. Accordingly, this book on its theoretical side focuses on psychodynamic forms of family therapy without neglecting other formulations and approaches. I see the psychodynamic and the systemic as equally necessary if we are to understand the experiential world of the addict.

Let us to return to the question from which we have long detoured, namely what is meant when addiction is said to be a family disease, or if you don't accept the disease concept of addiction, a family disorder. There are at least three meanings inherent in making the pathology familial. The first concerns the influence of the past on the present; the second is concerned with the present, with what dynamic sustains the addiction; while the third is both present and future oriented, focusing on the impact of the identified patient, the addict, on the rest of the family.

We have long known that alcoholism[1] runs in families. What was originally folk wisdom has become scientific fact (Bleuler 1955). It is a finding, unlike so many others in this field, that is not in dispute. So one meaning of "addiction is a family disease" is simply that it runs in families. The reason it runs in families is more in dispute. Some authorities believe this is a biological phenomenon, a genetically transmitted neurochemical vulnerability. Others see the running in families as more of a psychological phenomenon, citing such factors as the power of models, that is, the effect of social learning in alcoholic families; the effect of unconscious defense mechanisms, particularly identification with the aggressor; and the emotional damage growing up in an addictive household inflicts. Within the family therapy tradition, Bowen's (1978a) intergenerational approach speaks most directly to the influence of the past on the present and the psychological and social learning transmission of addiction and addresses its treatment to escaping, through differentiation, the addictive heritage. The various psychodynamic family therapies also highlight the present past, both in their understanding of etiology and in their treatment strategy, which originated as an individual treatment but is now a family therapy modality.

The second meaning of "alcoholism is a family disease" takes the focus off of the identified patient and looks at addiction as a symptom of dysfunction in the family. The addict may be seen as a scapegoat, as a deviant necessary to strengthen family cohesiveness, delineate family boundaries, and clarify "mainstream" values; as a target and focus of family aggression; as necessary to the maintenance of

---

1. Since, as noted in the preface, the scientific literature on alcoholism is far more extensive than the literature on addiction, I will frequently use alcoholism as a "model addiction." What is said of it can, with some caveats, be said of the other drugs of abuse. In so generalizing, the reader should be aware that the different pharmacologies, the different subcultures, and perhaps the different psychological—normal and pathological—correlatives of each drug impose the need to qualify such generalizations. Nevertheless, chemical addiction is a remarkably consistent phenomenon and most addicts are cross-addicted these days, so I feel justified in using alcoholism as a model disease.

homeostasis, that is, the stability of the family; as a distraction and defense against various other conflicts—intrapsychic and interpersonal, preconscious and dynamically unconscious[2]—coming into awareness; and as one component in the interactive, multicircuited, mutual feedback system that is the family. Alcoholism as a family disease in this sense is addressed theoretically and therapeutically by the strategic, structural, systemic, and psychodynamic schools of family therapy. Individual therapists may also conceptualize their patients' pathology in these terms even though they work in a dyadic format.

The third sense in which addiction is a family disease is the least controversial of its meanings. Few in the recovery, professional, or scientific (addiction) communities doubt that the presence of an addicted family member has profound effects, usually seen to be deleterious, on all the other family members, this being particularly the case when the addict is a parent and the family member is a child. (A few researchers deny this.) Hence every rehab center has a family therapy program (or did until the current emphasis on cost containment under managed care). The vast and growing pop and professional literature on ACOAs (adult children of alcoholics) as well as the ACOA and *codependency* movements attest to the saliency of this meaning of the family as the seat of addiction. Any and all family approaches as well as the individual approaches to psychotherapy can and are used to "treat" the affected family members. If the "patient" has left the family where the addiction took place, the treatment is usually individual; if both the affected family members and the addict are still together, one of the family modalities is usually employed, although individual treat-

---

2. Sigmund Freud made a distinction between the descriptive unconscious—everything of which we are not currently aware—and the dynamic unconscious—that which is kept out of awareness by repression and other psychological defenses. The descriptive unconscious includes the preconscious and the dynamic unconscious. We can gain access to the preconscious by a simple act of recall, which we cannot do with the contents of the dynamic unconscious. In Freud's usage, the unconscious without qualification includes both the preconscious and the dynamic unconscious, but in practice almost always means the dynamic unconscious. That is the way it is used in this book—unconscious means the dynamic unconscious.

ment is also common. In either case, structural, systemic, and psycho-dynamic family therapy theorizing can be used to illuminate the "pathology" of the nonaddicted family members.

GREGORY BATESON: CYBERNETICS OF SELF

Gregory Bateson, an anthropologist turned cybernetic theorist, was a seminal thinker whose analysis of human beings and their interactive aggregates constitutes a major theoretical underpinning of both the rationale of, and the practice of, at least some forms of family therapy. He is also the author of an equally seminal paper (1971), "The Cybernetics of 'Self': A Theory of Alcoholism." Bateson's unique dual contribution to family therapy and to alcoholism theory makes discussion of his work a logical starting point for our exploration of the family dynamics of addiction.

Bateson's central organizing principle is a reconceptualization of the nature of the self as a nodal point within a field of interactive, dialectically related and relating other nodal points. All is flow, the process is the reality, interaction is the name of the game, and the reification of the self as a hermetic entity enclosed in an envelope, somatic or psychic, is the fundamental cultural flaw of the West, responsible for both the disease, family dysfunction or addiction, and the misunderstanding of that disease. Let us try to elucidate this Batesonian vision of the nature of reality and of pathology and see how that vision became the foundation stones of the family therapy movement and the basis of an intriguing elucidation of the dynamics of addiction.

Since for Bateson the self as an autonomous, self-sufficient, sharply delineated and bounded entity is an illusion, his understanding of mental illness could not be and indeed was not intrapsychic. Rather the illness, in some sense, is precisely that illusion and the consequences flowing from it. What is real is the flow of information, the exchange, between the nodal points in the flow that we call persons. Each communication elicits a communication, some form of not necessarily linguistic feedback, that in turn affects the original communicator. The short term for this mutual influence is *recursion* and such an interactive process is said to be *recursive*. So Bateson moves the focus of pathology from the self to the interaction, from the intrapsychic to the communicative. Now we have two sources of pathology: an illusionary notion, not merely theoretical but existential and experiential, of the self, and disturbed communication between that misconstrued self and similarly misconstrued selves.

In common with most of the family therapy theorists, Bateson's original interest in mental illness was in schizophrenia. What he came to see was that the families of schizophrenics drove them mad without the least awareness that they were doing so. They did this by a pattern of communication Bateson called the *double bind*. In a double bind, there is no way for the recipient of the communication to "win," no way to be "right." It is a damned-if-you-do, damned-if-you-don't trap. The double-bind theory asserts that the continuous immersion in damned-if-you-do, damned-if-you-don't environments in which covert messages contradict overt ones leads to madness (schizophrenia), the only way out being to go "mad." Of course we all communicate double binds on occasion, but what makes the schizophrenic family different is the pervasiveness and persistence of this mode of interaction.

Bateson gives the example of the mother of a schizophrenic patient, who was doing rather well in the hospital, visiting her son. As she walked into the room the mother said, "Aren't you going to embrace your mother?" but when the "patient" embraced her, she said, "Stop smothering me." (An alternate nonverbal form of the double bind would be for the mother to stiffen and/or push away, a pattern that Bateson also observed.) The "patient" immediately began acting "crazy." It is essential to the double bind that it not be commented upon; that is, there is a level of *metacommunication* that specifies no communication about communication. In our example, if the "crazy" son could say, "Mother, you are telling me to get close and pushing me away at the same time," he would not have to "go crazy," but he cannot, either because he lacks the insight into the double bind in which he is trapped or because the "rules" of the family prohibit such an utterance. These possibilities are not mutually exclusive. Lack of insight and the prohibition reinforce each other.

A therapist, who does have insight into the double-bind situation, can comment on it, thereby breaking the double-bind impasse. Such an interpretation is not usually well received and is often not heeded, illustrating the inertia of the "system," its tendency to resist change and to maintain its *homeostasis*. The "crazy" son may be counter–double binding the mother or may come to do so to maintain the status quo. As has long been observed, human beings do not change easily or gladly. For example, the son may reach to embrace his mother while glaring at her hatefully, communicating "I love you" and "I want to kill you" simultaneously, so that the mother has a choice of accepting his love and being "killed" or of rejecting his love and eliciting his madness. Each double bind elicits the other. However, the early family therapists emphasize the family's driving the child mad. This was true of both Bateson and his co-workers (1956) at Stanford and the Palo Alto Veterans Hospital, and R. D. Laing (Laing and Esterson 1964) and his associates in England, who also wrote in very similar terms on schizophrenia and the family.

This kind of theorizing has been criticized from at least two perspectives: the biological and the feminist. The more dogmatic of the biological psychiatrists view schizophrenia as exclusively a brain disease caused by genetically determined abnormalities in neurotransmitters, and so view Batesonian double-bind theory as at best irrelevant to the understanding and treatment of schizophrenia.

According to the biological hypothesis, schizophrenia is caused by abnormalities (excessive activity) of the neurotransmitter dopamine, with this excess viewed as genetically determined, with environmental influences perhaps tipping the scale toward or away from manifestations of the genotype but not determinative of the illness. In today's climate, it would be hard to get a hearing for the double-bind hypothesis in most psychiatric circles. The double-bind theorists might reply, "It's not the dopamine, it's being called a dope and being expected to excel that drives people crazy."

The feminist critique sees the theory as essentially blaming the mother. The concept of the schizophrenogenic mother is actually a psychoanalytic, not a communications, concept, having originated with Frieda Fromm-Reichmann (1948), who described a cold, distant mother with a distorted communication pattern similar to Bateson's double-bind model who drove a son who lacked a strong father "mad." Bateson's concept is less gender specific, seeing more of a schizophrenogenic family than a schizophrenogenic mother. In fact, in Bateson's analysis, there are no villains; the problem lies in the nature of the communication in the system, and one can hold the view that aberrant communication characterizes the families of schizophrenics without denying a substrate of biological vulnerability.

A more sophisticated form of criticism of the double bind and other disturbed communication theories of the etiology of mental illness holds that the disturbed communication pattern that the various investigators observe is "post"; that is, it is the pattern of communication in the family *after* the illness develops, which may or may not have been antecedent to it, and therefore cannot be legitimately claimed as etiological. The communication theorists would respond, "Etiological or not, the double bind is sustaining the illness and must be therapeutically modified for healing to occur." As we shall see, similar debates characterize the substance abuse literature on psychopathology and familial pathology in addiction.

Whatever may be the case about schizophrenia and the double bind, Bateson has clearly made a magnificent contribution with his view of mental illness as disturbed communication. This disturbance in communication is both the cause of mental illness and the essential quality of the illness itself. Communication is essentially the exchange of information, and Bateson was vitally interested in and profoundly influenced by scientific information theory, or *cybernetics*. His principal work on mental illness, co-authored with J. Ruesch (1951), is titled *Communication: The Social Matrix of Psychiatry*. Since he drew so heavily on information theory in his studies of psychopathological conditions, it is not surprising that his essay on alcoholism is titled "The Cybernetics of 'Self': A Theory of Alcoholism" (1971).

Bateson believed that the experience of the self as a thing rather than as a process and as set in opposition to a disjunctive world is an illusion or, as he would prefer to put it, an *epistemological error*. There is no substantial self apart from its world; rather the self is interrelational, the pattern of its communications with its world. Bateson believed that Western culture makes this kind of cognitive or epistemological error in its understanding of self, world, and their interrelationship, and that the alcoholic is caught in a particularly intense form of this error.

Bateson was interested in the unreflective assumptions, sometimes conscious but mostly unconscious, that people use to construe a world. The human mind is constitutive of its experiences of the world, although people are usually unaware of their roles in shaping that experience. According to Bateson, these largely unconscious assumptions are a cognitive structure that one imposes on experience in an effort to organize and make sense of that experience. This cognitive structure consists of a person's unspoken ontologies and epistemologies, that is, one's understandings of and assumptions about the nature of reality and how one knows that reality. There is a dialectical relationship between one's assumptions about the nature of reality and how one comes to know that reality and how one actually experiences it. Cognitive structures tend to be self-validating, even though they may be wrong; that is, they may distort the data that filter through them.

Here Bateson echoes the philosopher Immanuel Kant (1787), who taught that we are not passive recipients of sense data and information about the world but, rather, active organizers of sense data and data from the "inner" sense. Knowing is an active not a passive act, and we can only know the world as we experience it, filtered through perceptual "categories of the understanding," rather than as it may be apart from our knowing it. We construct our experience of both self and world. The poet William Wordsworth (1805) put it somewhat differently when he said, "The world is half perceived and half created," but he was making the same point. For Kant, the action of the human mind in constituting knowledge is invariant; it is the same for all people. Bateson, however, believed that one's ontology-epistemology is personally and culturally determined. Bateson used the word *epistemology* to denote the whole automatic, reflexive process of understanding experience. Different cognitive structures or epistemologies result in different ways of construing the world. For Bateson the alcoholic suffers from *cognitive error*, from a false epistemology. Instead of being part of a (feedback) loop, the alcoholic gets looped.

What is the nature of this epistemological error? It is the error, first promulgated by the seventeenth century philosopher René Descartes (1642), that there is a subject, the "self," that knows an object or objects "out there." It is a radically disjunctive way of viewing human experience. In Bateson's view, this error leads to a disjunction between self and world that does not really exist. For him the "real" reality is a feedback loop in which information, or in his words, "transformations of differences," flow, and self and object are nodal points in that flow, mutually interactive and mutually interdependent. The radical disjunction of self and world predisposes one who lives by this epistemology to *objectify* (that is, to treat as objects) both the world and the people in it. This results in an attempt to totally control the world and the objects in it, as if destruction of the objects would have no effect on the destroyer since they have nothing to do with him or her. This leads to a kind of sadomasochistic relationship with the world. It is also a kind of pseudo–self-sufficiency.

An interactional, information-flow model of reality simultaneously connects knower and known and makes the known a center of independent, or better interdependent, initiative and does not lend itself to efforts at omnipotent control. It contains less epistemological error. According to Bateson, the sober alcoholic does not construe the world in this way, and alcohol offers a corrective to his or her epistemological error. Alcohol breaks down the barriers between self and world, here experienced as an object to be exploited, and reestablishes the alcoholic's interconnection with and interdependence on that object. In other words, alcohol dedifferentiates self and object representations. If such differentiations are too rigid, if the ego boundaries are too impermeable, the alcohol will be corrective. In Bateson's view, no matter how regressive the psychological consequences of this pharmacological process are, they result in a world picture that in some sense is more true or correct in that it allows the alcoholic to experience him- or herself as "a part of" rather than "apart from" the world. Alcoholism is then an attempt to correct an epistemological error. Unfortunately, the pharmacological qualities of alcohol are such that the attempt is doomed to failure. Like all other attempts to self-medicate with alcohol, the "cure" ultimately exacerbates the "illness" and the alcoholic winds up more disjunctive, more cut off from world and fellows than he or she was before drinking.

Bateson is fascinated with Alcoholics Anonymous (AA) and its twelve steps, which he sees as a noninjurious mode of correction of the alcoholic's false epistemology. Since drinking is here seen as a corrective to a deficient sobriety, the state of being of the sober alcoholic must be modified if that sobriety is to endure. Bateson argues that AA does just that by inducing an epistemological shift toward *complementarity* (the state of being in which disjunctive power relations are replaced by communicative interactions) through the "surrender experience" and the AA ideology in general.

Bateson is given to the creation of neologisms, which sometimes makes for a tough read. However, his conceptualizations illuminate. I would like to highlight some of them. Bateson spoke of *symmetrical* and *complementary* relationships and of *schismogenesis*. A symmetrical relationship is one in which an increase in one term of a relationship results in an increase in the other. A mathematician would say they are directly proportional. An example is an arms race. More missiles for nation A means more missiles for nation B. I am not clear if Bateson is saying that—to continue the example—unilateral disarmament by nation A would automatically result in a decrease in missile possession by nation B, which it should if it is a mathematically direct proportion. Be that as it may, Bateson is clearly defining a symmetrical relationship as one in which more of one results in more of the other. A complementary relationship is one that is indirectly proportional—the more of one, the less of the other. An example would be dominance/submission. The more dominant A, the more submissive B (less dominant). So far, nothing startling and innovative, merely a new slant and some new terms for some fairly well understood forms of relating.

Now to the originality in Bateson's notion of schismogenesis. A schismogenic relationship is one in which no negative feedback exists, negative here being a theoretical not a pejorative term. In a servomechanism such as a thermostat, there is a negative feedback loop between room temperature and the furnace turning off. In schismo-genesis, there is nothing but positive feedback. The temperature goes up and the furnace burns even more fiercely; the more fiercely the furnace burns, the more the temperature goes up, ad infinitum. It is a system run amok because it lacks a means for self-correction or sta-bilization at an optimum or maximum. Both symmetrical and comple-mentary systems can be schismogenic. Dominance may escalate until submission can go no further. Lucky and Pozzo in Beckett's *Waiting for Godot* (1954) come to mind.

Bateson applies this conceptual scheme to alcoholism. Here the relata are the alcoholic's will power, that is, illusion of control ("I can beat it"), and drinking. The more the alcoholic believes that he or she is in control, is master of his soul, the more he "slips," that is, goes on a bender, and the more he slips, the more he needs to believe he is in control, a classical schismogenesis that may end only in death. On the other hand, the theology, the epistemology of AA and the Twelve-Step movement offers an alternate stance: instead of me against the world, my will against the bottle, I come to see that I stand not against the world but rather am a part of that world, and in that insight, am able to relinquish my control and surrender. (Twelve Step refers to the twelve steps of recovery of AA, now widely imitated by other groups. The first step states, "We admitted we were powerless over alcohol and that our lives had become unmanageable" [Alco-holics Anonymous World Services, 1952, p. 5].) In surrendering, I move from a symmetrical, schismogenic relationship to the world to a complementary, nonschismogenic relationship to the world. My "humility" does not induce greater dominance in my "Higher Power," be that Higher Power my group, the anabolic forces of the universe, or a transcendent God. (If my higher power is my "sponsor," this is not so clear or so certain. A sponsor is a stably sober member of a Twelve Step group who acts as a mentor to a newly sober member, although it is recommended that members continue to have spon-sors even if they have many years of sobriety. The second step states, "Came to realize that a power greater than ourselves could restore us to sanity" [Alcoholics Anonymous World Services 1953, p. 5].)

Bateson believes that the complementary relationship between the now recovering alcoholic and the Higher Power is nonschismogenic, since the AA higher power wishes only that the member grow and be happy and that this is a more correct epistemology and has more truth in it than the one that the alcoholic could not live with. The self is now redefined as being in relation to the Higher Power, because for Bateson, the totality of one's relationship to the universe, which includes the individual as a part of that universe, is the correct understanding of the self. In his article, Bateson states that man's relationship to the universe is truer, is more congruent with reality, if it is complementary, yet he observes that human relationships are enriched by complexity and that we are optimally configured as both complementary and symmetrical but not as schismogenic. He expresses some doubt that recovering alcoholics can afford symmetrical relationships; for them, they all too easily become schismogenic. My first clinical supervisor, Claude Miller, used to say, "All of our lives we need mother's milk and corrective feedback, preferably from the same person." Bateson would agree.

Bateson founded family therapy by relocating the locus of pathology in schizophrenia in the communication pattern of the family of the schizophrenic and he elucidated a significant theory of the dynamics of alcohol addiction, albeit an intrapsychic one, one about change in the alcoholic's epistemology, but he didn't explicitly adumbrate a family therapy approach to addiction. It is true that both the dynamic that sustains the drinking for the Batesonian alcoholic and the dynamic of his recovery is intrapsychic; nevertheless, this experiential change in the self is a change from isolation to relationship, from being apart to being a part, and that change comes about through affiliation with and membership in an organization. In joining AA, the alcoholic joins a "family" (language frequently used at AA meetings), so that the "family therapy" consists in becoming a member of a new family.

Further, Bateson and his colleagues Jay Haley and John Weakland (none of whom, interestingly enough, had been trained in a mental health discipline, coming rather from engineering and anthropology) in effect founded a school of family therapy based on systems theory

and directed to the correction of impaired or pathological communication. Bateson borrowed the notion of feedback, negative and positive, from Norbert Wiener (1948), the cybernetic theorist. Systems
theory comes from von Bertalanffy. Bateson himself never practiced
family therapy, nor any other therapy, but went off to study the communication of dolphins.

LUDWIG VON BERTALANFFY: GENERAL SYSTEMS THEORY

Ludwig von Bertalanffy's 1968 book *General Systems Theory: Foundation, Development, Application* has become canonical in the family
therapy movement. I myself have not read von Bertalanffy, nor have
I ever met anyone who has ever read von Bertalanffy, yet it is not
possible to read an article or a book on family therapy which does
not cite von Bertalanffy. Now I have no reason to believe that von
Bertalanffy, who was a biologist, has not done work of the highest
quality and significance. In fact, I assume that he did so. Nevertheless, the genuflection to systems theory and its high priest seems more
ritualistic and religious than scientific. Once having mentioned von
Bertalanffy and systems theory, most authors do nothing further with
it. I will now do more or less the same.

However, as I understand it, general systems theory is a conceptualization in which the whole is seen as something greater than the
sum of its parts; those parts only being fully comprehensible, totally
understood, when they are seen as part of an interactional system. Each
part, or subset of the totality, is determinative of and determined by
the sum total of its interactions with all the other subsets of the system. Depending on the level of organization, an atom is constitutive
of a molecule, while participation in the molecular organization characterizes the atom, and a lion exists and has its reality only in the context of gazelles and wildebeests whose existence is in turn determined
by their cohabitation with the lion. In sum, everything is related to
everything else, their relationship being reciprocal, interactive, recursive feedback systems. The more gazelles, the more lions; the more
lions, the fewer gazelles; until some optimal equilibrium point is

reached. Levels of organization are hierarchical, for example, biologically atoms, molecules, cells, tissues, organs, systems, organisms, species, genera, phyla, and kingdoms form a system. Yet this hierarchy cannot exist apart from the physical environment, the energy of the sun, and the gravitational pull of the moon and stars ad infinitum. Von Bertalanffy's understanding of the embeddedness of biological systems rightly makes him the founding father of contemporary ecological theory and indeed spiritual father of the ecological movement.

Von Bertalanffy's cybernetic biological model was undoubtedly influenced by two European developments: in biology, ethnology; and in philosophy, phenomenology. The ethnologists speak of the *umwelt*, literally translated as the "around world" but usually translated as the "surround." The notion is that no animal exists nor can be understood apart from his or her surround. The surround is everything from the immediate natural environment with its physical qualities, climate, plants, and animals to the universe. The surround, however, in one of its meanings, is subjective; it is the animal's experience of its physical and biological situation. Thus a rabbit's surround in the more subjective sense may be primarily grass, hole, and predators, while the fox's surround; in exactly the same physical and biological situation, may be primarily rabbit, jumpable fences, and vixens. Thus the surround is both the surround for the organizer, organized in terms of his or her values, and the totality of the situation in which the animal exists. Extrapolating to the human family, the surround as constituted by other family members exists both as conscious awareness of relationships in that family and as the subtotal of all the unconscious transactions that occur in that family. The human surround consists of more than the family, encompassing social class, economic structure, political entity, and all of nature. Again the degree of awareness of this indeed infinite concatenation of interrelated complexity varies enormously both across and within persons; that is, different people have different levels of awareness of their environments and their interactive relationship to them and the same person's level of insight will change with maturation, education, and experience.

The phenomenological thinker Edmund Husserl (1929), the personally odious philosopher Martin Heidegger (1927), and existential psychoanalyst Ludwig Binswanger (1958) spoke of three structural components of human existence—the *umwelt*, the *mitwelt*, and the *eigenwelt*—using these terms differently than does the ethnologist. Heidegger spoke of humans as *Dasein*, as *being-there*. His notion is that we always exist as embedded; there is no disembodied, solipsistic mind contemplating an external reality disjunctive from itself such as Bateson criticizes in Descartes's metaphysics. Rather we are always there—somewhere, sometime—and exist as nodal points in a field of flux much as a quantum physicist sees physical entities such as electrons as nodal points in a field of electromagnetic energy. The convergence of Bateson's cybernetic theory, von Bertalanffy's ethnological theory, and Heidegger's *Dasein* is apparent. The degree of influence, mutual or unidimensional, is less clear.

What did Binswanger and Heidegger mean by *umwelt*, *mitwelt*, and *eigenwelt*? For them, the *umwelt* is the physical and biological surround and our embeddedness in it. The *mitwelt* exists only for human beings and is our contextual being with other human beings. It might be translated as community, as long as community is understood as a mutually interactive system. *Mitwelt* is the whole nexus of meanings, feelings, expectations, obligations, and traditions that exist between us and others. The *eigenwelt* is the own world or value world, and it is the self's relationship to itself apart from its relationship to surround and others. It is what is often called the self, not here reified as a disjunctive entity but rather seen in its relationship to itself. It is the internal psychodynamic aspect of being there, of being human. Of course there is only one *Dasein*, one person, who is constituted by *umwelt*, *mitwelt*, and *eigenwelt*.

The relevance of all this to the family therapy of the addictions may seem obscure, but I don't think it is. Binswanger's analysis of the nature of the self clearly posits the need to intervene at different levels, to work systemically with *mitwelt* issues and interpsychically with *eigenwelt* issues. Substances constitute increasingly exclusive (as the addiction progresses) *unwelten* of addicts; that is, the addict's entire relational surround becomes his relationship to his drug of choice.

An important word on hierarchical organization of systems. One can view higher level, that is, more complex, organizations, as epiphenomena of lower level organizations, for example, Darwin's nineteenth century popularizer Thomas Huxley's notion that consciousness was an epiphenomenon of material processes in the brain. An adequate account of neurochemistry would be an adequate account of consciousness. All the causal vectors go from the bottom upward to the top. You could have an account of group phenomena or family phenomena that recognizes the interaction of the group or family members and the mutual feedback that each elicits from the others that nevertheless maintains that there is nothing more to be said or accounted for at the family level once the sum total of individual dynamics and their interactions have been explicated. Such an account would be recursive, yet remain reductive. Nothing new emerges at the group or family level.

Most family thinkers do not want to be reductionistic in their accounts of the relationship of various levels of hierarchies. That is, in some sense or another, they want to assert that the whole is greater than the sum of the parts. There are two important notions here: *emergence* and *top-down* causality. What emergence theorists assert is that something novel that hitherto did not exist comes into being at higher levels of organization. For example, water has properties that its constituents sodium and chlorine do not have. Nevertheless, water can be exhaustively explained by an account of its chemical composition. So we have emergence and reduction in this example. It is a weak emergence. A strong emergence theorist asserts that the novelty that comes into being at the higher level of complexity, here molecular rather than atomic, cannot be accounted for in terms of its lower level constituents. To take an example from a more commonly held form of strong emergence theory, consciousness may occur if and only if certain neurochemical events occur in the brain in particular patterns and places, yet consciousness may be something that cannot be explained by an account, however exhaustive, of those neurochemical events, their patterns, and interactions. Something has emerged that simply is not a neurochemical event or a combination of neurochemical events and cannot be reduced to them. The higher level systems in the hierarchy of electromagnetic events, atomic events, molecular events, biological events, and mental events cannot be reduced to lower levels of the hierarchy, although they depend for their existence on conditions in the lower levels of the hierarchy. Seen from this perspective the group or the family cannot be reduced to the group or family members.

One may be a strong emergent theorist without subscribing to top-down causality, although the two beliefs generally go together. The top-down theorist Roger Sperry (1993, 1995), the psychologist who first described split-brain phenomena resulting from severing the corpus callosum, a band of nerve tissue connecting the right and left hemispheres of the brain, held that the causal vectors are not unidirectional. In Sperry's discussion of consciousness, it is not only the case that electromagnetic and neurochemical phenomena cause states of consciousness (which he does not deny), but states of consciousness assert their top-down control, that is, they have causal efficacy, on lower-level phenomena. This is a new wrinkle on the age-old mind–body problem. But the new wrinkle is indeed new—Sperry, a "hard data," rigorously empirical scientist who has made a magnificent contribution to neuroscience, argues that mind (consciousness) influences the "material" (although quantum physics tells us the material is not so material anymore). In Sperry's view mind influences matter just as much as matter influences mind.

In terms of our topic, not only is family inexplicable, because of emergence, in terms of the dynamics of its members, but family exerts top-down control over its members. Is this mystical nonsense? Or does indeed the group, the family, the culture, society, have a reality superordinant to its constituent parts and their recursive or linear relationships? This is a question that has vexed the best philosophical minds for centuries, and I will not try and answer the question on an ontological or metaphysical level. Whatever the ultimate reality—nature—of groups and families, I do not know it, but I can say that my experience of organizations, of groups, and of families is that they are not only emergent phenomena but that they do exercise top-down control. Experientially they have a reality different from the sum of their parts.

The philosopher Immanuel Kant taught that we can never know the *ding-an-sich*, the thing-in-itself, but can only know the world as it appears to us through the screen of our perceptual and cognitive processing. He was undoubtedly right. Accordingly, I cannot know the *ding-an-sich* of families or couples, but I do know that my experience of them is that of superordinant organizations. This is not to say that bottom-up causal explanations have no validity; quite the contrary. What I wish to say is that there is a complementarity, in the sense that the physicists speak of waves and particles as being complementary explanations of electromagnetic phenomena, between bottom-up and top-down influences in human organizations of all kinds.

The philosopher, who surprisingly is almost never cited in the family therapy literature, whose metaphysics is most congruent with systems theory is Alfred North Whitehead. Although Whitehead's philosophy seemingly takes us far afield from family theory of the addictions, I think his system is of significant interest to warrant its exploration here. Whiteheadian metaphysics can serve as a metastructure for most of family therapy theory and may have some practical implications. However, before discussing Whitehead there is another concept, *homeostasis*, that plays a central role in family therapy theorizing and that needs to be defined.

HOMEOSTASIS

Homeostasis is a term that systems theory borrowed from physiology. It was coined by Walter Cannon (1932), one of the great physiologists, in his book, *The Wisdom of the Body*. As Cannon defined homeostasis, it refers to the body's mechanisms for maintaining reasonably constant and optimal levels of such biological necessities as glucose, oxygen, temperature, and respiration rate. Homeostasis is essentially a principle of inertia; any change in the system will be resisted and mechanisms will be invoked to restore the system, or a subset of it, to the optimal level, this being essentially accomplished by negative feedback loops. To use glucose level as an example: if following a meal, the concentration of serum glucose, more commonly called the level of blood sugar, goes up, glucose molecules signal the liver to convert the excess glucose into glycogen (animal starch), where it is stored until needed. If blood sugar then falls below a set point (optimal level) the liver is then signaled to convert its stored glycogen back into glucose and return it to the bloodstream. In either case, a change in glucose level is compensated for and the blood level remains within fairly narrow parameters. The body's mechanism for controlling serum glucose level is far more complex than this illustration would suggest, but the basic principle—change is resisted—is equally the case if all of that complexity is taken into account.

Family therapy has extrapolated from Cannon's physiological homeostasis to state as a more or less general principle that families resist change, and that they too have mechanisms to maintain the status quo whether that status quo be defended in terms of rules, or power relationships, or of substance use. The system—here the family—no matter what its conscious desires for change, always attempts to restore the status quo ante as roles and power relationships shift. There is inertia in the system; it "works" to keep on running in a straight line at the same velocity just as in Newton's first law, a body will continue at rest or in motion in a straight line unless a force acts upon it. We particularly see this in substance abuse when a family member gets "straight," which has long been the stated wish of the other family members, and then all hell breaks loose. Put simply, human beings and their aggregates do not change gladly. So the family, or the group, or the organization has a strong homeostatic tendency that requires an equally strong countervailing force to overcome.

The principle of homeostasis as extrapolated to the family is well illustrated by the story of the man who goes to the psychiatrist desperate for help for his son who believes that he is a chicken. The psychiatrist listens to the father's story and tells him, "Delusions like your son's are common but fortunately we psychiatrists can rather easily cure them. Talk it over with your son and call back for an appointment and I am sure I can help him relinquish his belief that he is a chicken." A month passes and there is no call from the father, so the psychiatrist calls him and says, "I was expecting to hear from you. I wonder why you haven't called me." "Well, doctor," says the father, "I haven't called because the family talked it over and we decided we need the eggs." There are many families with substance-abusing members who decide that they need the eggs. Homeostasis is to family dynamics and therapy what resistance is to individual dynamics and therapy.

Homeostatic forces are not the only forces at work in families. If they were, change would not be possible, at least not without leaving the family, and indeed this is sometimes the case. But most families and most couples do find ways to accommodate and even initiate change. Therefore, some family theorists hypothesize that there are innate growth-promoting mechanisms as well as inertial ones in family systems. Be that as it may, growth does occur whether as a manifestation of an inner drive or as a result of external forces, and we as therapists need to be equally aware of homeostasis and of evolutionary forces in the families we work with. That brings us to Whitehead.

ALFRED NORTH WHITEHEAD: PROCESS PHILOSOPHY AND THE FAMILY

Whitehead (1929) is best known for his statement, "The process is the reality." Bateson, who wanted a bumper sticker "*STAMP OUT NOUNS*," would heartily agree. Whitehead, along with many other philosophical critics of language, maintained that the subject-predicate syntax of Indo-European languages falsifies reality and concretizes fluidity and process into solidarity and stasis. This is a good enough approximation for the purposes of common sense and everyday living; after all, there are relatively stable enduring objects—things— in our experience. It is no accident that our languages have a subject-predicate grammatical structure; it is serviceable, yet so misleading as a guide to ultimate truth. Metaphysically grammar deceives. And so it is with the family. We reify and substance-ize, turning process into a thing, losing history and our sense of the historical in present-ness, which paradoxically costs us true presentness since the unacknowledged influence of the past asserts baleful influence on the present. In holding on, we lose the now as well as the then. The great seventeenth century empirical philosopher John Locke (1690) wrote that "time is perpetual perishing," a statement that strongly influenced Whitehead. His philosophy is, in part, an account of how that which is perpetually perishing is incorporated into the ongoing process that is the universe and ourselves. Whitehead's highly abstract metaphysical speculations address these very issues.

Whitehead started out as a mathematician who remains best known for his collaboration with Bertrand Russell from 1910 to 1913 on the *Principia Mathematica*, an attempt to derive all mathematics from the few logical categories and rules of inference. Relatively late in life he turned to philosophy and metaphysics, which he defined as an extremely general account of the nature of things. I would like to highlight his discussions of perception, logical fallacies, and metaphysical vision. Let us start with his analysis of perception. According to Whitehead there are two modes of perception: presentational immediacy and causal efficacy. *Presentational immediacy* gives us a display, almost in a sense of a computer display. It is vivid, colored, sharply defined, at a distance, and representational; it is also cold, empty, and intrinsically meaningless. It is a projection of a bodily state. Sight is a paradigmatic exemplification of presentational immediacy. There are no internal connections, no necessary connections between the bright bits of color or the sounds or the smells of presentational immediacy. Causal connections are not part of the display. Presentational immediacy is never so effective as in a state of alertness. It has been built into the higher organisms in the course of evolution because its symbolizations and their interpretations, although fallible, have, on the average, survival value. It is an instrument of great practical utility but not necessarily the best source of insight into the ultimate nature of things, not the best tool with which to do metaphysics or perhaps therapy. If we limit ourselves to presentational immediacy, the events of the world have only external connections, if any; it reveals no intrinsic linkages or causal sequences. It simply displays that which is contemporaneous.

Not so for what Whitehead calls *causal efficacy*. Causal efficacy is just as much a mode of perception as is presentational immediacy. In fact, it is more basic in the sense that it characterizes lower grade organisms and dimmer states of consciousness. It is causal efficacy, not presentational immediacy, that is the preeminent mode of perception in the sense that it gives us our experience of the causal nexus, which is the world. It is the source of our sense of the power of things, of their ability to impinge on us, of their agency and activity. As such, it has great survival value, and it too was built in by the evolutionary process. We get our experience of causal efficacy by defocusing; it is vaguer, more premonitory, more likely to be felt in the dark, in states of semiconsciousness as upon awakening, or in the hypnagogic state preceding sleep. It is the sensation that there are powers around us, and that they can act on us, that they have causal efficacy. The paradigmatic case of causal efficacy is the sense of the brooding presence of things in a dimly lit room as we emerge from sleep. Whitehead says that the data of philosophy, at least of cosmological metaphysics, must include all of our experiences, waking and sleeping, going to sleep and awakening, rational and insane, scientific and religious, ill and well, sharply focused and dimly perceived, highly abstract and irredeemably concrete, and brute fact and flight of fancy.

These are precisely the data of analytic therapy. The vivid is the most disconnected; it provides (potentially) aesthetic pleasure but not a demonstration of the power of events to affect one another. That is only revealed in the philosophically disavowed, vague, dim, unfocused, lower level experience of the power of things to affect us. Whitehead's turning to the philosophically disreputable is reminiscent of Freud's and psychoanalysis's attention to the "sordid" details of life, and to such "unscientific" data as dreams and jokes.

The experience of causal efficacy is the closest we get to direct experience of the unconscious. In being a member of or working with a family, it is the felt experience of our sense of the unconscious influences in that family—the power relations, the projections, the identifications. What is suggested here is the therapist (paradoxically) attend to the unfocused, the vague, the felt processes and presences, the peripheral as opposed to the central as a way of tapping into family process. Whitehead's mode of causal efficacy resonates with Freud's injunction for the analyst to maintain an "evenly hovering attention."

Perception is not the exclusive property of higher organisms like man, although the perceptual mode of presentational immediacy is.

Perception in the mode of causal efficacy is the property of all "actual occurrences," the ultimate "real objects" of the universe. Whitehead's universe is a universe of organisms interactive with one another. Such perception does not necessarily involve consciousness. There are grades of awareness and of self-consciousness in the real entities, or real events that constitute the universe.

There is an interesting parallel between Whitehead's modes of perception and the psychoanalytic developmental psychologist Rene Spitz's distinction between coenesthetic sensing and diacritic perception. Spitz (1965) conducted some of the first infant observational research and concluded that the earliest mode of perception was *coenesthetic sensing*, experiencing on a level of deep, primarily visceral, global, or totalistic sensibility, which is largely superseded in adult life by the mode of *diacritic perception*, which is perception at a distance through the specialized sense organs of discrete sensa—colors, sounds, tastes, and smells. The vague intimation of coenesthetic awareness of presence is clearly a close relative of Whitehead's causal efficacy, and diacritic perception is clearly a close relative of presentational immediacy. Spitz believes that those adults who retain the greatest capacity for coenesthetic sensing are the artists and creative thinkers. Coenesthetic sensing is the basis of intuition and of feelings of connectedness and interaction, of causal efficacy. It is preeminently an affective mode of perception, while the diacritic is preeminently a cognitive mode. Feelings rather than high-level abstract thinking give us our most intimate and veridical experience of the ultimate nature of things, that experience being grounded in the experience of connectedness, indeed, of oneness with Mother, as well as apartness and separation from her. The bridge between the coenesthetic and the diacritic is the experience of being held on the breast with nipple in mouth and looking at Mother's face. The vague, richly affective sensations of tactile merging with Mother are coordinated with the more cognitive presentation at a distance through sight of Mother's face. Affect is the bridge. Whitehead too writes of the interaction of the two modes of perception, but it was Spitz who found the biological, developmental linkage in the nursing experience.

Whitehead also wrote of two cognitive errors characteristic of much of Western thought. He called them the fallacy of misplaced concreteness and the fallacy of simple location. In a sense, both stem from the naïve and uncritical assumption that the subject-predicate syntax of the Indo-European languages is isomorphic to, and an adequate guide to, reality and its ultimate nature. Subject-predicate syntax and its philosophical derivatives see reality as comprising some sort of solid stuff or substance that has enduring qualities, attributes, or characteristics that somehow adhere in that enduring substance. Substances and their accidents (i.e., individual characteristics) are the ultimate. The idea of an underlying substance that is the permanent substrate of the surface flux of things stems from the pre-Socratic Greek philosopher Thales's statement that "all things are water," water being the permanent underlying substrate. Thales's water becomes Anaximander's air; Empedocles's air, earth, water, and fire; and Democritus's atoms. In one way or another, the basic model of underlying stable stuff of some sort having qualities that endure "beneath" or "behind" the ever-changing surface resurfaces repeatedly in the history of philosophy. Whitehead is aware that the subject-predicate mode of construing reality has great pragmatic utility, that it is a rough-and-ready yet adequate guide to action, and that is why it is incarnated in the syntax of ordinary language. Like Newtonian physics, it is not so much untrue as true only under restricted circumstances.

The *fallacy of misplaced concreteness* is the error of eating the menu instead of the steak (or these days, the menu instead of the sushi). It is mistaking our abstractions for the individual concrete existents, or mistaking conceptual analyses for the realities. We take substance, either naively, from the grammatical structure of our language, or sophisticatedly, from the high-level abstract reasoning of philosophy, as a given, as a concrete reality when it is not. In Whitehead's view, a good deal of philosophical error and puzzlement comes from taking our abstractions from the concrete givens of experience as the concrete things themselves. Symbol systems are not the symbolized. To abstract is to take away from, to strip down, and a metaphysics based on mistaking abstractions for direct experiences ineluctably results in a picture and understanding of reality that lacks meaning and in which connectedness and causal sequence is problematical.

The *fallacy of simple location* is the error of assuming that events are things that exist only at a place specifiable by a system of coordinates, when the reality is that events are *field phenomena* in the same way in which electromagnetic events are field phenomena. They are in fact emanating throughout the universe. It is the pebble-in-the-pond phenomenon. Its waves radiate asymptotically throughout space-time. I am the energy radiating from my epicenter into that world. The Whiteheadian self is self as flow of relatively but not permanently enduring patterns, and self is not so much embedded as it is interactive energy exchanges.

This brings us to a discussion of Whitehead's metaphysics per se. His is an exceedingly complex system, and I will not attempt to present that complexity. According to Whitehead, metaphysics is not a deductive procedure in which truth is inferred from a few apodictically certain premises. That is the way in mathematics, which has seduced and deceived philosophers. What metaphysics should do is to give an extremely general account of experience. "Speculative philosophy is the endeavor to frame a coherent, logical, necessary system of general ideas in terms of which every element of our experience can be interpreted" (Whitehead 1929, p. 4).

Whitehead's ultimately real are "actual occurrences," also called "actual entities" and "actual events." Such "a real individual is an organizing activity fusing ingredients into a unity, so that this unity is the reality." Events are interdependent and mutually immanent. But in perishing, actual occasions are preserved by being "prehended" by other actual occurrences, by new events. The living are alive in virtue of incorporation of the dead. Whitehead calls this *objective immortality*. But all is not determined by the past; there is a "creative advance" of the universe; novelty is real. The universe strives for vividness and value. What is, is the "consequent nature of God"; the creative advance in novelty is the "primordial nature of God."

An actual occasion is the prehension of its real antecedents, and of *eternal objects*: permanent possibilities waiting to be actualized in actual occurrences. This coming together of antecedents and eternal objects in actual occurrences Whitehead calls *concrescence*. Eternal objects are Whiteheadian, disembodied universals; they do not exist anywhere until they are actualized. Actual occurrences or events prehend each other, so that the universe is a mutual grasping of the contemporaneous, a mutual immanence, and a successive incorporation of those events that are perishing. So is a family.

Self is a "society" of actual occurrences, a patterning of those that are contemporaneous and a patterning of those that are successive. The creative advance of the self is that of coming into being by reaching back and grasping—prehending—that which is perishing, thereby making the dead part of the living. In so doing, the actual occasions that constitute the society that is the self both change (perish) and endure. Thus the self can be the same yet different. *The process is the reality.* In the course of emergence of new actual occasions, permanent possibilities of organization and of quality come into being as part of that which is prehended by those actual events. Experience is experience of an enduring organism in a world of organisms.

Our most immediate environment is constituted by our body. Experience is activity, and Whitehead's self is activity, activity initially aware of its own organism and sequentially of the organisms that constitute the universe. The self is a society of actual occasions, or societies of societies of actual occasions, depending on the level of complexity from which we view it. The self is a real individual and a real individual is an organizing activity fusing ingredients into a unity.

What Whitehead says about the universe and the self can just as easily be said of the family, which is also an *entity* or Whiteheadian *real object* at a higher level of complexity. It seems to me that Whitehead's ontology provides a metaphysical basis, if it needs one, for the practice of family therapy. His view captures ongoingness, evolutionary process, novelty, nexus, stasis, permanence, and the living influence of the past in the constitution of any actual entity: self, family, or universe. It is the interactive process model Bateson and the other family therapists have sought. Its practical application includes attendance to the rich contribution of the mode of causal efficacy to the therapist's data and the defocusing necessary to attend to that mode. Awareness of the dangers of the fallacies of simple location, for example, believing the problem is in the patient, or that the patient is in (bounded by) his or her skin, and of misplaced concreteness, for example, taking the verbalization and other symbolic activity of the family members for the reality of their felt worlds helps the therapist stay close to the experiential and affective reality of the system. A sense of the infinite nexus of interconnections contemporaneous and prehensive of the past of each of the nodal points, that is, members of the family system, helps keep the focus on the necessity for the therapist to engage in an ongoing struggle to stay with process, rather than reifying it into structure. The pre-Socratic Greek philosopher Heraclitus wrote, "You cannot step into the same river twice." Whitehead might say, "You cannot even step into the same river once—there is no river, only flow."

As I think about Whitehead's process philosophy, Sally, a deeply troubled, extremely angry patient with strong feelings of entitlement and surprisingly good survival skills comes to mind. Sally, a long-term client of the State Office of Vocational Rehabilitation (OVR) had dropped out of her tenth vocational program. She approached her counselor highly enthusiastic about yet another training program (I think it was electronics). Mrs. Dwight, the OVR counselor, explained that the agency couldn't possibly sponsor her in yet another program since she had dropped out of one after another. Sally summoned up all of her considerable self-righteousness and indignantly proclaimed, "What do you mean? I'm in the process of *becoming*." Sally went to electronics school. I'm not sure how Whitehead would feel about Sally's continuing OVR sponsorship, but surely we have to concede that Sally has an excellent grasp of process philosophy.

Major Family Therapy Approaches

Let us move from Whitehead's extremely general notions of what constitutes an individual (or as he would say, an "actual event") and a society (family) of such events to more specific systems of family therapy. Before doing so, we might ask what is the therapeutic implication of Whitehead's process philosophy? The main implication would seem to be that anything that attempts to arrest the flux—freezes the process—is incongruent with reality and doomed to failure in the sense of ineluctably exacerbating conflict, and there is nothing as solidified as an addicted family. Paradoxically, Whitehead also teaches us that the incorporated, assimilated "dead" past is an ineluctable component of the living process, which is the present. Therapeutically, this means that individual, couple, and family are only and can only be fully in the present when they have successfully assimilated the past.

The major theories of family dynamics and systems of family therapy considered here are the family as group (Freud and Bion), strategic family therapy (Haley), structural family therapy (Minuchin), experiential family therapy (Whitaker), intergenerational systems family therapy (Bowen), psychodynamic family therapy (Ackerman), object relations family therapy (Jill and David Scharff), and self-psychological family therapy. Behavioral family therapy, which virtually all of the family

therapy schools incorporated into their techniques even if not into their
theories, will be considered more briefly.

FAMILY AS A GROUP

One of the most obvious things about the family is that it is a group.
As such, it can be treated by group therapy just like any other
group. But there are important differences. In constituting a therapy
group, the therapist is able to select the members according to criteria
ranging from availability to level of object relations, to verbal skills,
to commonality (or heterogeneity) of problems. The family therapist has no such freedom; he or she has to take the family or couple
as they come. Most therapy groups are not multigenerational; families
are. Having said this, the fact remains that a family is a group. There is
a vast literature on family dynamics: Lewinian field theory, socio-
metric theories about how groups make decisions, studies of group con-
formity, and many others. Having taught group dynamics several times,
I have worked through a goodly portion of that literature; very little
of it sticks. I don't really wish to demean these studies and theories;
however, they just don't speak to me, with the exception of the findings on group polarization. Put simply, the theory of group polarization states that groups make extreme decisions compared to individuals. Empirical research shows that on the average, group discussion
of an issue results in the group taking an extreme position. The implication of this for family dynamics is obvious: discussion does not
necessarily lead to rational insight, but on the contrary may well be
inflammatory, moving the family to progressively more irrational
decisions. Of course, not every family enclave results in polarization,
but the tendency is there. In general, the group dynamics literature
points to the power of emotional, irrational, or at least nonrational
components of group process. For readers so inclined, I recommend
any standard text on group dynamics. There are, however, two psychoanalytic works on groups that illuminate what drives group behavior: one by Sigmund Freud and the other by Wilfred Bion.

Sigmund Freud

Almost all of Freud's work is about individual psychology, yet for all his emphasis on the intrapsychic, he was very well aware of the effects people have on one another. The Oedipus complex is about family dynamics. The notions of identification, introjection, and internalization are bridges from the interpersonal to the intrapsychic, and the analysis of Little Hans (1909) is a family therapy case. Yet Freud wrote almost always about the family drama within, rather than about the struggles between people in the external world until rather late in his career. There was something about the incredible destructiveness of World War I and the rise of mass political parties after the war that turned Freud's attention to the dynamics of groups.

In 1921, approaching the age of 70, he published *Group Psychology and the Analysis of the Ego*, in which he analyzed group behavior. In congruence with the polarization literature, Freud concluded that men in groups undergo regression and deindividuation. Starting as he often does with a selective review of the literature, Freud summarized the work of LeBon (1895) on what we might call a crowd or even a mob—short-lived aggregations of men—in terms reminiscent of Shakespeare. LeBon describes the crowd as fickle, intellectually regressed, primitive, and driven by emotion. Affectivity is heightened and rationality all but disappears in the group or crowd mind. Freud keenly endorses LeBon's phenomenology but finds it incomplete. Lacking a highly developed notion of the unconscious, LeBon has difficulty accounting for the group's regression. Freud extends his criticism, making two points: LeBon's crowds are leaderless, while most natural as opposed to theoretical groups have leaders, and the crowd's relationship to the leader is of the essence; and that LeBon sees only the negative side of group consciousness. Freud, on the contrary, believing that the individual is always driven by narcissistic self-interest, thinks that the highest moral achievements and acts of self-abnegation are group achievements, in contradistinction to intellectual achievements, which are solely the province of individuals. So Freud with his usual exquisite sensitivity to the tragic dilemmas of human choices posits the horns of a developmental dilemma: the choice seems to lie between the utterly egotistic narcissism of the individual ideally motivated by a pure rational self-interest and a regressive, affective, and possibly morally debased, even bestial, yet possibly morally sublime sacrifice that comes with participation in a group and its "mind." Reminiscent of the stark choice between murder and suicide implicit in his dynamics of the vicissitudes of Thanatos in *Beyond the Pleasure Principle* (1920), here we have the stark choice of unvarnished narcissism or the unthinking emotionality of the herd.

LeBon's transient moblike crowds appear to have little to do with the dynamics of the family. And yet the heightened emotionality, diminished (or augmented) egoism, and lowering of intellectual level is certainly not unknown in the cauldron of family conflicts.

Freud goes on to look at McDougall's (1920) theory of the highly organized group, which seemingly is more isomorphic with the family. Such groups are characterized by continuity; clear ideas about the nature, composition, function, and capabilities of the group; interactions with similar groups with which it is nevertheless differentiated; traditions, customs, and habits; and a definite structure that provides for specialization and differentiation of functions. Freud points out that McDougall's highly organized groups have many traits of the individual. They also have many parallels to the family. In fact, McDougall's descriptive analysis of group behavior could clearly be converted into a normative theory of the "healthy" family. Again, Freud agrees with the renowned author descriptively but objects to a lack of a dynamic explanation of the organization McDougall depicts in a stable group.

Freud then turns to Trotter (1916) and his theory of a "herd" instinct or innate gregariousness in man. Although Freud sticks to his dual instinct theory—at this stage in its development, Thanatos and Eros—and will go on to give an account of the herd instinct in terms of libido, he agrees with Trotter "that the tendency towards the formation of groups is biologically a continuation of the multicellular character of all higher organisms" (Freud 1921, p. 87).

McDougall's delineation of the qualities of the enduring group have clear implications for family therapy. Structure, boundaries, clearly defined roles, purposes, and expectations all contribute to "stability." Of course, as we have seen, the inertia of the system, the forces making for the maintenance of homeostasis may ossify roles and structures into an all too stable stability characterized by pathology. Roles, purposes, and expectations may be all too clear, albeit "sick." Some addictive families may be too chaotic to be stable in McDougall's sense, while others may go on forever in the same ruts. Paradoxically, there can be stable chaos. One wonders what this theory of group dynamics implies for the more democratic family structures characteristic of some educated contemporary families, since McDougall (and Freud) imply that hierarchy is necessary for stability. Perhaps we are now evolving more egalitarian family structures than can work, but perhaps the egalitarian family is a contradiction in terms and that lack of clear power differentials simply does not work. One could argue that our divorce rates are evidence of this.

Trotter's "herd instinct" reminds Freud of Schopenhauer's parable of the freezing porcupines who cuddle together seeking warmth only to prick each other with their quills, moving apart, again freezing, and then drawing close once again only to feel those quills. We are kind of like that, neither able to subsist without others nor to sufficiently blunt our quills to be comfortably close. Whether secondary to libido or primary, Trotter's herd instinct certainly underlies man's enduring gregariousness. There is no escaping the need for others, in the family or otherwise, no matter how much pain that need may cause.

Having borrowed from LeBon, McDougall, and Trotter, Freud develops his own theory of group psychology. Freud notes that individual psychology is always group psychology. This is true both intrapsychically and interpersonally. Perhaps Winnicott (1956) made the point most succinctly when he wrote, "There is no such thing as a baby." Similarly, there is no group psychology that is not an individual psychology. Freud is essentially concerned with the dynamics of the process by which primary narcissism, which he regards as innate, evolves into feelings of solidarity with fellows, into social feeling. Although the language is foreign to Freud, he is concerned with the socialization process whether he is talking about individual development, family constellations, or group psychology. It is a bum rap to portray Freud as solely concerned with the intrapsychic understood as the unfolding of a biologically given developmental sequence of the distribution of individual energy. That is certainly in Freud, but what makes him so exhilarating is the broadness of his vision—even when his formulations are most dubiously speculative—the integration of the vicissitudes of individual development with his understanding of the forces driving human history. Too grand, too excessive, too wrong in its details, there still is nothing comparable in modern thought, no other thinker who looks at the family, at the foundations of morality and religion, at humor, at everyday errors, at dreams, at the internal world of men and women and puts them into a unified explanatory system. Freud himself compared his thoughts to the systematic delusions of a paranoid; no matter what objection you raise, it gets incorporated into the system. Freud's system is indeed too powerful, too systematic, too seamless, yet so suggestive and so fruitfully heuristic.

To return to his theory of group psychology, Freud decides to concentrate on groups with leaders and in doing so, meditates on situations in which one human being asserts strong influence on another. Three situations he comes up with are falling in love, hypnosis, and group formulation. His explanations are all in terms of drive theory, of the vicissitudes of libido. Harking back to the distinction he made the previous year in *Beyond the Pleasure Principle*, he equates his libido to Plato's Eros, the cosmic force which strives for unification and pits libidinal energy, the life force, against Thanatos, the death instinct. In group formation, in hypnosis, and in falling in love, Freud sees primarily libidinal forces at work. One is reminded of his reiterated insistence that "love is the great teacher." In falling in love we transfer our ego-libido, the primary narcissism with which we come into the world, onto another person. Ego-libido becomes object-libido. Developmentally we start in a state of autoeroticism in which there is as yet no ego (in the sense of a self), but only isolated experiences of bodily parts and states, and progress to the narcissistic stage in which all of our libidinal energy cathects—attaches to—our nascent selves (rudimentary egos), and then develop the capacity for object love in which libido flows outward to attach to objects in the world. If this process is blocked or if we are so disillusioned with the world and the objects in it that we take our marbles and go home (redirect our libido onto ourselves, a process Freud calls secondary narcissism), then we fall ill. "We must love or grow ill," says Freud. Meanwhile, a grade or graduation has been established in the ego (self) between ego and ego-ideal, between what we are and what we wish to be. When Freud develops his structure model in 1923 in *The Ego and the Id*, the ego-ideal will become a component of the superego. In falling in love, we project our ego-ideal onto the beloved and fall in love with what we wish to be. (At least, that is one important way in which we love.)

But we risk depleting our egos, impoverishing ourselves, for if we do not leave enough of a reserve of primary narcissism, of ego libido, the loving attachment to ourselves, and all of our energy goes out to cathect—literally to occupy—the loved object; there is little left to maintain our self-esteem. If our love is unrequited, we are in trouble, set up for melancholia and depression. If the love object, which may be an ideal, a social cause, or an abstraction as well as a person, dies or abandons us, then we introject the lost object, take it within ourselves, make it a part of our egos, and our rage against the abandoning object, the rejecting object, is now rage against ourselves. In Freud's poignant phrase, "The shadow of the object falls on the ego." What started out as an instinct theory about the vicissitudes of libido has become an object relations theory. So will Freud's theory of group formation.

Most explanations of hypnosis have relied on suggestion and the power of suggestion to account for the phenomenon. Freud had long been familiar with explanations using suggestion. As a young man he had translated the French hypnotist Bernheim's work into German. Even then, Freud found all this too similar to the Molière character who explains the effect of sedatives in terms of their dormative power. The issue is important because Freud finds explanations of group cohesiveness in terms of such notions as McDougall's "contagion of emotion" to explain group solidarity as equally circular and vacuous. That is why Freud wants to offer an alternate explanation, an explanation couched both in terms of the dynamics of energy—the vicissitudes of libido—and of transference, which is at bottom an object relational notion. Essentially Freud analyzes hypnosis in terms of two kinds of transference: a mother transference motivated by love, and a father transference motivated by fear. As in falling in love, libido moves from self to object, and Freud invokes unconscious ideation to account for the absence of conscious thoughts about the hypnotist in the hypnotized. It is a short step from both the transfer of libido to the loved object, and the submission to the power of the father-hypnotist, to group psychology. Note the ambition, the broad sweep of Freud's account. To be part of a group is to fall in love; to be part of the group is to be hypnotized, just as love and hypnosis are themselves group phenomena, albeit dyadic ones.

To analyze what is unique about the group psychology of enduring groups with structure and leaders, Freud examines two "artificial" groups: the church (here preeminently the Catholic church) and the army. He concludes that they work because all of the members feel equally loved by the leader: Jesus Christ and the commander-in-chief, respectively. This condition of equality reduces sibling rivalry and makes possible strong feelings of solidarity with fellow congregants/soldiers. Egotism is forsworn and one "loves one's brother as oneself." Being (or feeling) equally loved by the "father" leader is the sine qua non of group cohesion. Cain and Jacob, who murder and swindle their brothers, respectively, and who are our mythic cases of sibling rivalry, did not feel equally loved by their father-leaders. One loves one's fellow group members, feels a libidinal tie to them, one in which the original sexual aim of libido has been deflected or sublimated. It is Eros that makes group cohesion possible. An aim diverted Eros, but Eros nonetheless.

Is this libidinal bond homosexual? Freud says it doesn't really matter; the point is that it is an aim-inhibited libidinal energy. Centuries earlier, Plato (375 BC), in his great dialogue on love *The Symposium*, had suggested that homosexual love was good for the army because the lover would act heroically to win the praise (love) of his beloved. Be that as it may, love holds groups together.

Freud continues his analysis. What is it about the group leader that enlists the devotion of the group members? First he is a love object—

the beloved. All members of the group are in love with the leader. Their libido is invested in an *ideal* object; what libido is left is invested in one's "brothers in Christ" or one's "comrades in combat." Like the hypnotist, the leader exercises enormous power over the led. Here what is at work is a father transference. Freud speaks of the "lust for submission." Finally, and perhaps most important, the leader becomes the ego-ideal of each and every group member. This is partly a matter of projection, the individual projects his ego-ideal onto the leader, but much more it is a matter of introjection or identification. The member brothers identify with the ego-ideal of the leader and make it their own. This primary identification with the leader, who is internalized as the ego-ideal, makes possible and relatively facile the secondary identification of the brothers with each other.

Although Freud's analysis is in terms of father and brothers, there is no reason why the same analysis cannot be applied to mother and sisters, or leader and brothers and sisters. Something like this happens in twelve-step groups in which the Program/Higher Power becomes the common ego-ideal and the band of recovering brothers and sisters in sharing this ego-ideal identify with each other. Twelve-step puts tremendous emphasis on identification as a curative mechanism.

Let us summarize Freud's group psychology: groups function differently than individuals, their very essence entails a relinquishing of primary narcissism and a transformation of ego-libido into aim-inhibited object-libido; short-term leaderless groups demonstrate instinctual and ego regression operating at a debased intellectual level, are driven affectively, and are capable of both unmitigated savagery and the highest levels of self sacrificing morality. Enduring groups are highly structured and have leaders who serve as the common ego-ideal of the group members, who in turn identify with and love each other while hating those outside of the group. Such groups are naturally democratic (since each member is equally loved or feels equally loved by the leader) and capable of high levels of cooperation and mutuality. Freud is aware that such artificial groups as the church and the army are organized hierarchically, but sees each level of the hierarchy as exhibiting the "leader-equally loved followers" structure, so the essentially democratic nature of such groups is preserved within their hierarchical structures.

The implications for family dynamics of Freud's group psychology are fairly obvious. "Leaderless" families, if any be such, will be more primitive, more emotional, less rational, and more erratic and unstable than those with a strong leader, and paradoxically the strongly led group, provided that the leader (parent) loves the followers (children) equally, will be more democratic, or at least more egalitarian within the sibling system than one with diffuse leadership. Further, group cohesion is only possible through the relinquishing of narcissism, or since there is conservation of psychic no less than physical energy, the transformation of a significant part of ego-libido into object-libido. The family will share an ego-ideal, which is an identification with the parent(s), and this shared ego-ideal facilitates their mutual identification. The conversion of the sexual into the affectionate, that is, the aim inhibition of libido is a necessary condition of group solidarity. It follows from this that whatever else incest and sexual abuse do, they make family solidarity and cohesion impossible.

There is another aspect of Freud's thought on group formation expressed a decade earlier in *Totem and Taboo* (1913b), which has possible relevance to the family therapy of the addictions. There Freud expounds his "scientific myth" of the horde—primitive band—of brothers led by a ruthless, utterly narcissistic primal father who maintains exclusive possession of all of the women—mother and sisters—forcing the brothers' libido into aim inhibited bonds with one another. Eventually, perhaps under the leadership of one of them, they rebelled and slew the father, ripping him into shreds and consuming him in a totem meal, thereby demonstrating their "devouring affection" for him. Here identification becomes literally incorporation, enacting its originally biological basis in oral "love" for the object (cf. Christian communion and Jewish *kiddush* as incorporation-identification ceremonies).

This cannibalistic, manic feeding frenzy deepens the bond between the brothers, who now share their guilt. The manic high is followed by the depressive fear, guilt, and shame. In a reaction formation, that is, a turning into its opposite, against their murderous and cannibalistic thoughts (and enactments), the slain father is transformed into the deity (or totem animal) and worshiped. Now the band of brothers once more shares an ego-ideal of the now deified leader-father. In this drama, Freud sees the basis of religion and morality. Morality is at base a reaction formation to parricide. Poor anthropology perhaps, but brilliant psychology, whatever it may say about Freud's feelings toward his own father.

I would like to suggest that Freud's scientific myth may give a pretty good account of one dynamic of (particularly although not necessarily exclusively male) addiction. In the ingestion of the drug during a drug orgy, the unconscious fantasy of the drinking/drugging frantic, manic participants may indeed be the murderous cannibalistic identification with, incorporation of, the loved/hated father. Taking him in in this way not only tears and shreds him into bits, assuring that the dangerous, ingested object is now safely within, safely under control, but also makes his strength available to the orgyists. "Not only have I destroyed father by getting high, I have become him." The well-known phenomenon of intense feelings of camaraderie during the drinking/drugging bout can be partially attributed to the sharing of the "totem meal" with all of its possibilities for mutual identification. Then comes the crash/hangover and the guilt/fear of retaliation for the manic cannibalistic act. It may be the case that the extraordinary curative power of sharing guilt at twelve-step meetings may be in part attributable to just such an unconscious drama; *mutatus mutandis*, something similar can be attributed to the dynamics of female addiction. If there is anything in my fantasy, it may be usefully interpretable in either individual, group, or family therapy. Although what is described here is a group activity taking place with actual others, whatever the accompanying unconscious intrapsychic fantasy, the same dynamic may be acted purely in unconscious fantasy by the solitary drugger/drinker. Since addiction usually leads to progressive isolation, the fantasy necessarily replaces reality as addiction progresses.

Wilfred Bion

One of the most clinically useful as well as conceptual powerful analyses of group behavior was made by Wilfred Bion, an English psychiatrist and analyst. As a young psychiatrist before the Second World War, Bion came under the influence of Melanie Klein and became a Kleinian analyst. As a military psychiatrist during the war, he found his analytic skills of limited utility. More out of necessity than conviction, he started conducting therapy groups. He found group therapy highly efficacious in treating his shell-shocked patients. After the war, he continued group work, understanding group dynamics from an object relations perspective.

In 1961, he published *Experiences in Groups*, a slim volume chock full of insight. Bion saw that every group operated on two levels simultaneously: a realistic *task* or work level and an unconscious or *basic assumption* level. There is a clear parallel here to the distinction between conscious and unconscious motivation and mentation in individuals. Every group is a work or task group including the therapy group (or family therapy group) whose task is the acquisition of insight into its own process. Every group simultaneously pursues its basic assumptions—its unconscious aggressive, sexual, and dependence needs. Aggression is expressed by fight or flight fantasies and action, dependency needs by dependent fantasies and behavior, and sexual needs by *pairing*; the unconscious fantasy of both the group and couple doing the pairing is that they will conceive the Savior or Messiah. It is only because the group believes that the pair will conceive the Messiah that it tolerates pairing. Freud considered sexual pairing as antithetical to group cohesion, seeing it as an expression of individual libido and as such representing withdrawal of the aim-inhibited libidinal energy that Freud believed bound the group together. Totalitarian and totalistic groups (societies) of various sorts have tended to agree with Freud and severely restrict pairing. Of course, every group that wants biological continuity has to make some provision for pairing and indeed for the family. David Scharff (1992) has added a fourth basic assumption: fusion-fission, the need to fuse (merge) and the need to isolate (fragment).

Families are very usefully viewed as simultaneously pursuing tasks—raising children, mourning losses, earning money—and pursuing the unconscious basic assumptions of fight/flight, dependency, pairing, and fusion/fission. The basic assumption may contribute to the work of the group or it may undermine it, but in either case it is a mostly unconscious process. Addicted families tend to do poorly as task groups and to be driven, more than most, by their unconscious basic assumptions.

For the moment, let us move away from analytic and dynamic theories and practices, and take a look at Jay Haley's strategic family therapy, Salvador Minuchin's structural family therapy, Karl Whitaker's experiential family therapy, and Murray Bowen's intergenerational systems family therapy.

STRATEGIC FAMILY THERAPY

You will probably not be amazed to learn that strategic family therapy is about *strategies*. The strategic family therapist self-consciously tries to contrive a strategy to bring about change. Such strategies are by their very nature ad hoc, designed to fit a particular situation and in that sense, are spontaneous and creative. They also tend to be manipulative and gimmicky. Although there are some underlying assumptions such as the saliency of communication and miscommunication in family dysfunction and a clear view of the ubiquity of power struggles and differentials, strategic thinkers are generally aggressively atheoretical, particularly if the theory purports to explain underlying causality as does most dynamic theory. Metapsychology is anathema to this school. Its whole emphasis is on what, or perhaps how, rather than why whatever goes on goes on. Although there is no reason that a strategic approach could not be taken in individual psychotherapy and in fact often is without being labeled such, the term *strategic therapy* means strategic family therapy. Strategic therapy grew out of Bateson's and his associates' work on the double bind and thus was paradoxically originally theory-driven, that theory being a theory about communication. Strategic therapy is largely the creation of Jay

Haley (1976, 1984, 1990), who was one of the original members of Bateson's group at Palo Alto and he, like them, started by analyzing the communication patterns of couples and families. Pathology was garbled communication and the task of the therapist was to improve communication by making the covert overt, by clarifying, by disturbing double binds by commenting on them, and by pointing out various language games people play. To try and improve communication is to be on the side of the angels and all therapists do it when analyzing the communications of the individual patient to the therapist or commenting on the communication patterns of the family.

One of the most effective interventions that I can remember making was to a recovering alcoholic woman who referred to "it," "that," "them," "the book," "the event," and so forth, without stating the antecedent of these unqualified pronouns or unspecified nouns. For a while I guessed, then I began telling her that I didn't know what "it" was or to which book she was referring. Sue experienced my comments as narcissistic wounds and angrily replied, "I know I stink at communication." She was a person who experienced herself as radically different from others, a perception that was a source of both pain and pride. In fact, she thought that she was crazy. I empathized with her hurt at my telling her that she wasn't communicating, but I stuck to my guns calling her on it whenever (unless some affectively significant process was under way I didn't wish to interrupt) she failed to communicate. Although this was individual therapy, my interventions were strategic ones. I didn't analyze the defensive purpose of her evasiveness nor its genetic roots in defense and in deficit, although we eventually got to that too. Slowly listening to her became less mystifying and "it" became concrete happenings or definite feelings. As time went on, she experienced herself as less and less "crazy."

Yes, improving communication is certainly work fit for the gods. Yet it has become such a cliché. I haven't seen a couple in years in which at least the wife, and often both of them, didn't say, "We are having trouble communicating." Sometimes that is true, maybe even often, and the couple doesn't exist whose communication can't be improved, but very often communication isn't really the problem. Communication has become another place to hide, another defense. The real problem isn't the *lack* of communication, it is the *content* of the communication, a content one or both of the partners don't wish to hear. "He doesn't know how to communicate" often means "He is telling me that he doesn't love me and I don't want to hear it." A very effective, albeit painful, intervention is to point out that the problem isn't lack of communication but the content of the communication. Communication is more than verbal, and the husband who "doesn't talk" to his wife is sending a powerful message. Gesture, tone of voice, and silence are all meaningful means of communication.

Haley, along with the rest of the Batesonians, was fascinated by paradox. *Paradoxical communication* is a kind of weak double bind. It doesn't drive you crazy, but it obfuscates and confuses. The analysis of paradox and paradoxical communication led to a view of language as simultaneously operating on two levels: content and qualification of content. Bateson and his associate Watzlawick called this second level metacommunication. I prefer to reserve the term *metacommunication* to communications about communications, which is much closer to its usual meaning, but not consistent with Bateson's usage. For Bateson metacommunication is part of the communication and a structural component of all communication, while in my usage it is simply comment on language and may be made by the speaker, by a scientific analyst, by a therapist, or by any other observer. Many strategic thinkers have commented on the multilayered nature of language and communication, making such distinctions as overt and covert, content and relationship, and surface and depth.

Overt and covert is fairly clear; content is just what it says, while the relationship aspect of the communication is always a command. In other words, behind every communication there's a power struggle. Somebody is trying to be top dog. Language here is a weapon and what is said is the least of what is meant. The issue is always control. It is interesting that the atheoretical strategists, at least here on their

communication side, sound so much like Freud talking about unconscious motivation. The dynamic unconscious simultaneously
atemporal and driven by the past, personal and (racially) historical,
becomes a covert here-and-now power message (in its relationship
aspect) of the content of a communication, and, much like the
analyst making the unconscious conscious, the strategic therapist
makes the covert power struggle contained within the linguistic
exchange overt.

Watzlawick (1978) developed a technique or strategy of the *therapeutic double bind*, which often takes the form of prescribing the symptom. Bateson in his paper on addiction alludes to AA members telling a recalcitrant drinker to "go out and tie one on." If the drinker
follows the "prescription," John Barleycorn himself may convince the
drinker the game isn't worth the candle, and if he doesn't follow the
prescription he gets a chance to try sobriety. Ideally the therapeutic
double bind sets up a win-win situation. In "I want you to become
'more anxious,'" the anxious person may increase his anxiety only to
discover that he can control his anxiety, or he may refuse, similarly
learning that he can control his anxiety, thereby changing if he does
and changing if he doesn't. The languages of change seem to be right
hemisphere stuff—analogy, paradox, symbol, ambiguity—rather than
logical, sequential left hemisphere stuff. Again the atheoretical fellows can't seem to get away from theory. A communication theorist
like Watzlawick would not see it that way, but he is talking about
tapping primary process rather than using secondary process thinking to affect change. Strategists use the unconscious, rather than trying to understand it. Manipulating dragons is an inherently risky business, but the therapeutic double bind has its successful moments. Like
most therapists, I occasionally use paradox, therapeutic double binds,
and prescribing the symptom; I only wish that I had found these techniques (strategies) as efficacious as their advocates would have it.

Another strategy is *reframing*, also called *relabeling*, which usually
means putting a positive spin on a symptom or symptomatic behavior. To the pot-smoking college student who angrily says to his furious mother, "You really don't want me to stop or you wouldn't have
given me that bottle of whiskey for Christmas," the therapist says,

"She was trying to save you money so you could put it toward tuition." An absurd example, although I've heard worse, but relabeling or reframing can be highly mutative. A more dynamic take on reframing is to interpret the adaptive function of the symptom or behavior. "Your drug use is your way of asserting your identity" is both a reframing and an interpretation of the adaptive meaning of the patient's use.

The surface versus depth analysis of language use is essentially the creation of Noam Chomsky (1957). Chomsky developed his theory of *generative grammar*: innate, preprogrammed grammatical and syntactical structures that are universal and underlie all language acquisition and use. It is the indwelling of these generative grammatical structures in all people that makes communication possible. Chomsky's work was ingeniously adapted by Leonard Bernstein, in his Norton Lectures at Harvard, to argue that music is characterized by an aesthetic surface and an innate depth structure that make possible the universality of music. As far as I know, Chomsky's version of language and metalanguage has not come to the attention of psychotherapeutic observers of communication. Its therapeutic implication would seem to be that every communication, no matter how "crazy," has to be meaningful because the underlying structure is a variant on the universal one that makes communication possible in the first place, and that if the therapist can get to the depth structure, the latent meaning can be made manifest. The essential notion here is that all communication, including the nonsensical, contradictory, and paradoxical can be decoded and understood.

Haley went on from his Batesonian communication therapy approach to work with Minuchin at the Philadelphia Child Guidance Center and then to develop his own approach. Like so many of the founders of family therapy schools he is a highly charismatic figure whose techniques are not easily transferable or learned. But some learning is possible. Haley does many things, all of them *directive*. Let us examine some of his techniques and his rationalizations for them.

Haley's central insight is that all relationships, including, in fact especially including, that between therapist and patient, are *power relationships*. Whether through our use of language, our gestures, our body postures, or our overt behavior, we are always trying to establish dominance and control. If we fail, then it is we who are being dominated and controlled. Of course one can control through one's weakness, and no one is more attuned to the power of passive aggression (although that wouldn't be his terminology) than Haley. As an immediate corollary of the ubiquity of power in human relations, Haley stresses the absolute necessity of the therapist's taking control, and his entire thrust is directive.

Haley's (1990) *Strategies of Psychotherapy* views both Carl Rogers's nondirective therapy and Freud's evenly covering attention and therapeutic neutrality as acts of bad faith or at best manifestations of naïveté. According to Haley all therapy is, in reality, directive, and there is always an enormous power differential between therapist and patient. Whether acknowledged or not, the therapist controls the patient and that is exactly the way it should be, only the control should be overt and self-conscious. The intervention, "I am not going to tell you what to do," is paradoxical. If the patient finds his own solution he is following the therapist's directive, and if he refuses to follow the directive of the therapist and goes his own way, he is doing exactly what the therapist implicitly directed. So the nondirective therapist or analyst, in refusing to direct, is actually ineluctably directive. Haley and the strategists in general love such paradoxes, seeing their masterly use as the epitome of strategic therapy. Paradox and dialectical reversal there certainly is, but somehow Haley is simply too clever; everything is turned into a therapeutic paradox, and his solutions are a little too facile. Without suggesting any dishonesty on his part, I don't quite believe his cures.

Haley (1973) was particularly influenced by Milton Erickson, the hypnotist (how does one relate to a renowned hypnotist except by being influenced by him), and curiously like Freud made hypnosis a model for understanding human relations. As we have seen, for Freud, hypnosis is to be explained by displacement and projection of libido onto the hypnotist, by displacement of the ego ideal onto the hypnotist, and by both father and mother transferences. Haley, atheoretical (at least in theory) and here and now, will have none of libido or transference, and he sees hypnosis purely in terms of one human being gaining control over another. Again control is the issue. What Haley is interested in is the technique or strategy of gaining control, while Freud wishes to understand the dynamic whereby the therapist gains power. Haley wants to know how; Freud why. The Ericksonian how that Haley was to incorporate into strategic family therapy was oddly enough *indirection*. Erickson controlled by not controlling in the sense that he joined (or circumvented) the resistance. For instance, he sometimes lulled people into a hypnotic state by gently talking to them. But once he did he was highly directive, his directive often assuming the form of prescribing the symptom. One of Erickson's most famous interventions occurred in his work with a paranoid schizophrenic who believed he was Jesus. Erickson hypnotized him and gave him the directive that he was to become a carpenter. Being congruent with the patient's ego ideal, indeed with his identity, he learned carpentry and greatly improved.

Haley was hardly the first to see that all human relations have a power dimension. His work is reminiscent of Hegel's, Sartre's, and once again Freud's. In Hegel's *Phenomenology of Mind* (Spirit) (1807), his account of the adventures of mind as manifested in human thought, art, religious institutions, and philosophy, one famous chapter is on the "Dialectic of Master and Slave." Hegel's analysis is an analysis of paradox. The master can only be master by being master of the slave; hence, he is dependent on the slave for his identity, as well as for his service, and the slave becomes in some sense the master of the master and the master the slave of the slave. The relationship between master and slave is inherently paradoxical or to use Hegel's word, *dialectical*. The remark of the sadist to the masochist to the effect that "I refuse to beat you" comes to mind. The master and the slave are inextricably intertwined, neither having definition or reality without the other. Haley could not agree more.

Jean-Paul Sartre, the existential philosopher, is heavily indebted to Hegel for both his terminology and his conceptual scheme. The Sartrian dialectic between *Being and Nothingness* (No-thing-ness) (1956) comes out of Hegel and the *Phenomenology*. In Sartre's ontology (catalogue of the types of being) there are being-in-itself and being-for-itself. *Being-in-itself* is substantial, solid, enduring—in short, thingness, while *being-for-itself* is consciousness which is precisely no-thing, insubstantial, pure negativity. According to Sartre, all human beings are driven by the need to be the in-itself-for-itself, a thing that is conscious of being a thing and a consciousness that has the solidity of a stone. But the in-itself-for-itself cannot be; it is a self-contradictory notion. From this Sartre concludes that "man is a futile passion." Futile passion or not, we each have a "project," or as Haley would have it, a strategy to become the consciousness substantial and the solidity conscious of itself, and we carry out that project among other ways in our human relations.

In his famous analysis of the gaze, Sartre postulates that when one person meets another there is an immediate struggle to see which of the two will turn the other into an object of his consciousness, to ob-jectify and control the other, thereby achieving a simulacrum of the impossible state of being in-itself-for-itself. If I reduce you to an object of my gaze—consciousness—then your solidity becomes the thingness my consciousness seeks, and conversely the one reduced to objectivity now becomes the objectification of the other's consciousness and as such a representation of the impossible project of becoming the in-it-self-for-itself. But, says Sartre, this is "bad faith" because one can only be reduced to an object by consciously choosing to be reduced and stones don't make conscious decisions or have consciousness. So much like Hegel's master the winner of the gaze game can only be the win-ner through an act of the other's consciousness. Both the dominance and submission strategies fail and man is indeed a "futile passion." Haley would say that both Hegel and Sartre are completely right in their emphasis on strife and the struggle to control in human relations, but would contend that both Hegel and Sartre lose the reality of power in psychological subtlety. After all, the master can beat or even kill the slave, and the slave, no matter how "dialectically" in control, cannot beat the master. Similarly the one reduced to the object by the other *is* in some sense objectified no matter how consensually.

Certainly none was more attuned to the emptiness of convention-ality and the reality of the underlying instinctual motivation than Freud, and Haley's analysis of power sounds surprisingly like psycho-analysis stripped of libido and historical reference. Haley is, so to speak, a here-and-now single drive therapist, that drive being the quest for power, otherwise known as aggression.

Haley's analyses of symptoms also center on control. The purpose of a symptom is to control others. What Freud saw as the secondary gain from an illness is for the ahistorical asymbolic Haley the primary gain. Further, the symptom may serve as a control device or power advantage for other members of the family. Thus a symptom cannot be understood as an intrapsychic (or biochemical) event but only as an interpersonal (or better systemic) one. The clear assumption behind this understanding of a symptom is that the patient has control; that, as Sartre said, man indeed is "condemned to be free."

The implications of this concept for drug addiction treatment are clear. Drug use being a symptom like any other, it must have some interpersonal significance; let us say to be taken care of by the other family members. (The disease concept of addiction is clearly taboo to this school.) Haley would not interpret as might a dynamic therapist, but would urge the family members to continue to caretake on the assumption that they will resist him and cease caretaking, which will deny the drugger his or her payoff and presumably put an end to the symptom.

Not all strategic therapists are as highly directive and manipulative as Haley. His wife, Chloe Madanes (1984), has developed a softer edge, "playful" version of strategic therapy.

Haley makes an extreme statement to which I take exception, namely that the "patient" cannot get "well" unless the family does. Since the function of the symptom is to control the rest of the family it is logical that there would be absolutely no reason to change if the family continued to let itself be controlled, and conversely if the family were threatened by the patient's changing and its homeostasis put in jeopardy, it would undermine the patient to make sure no change occurred. From a systems viewpoint, Haley is right, but people flee systems and they change in spite of environmental resistance to that change. If they could not and did not, there would be no hope for the myriad of addicts who live in dysfunctional, usually heavily drug or alcohol involved, families. I have treated many patients who lived in just such environments who recovered nevertheless; so Haley's claim is contrary to fact. What does frequently happen is that the dysfunctional system literally disintegrates when one member, usually the identified patient, recovers.

Although Haley overstates his case, it is true that it is extraordinarily difficult to change when everyone around you is fighting that change, even as they loudly advocate it. If the patient is a child or otherwise totally dependent, the situation may indeed be hopeless unless the system can be broken up. The most powerful implication of Haley's claim is that family therapy is the only way to go, since change is only possible if all family members change.

To summarize strategic therapy, it (1) establishes the therapist's control; (2) is highly directive; (3) believes that the whole system needs to be changed; (4) devises strategies to bring about the required change; (5) relies heavily on reframing, paradoxical interventions, and prescribing the symptom; and (6) views symptoms as having covert, interpersonal purposes that are under the control of the patient.

MILAN SCHOOL OF SYSTEMIC FAMILY THERAPY

The Milan school of systemic family therapy shares many elements of the strategic approach. However its members, the best known of whom is Mara Selvini Palazzoli, all started as analysts and their analytic training influenced their work. Working with families with anorexic or psychotic children, the Milan group (Selvini Palazzoli et al. 1978) turned a logistical problem, the great distances many of their families had to travel, into an asset by deliberately scheduling infrequent therapy sessions. Typically, they would see a family once a month for a total of ten or so sessions. They call this "long brief therapy." The reason they do this is to allow families time to do their "homework" and reflect on both the session and the consequences of the homework. It also gives the family the idea that they can solve their problems. The Milan group so strongly believes in this structure that they refuse any contact with the family between sessions and will not schedule an emergency session.

Like Haley, they are highly directive, but in a sort of nondirective way. The Milan group works as a team. Two therapists, usually a man and a woman, work with the family while colleagues observe from behind a one-way mirror. At regular intervals the observers meet with the therapists to generate hypotheses about the symptom and its function. The therapists then return and question the family in such a way as to confirm or disconfirm the hypothesis. The questioning is "circular," that is, intended to lay bare the feedback loops maintaining the behavior. Unlike Haley, the Milan group stresses the necessity of the therapists' maintaining neutrality, never being for or against any family member. This is undoubtedly a legacy of their psychoanalytic training. Milanian therapy makes heavy use of *positive connotation*, that is, reframing in such a way as to put a positive twist on the symptom(s). This goes with a gentle, nonconfrontational style in which the therapists supply information (a reframing of the psychoanalytic notion of interpretation) about family functioning and dysfunctioning and prescribe family rituals, for example, the parents are to go out once a week together, without telling the children where they are going, as a way of disengaging an enmeshed family.

The Milan group believes that much symptomatic behavior results from a false epistemology, that is, a mistaken belief system, and that information will change this. That aspect of their treatment is rational or cognitive, while the prescribed rituals are experiential—change through doing. Through hypothesizing and circular, that is, systematic, questioning, the Milan group generates strategies, making their therapy a variant of strategic family therapy. Essentially agreeing with Socrates that sin (dysfunction) is ignorance, the Milan group tries to enlighten, putting much less emphasis than Haley on power as the dominant human motivation.

The Milan group's emphasis on therapeutic ritual is especially interesting in light of the claim in the alcoholic family literature that families whose rituals around holidays, birthdays, vacations, and so forth are intact are immune from pathological consequences to the nondrinking family members. This is to some degree tautological since the families with intact rituals may simply be the least pathological ones *and* it is contrary to my clinical experience, but it does suggest that the prescribing of ritual in and of itself, apart from the content or nature of that ritual, may be therapeutic.

The Milan group also relies heavily on counterparadoxes, which are similar to Haley's therapeutic double binds. Selvini Palazzoli claims great success with this method. The original Milan group no longer exists as such and its members have gone their own ways, but many family therapy institutes teach the Milan approach.

Selvini Palazzoli no longer believes that families are primarily driven by the need to maintain homeostasis or at least are not exclusively so. Her view of homeostasis is the notion that pathological families are stuck in unrecognized destructive patterns of interaction. Accordingly, she agrees with Haley that change is only possible if the whole system changes. Milan's prescriptions are intended to change the family rules, the unacknowledged, or for me unconscious, games the family plays. Like Haley, the Milan version of strategic therapy relies far more heavily on counterritual, countergames, and paradox than it does on information giving. It is essentially a form of family insight therapy, with insight being seen to be too weak to do much without the reinforcement of prescriptions. As the Milan group and its members have evolved, they are more and more seeing families as driven by the need for growth as well as pathologically resisting change. In the United States the foremost exponent of the Milan approach has been Lynn Hoffman (1981) and the Ackerman Institute in New York City.

Strategic therapy in all its variants—communication, Haleyian, and Milan systemic—although it borrows much more from psychodynamic theory than it would care to admit, has many overlaps with both cognitive and behavioral therapy. Its directive, here-and-now approach is often useful in substance abuse. However, its gimmicky, not-quite-straight quality is, to me, off-putting. But the distasteful may nevertheless be effective and the countermanipulation of the manipulative has a place in addiction treatment.

STRUCTURAL FAMILY THERAPY

If the point of strategic therapy is the development of strategies to effectuate change, the point of structural therapy is to elucidate the structure of the family—its recurrent patterns of interaction, its hierarchies (or lack of them), its boundaries and their degree of rigidity or permeability, its subsystems, and its coalitions, and to use this information to change the structure. The structuralists largely agree with the strategists that no change is possible unless the structure is modified or it will fight any change. There is a great deal of overlap between the schools, and Haley spent considerable time as a structuralist.

As with so many of the schools, structural therapy is associated with a charismatic leader, in this case Salvador Minuchin. Minuchin is a genuinely colorful and interesting person. An Argentine specializing in pediatrics, he emigrated to Israel after medical school to fight in Israel's war of liberation as an army doctor. He later moved to the United States where he retrained as a child psychiatrist with a heavily dynamic orientation. Minuchin entered analytic training but left to work with children who had survived the Holocaust and with Sephardic immigrants in Israel. Returning once again to the United States, he entered into what was perhaps his most formative experience, his eight years as a psychiatrist in the Wiltwych School for Delinquent Adolescents. Wiltwych had an illustrious pedigree, having attracted the attention and support of such notables as Eleanor Roosevelt; it also had a treatment-resisting, highly recalcitrant population of mostly black and Puerto Rican children from the worst neighborhoods in New York. Most of what became structural therapy came out of Minuchin's Wiltwych experience. He found that the insight-oriented, dynamic approach he had been trained in simply didn't work. He found that individual therapy per se was ineffectual, since participation in the family structure quickly undid whatever gains came out of the milieu and individual therapy of the training school. Never one to be daunted or to let an opportunity pass him by, Minuchin started to work with the families as well as with the kids, and soon modified Ackerman's (1994) psychoanalytic approach to family therapy to suit his temperament and population, evolving structural therapy as he went along. His efforts culminated in what came to be considered a classic book, *Families of the Slums* (Minuchin et al. 1967).

Having solidified his new technique, Minuchin left Wiltwych to found the Philadelphia Child Guidance Clinic, catering almost exclusively to an impoverished black population. It was a huge success and was affiliated with Children's Hospital, a University of Pennsylvania teaching institution. Here Minuchin's attention turned to the structural family therapy of psychosomatic illness, anorexia nervosa in particular. As we shall see in Chapter 4, Stanton and Todd developed one of the first family treatments expressly designed to treat addictions at the Philadelphia Child Guidance Center by modifying Minuchin's structural approach. Edward Kaufman (Kaufman and Kaufmann 1992), another pioneer in family work with addicts, also acknowledges his debt to Minuchin. It is no accident that Minuchin and colleagues (1978) entitled their book on the psychological treatment of diabetes, asthma, and anorexia *Psychosomatic Families*. The identified patient might be the somatizer, but the·"illness" resides in the family structure.

Leaving the University of Pennsylvania in 1981, Minuchin went on to become a superstar, giving compelling lectures and demonstrations to a worldwide audience. Such activity suits his flamboyant, theatrical style, and he puts on an extraordinarily compelling show. Unlike so much of the family literature (Haley's writing has clarity, organization, and a clear thrust, but tends to be dull and rather unexciting), Minuchin is a good read. He comes across as having conceptual power and literary skill and his sometimes gimmicky, manipulative clinical style is nowhere in evidence in his professional writings. A fascinating and no doubt well-lived life, but what can it tell us about families, addiction, and their treatment? Can a charismatic style be learned? Or should it be? I am not sure, but there is some solid stuff underneath the theatrics that can be incorporated by therapists taking different paths.

What Minuchin has to teach is analysis of family structure and technique. I find the analysis more valuable than the technique. Minuchin (1992, p. 6) states, "The therapeutic process will be that of changing family members' psychosocial position vis-à-vis each other." So the therapist is going to actively assert control to change the role relations within the system. The family structure is the sum total of the customary interactions within the system. They are relatively enduring (some may be short-lived, ad hoc arrangements), but in health not invariant or inflexible. Within that structure are subsystems—spousal, parental, sibling, and individual; the self is seen as a subsystem of the family. In health the subsystems are organized hierarchically. They also stand in reciprocal, complementary relationship to one another. One cannot be a father without a child. Boundaries are of the essence. If boundaries between subsystems are too rigid, the result is disengagement, a family characterized by lack of cohesion, support, and warmth; at the opposite pole is the enmeshed family characterized by all-too permeable, diffuse boundaries, intrusions, and lack of differentiation.

A healthy, nurturing environment both meets the needs of its members for affiliation and bonding, and provides the matrix out of which differentiation and individuation occur. As Minuchin (1992, p. 2) puts it, "Dependency and autonomy are complementary, not conflicting, characteristics of the human condition." The object relations family therapist David Scharff makes exactly the same point when borrowing Winnicott's term. He says that the healthy family provides the *holding environment* necessary for maturation, separation, and individuation. Here analyst and systems theorist concur. Paradoxically, the disengaged family disables the development of autonomy no less than the enmeshed one. It is interesting to compare Margaret Mahler's (Mahler et al. 1975) ego-psychological description with Minuchin's systems perspective and Scharff's object relations focus. She too sees individuation as coming out of a matrix of connectedness, stressing the importance of being able to return home safely (re-merge with mother), in what she calls the rapprochement stage of separation-individuation, if a healthy sense of autonomous self is to be achieved. Mahler is saying exactly the same thing as Minuchin, only in a dyadic field of mother and child rather than from a broader systems viewpoint.

Minuchin, unlike Haley and the communications people, focuses on self and its social determinants. Self to him is an accustomed set of responses learned in the family that slowly takes on an individual color. Self, like family, is challenged by too rapid change and may not be able to integrate new relations, values, knowledge, or demands. When it cannot, it becomes "sick." The Minuchinian self in no way lacks individuality, yet always exists within and is defined by, no less than it defines, the *family*.

Minuchin sees family pathology as rigidity, a rigidity that sets in if the stress is too great for the resources of the system. Pathology is a response to overload. His view of homeostasis differs from that of the Batesonians. Healthy families are basically open; they have conservation mechanisms that guarantee stability and ongoingness, but they are also flexible, protean, and responsive to internal and external change. The inherent homeostatic mechanisms do not ossify. But when the resources of the system are depleted and overloaded, a defensive rigidity sets in and the homeostatic mechanisms go into overdrive. There is a curious parallel here with the notion of Peter Kramer (1993), author of *Listening to Prozac*, to the effect that much psychopathology is a depletion phenomenon, the depletion here seen as proximally neurochemical but distally the result of stress. That is, working from the perspective of individual therapy, Kramer sees much psychopathology as a consequence of a nervous system depletion of optimal levels of neurotransmitters by trauma, or as he puts it, there is a neurochemical as well as an ideational memory, and trauma is encoded in neurochemical vulnerability.

Minuchin, from a systems approach, sees the same phenomenon only differently: a system functional yet vulnerable by virtue of boundary problems, weak hierarchies, and blurred role expectations encounters stress—developmental or otherwise—and cannot accommodate to it. Instead it rigidifies and becomes symptomatic. Just as Kramer has scant interest in the traumatic antecedents of the neurochemical depletion intervening pharmacologically in the present, Minuchin has little interest in the historical roots of the dysfunction, claiming that, in most cases, insight into how things got to the present impasse is not necessary for change to take place, and attempts to modify the present structure to enable growth.

In trying to understand the family structure, Minuchin pays particular attention to alignments and coalitions. Is the son in alignment with the mother? Do the children form a coalition against the parents? Clearly related to concern with coalitions is making overt the power relationships in the family. For Minuchin as for Haley, power is primordial and ineluctable. Far from seeing power as malignant, Minuchin sees much pathology as flowing from weakness, from lack of power, particularly of parents. One of Minuchin's more useful technical terms is the *detour in coalition*, a condition in which the problems within a natural coalition, say of the spouses, is evaded by one or the other parent forming a detour in coalition with one of the children. This results in triangulation, in which the child is drawn in as an ally of one parent against the other. This is always detrimental. The notion of triangles as avoidance mechanisms and of the multitudinous varieties of triangulation was developed much more fully by Murray Bowen (see below).

Minuchin creates structural maps as heuristic and didactic devices that make immediately clear the structural relations in the family— its hierarchies; subsystems; clear, diffuse, or rigid boundaries; and affiliations, conflicts, coalitions, enmeshments, and detours. A structural map is illustrated in the Baker case (see Chapter 4).

The structuralist is active, directive, and provocative, challenging frozen dysfunctional patterns, and insisting that parents exercise parental authority (use their power) and that subsystems be differentiated. One form of that challenge is a reframing, not in terms of putting a positive twist on the symptom, but by redefining the symptom as a systemic one. The identified patient ceases to be the patient, and the structure is put on the couch. This approach in itself radically changes structure. There is no attempt at insight; action precedes understanding, but insight may follow the change. Of course, the switch from an intrapsychic to systems viewpoint, from looking at the sick kid to asking what's going on to keep the sick kid sick, is a form of insight, but the structuralists would deny this. Change relationship patterns and the "cure" is here. This makes structuralism a close ally of behaviorism.

All this is very well; just get the parents to be parents, engage but disenmesh, establish clear boundaries, and all will be well. Maybe, but how? Minuchin's method shares much with Haley's; the therapist must be a commanding presence. He gets to be that commanding presence by *joining* the family. He does this by adopting or accommodating to the family's style, imitating their speech patterns, pace, and idiosyncrasies. The therapist must be a superb actor, because to do this poorly is to be perceived as mocking. But Minuchin, master that he is, does it smoothly and compassionately. Having joined the family, the therapist can now participate in and take a control stance toward the family interactional pattern, that is, toward its structure. But the therapist is not a family member, so he or she simultaneously is in and out of the family and as an out, can command.

Much like Haley, Minuchin likes conflict. Minuchin does such things as meeting an "anorexic family," that is, one with an anorexic daughter, for lunch at which he encourages the anorexic to openly defy the family members who are trying to control her by getting her to eat, or making enmeshed members literally move away from each other by changing chairs, and by taking sides often with the weak against the strong. This is sometimes called *unbalancing*. The chair game in which the family relationships are seen to be expressed in their physical deportment has been generalized into an important family therapy technique, *family sculpture*, in which the family is asked to represent their relationships by the placement of their bodies by one (or more successively) member(s) of the family. The active form of this is called *family choreography*. Minuchin's technical term for imitating manner, style, and content of communication, is *mimesis*. He also uses *tracking*, that is, following up on the family concerns as if he were a family member using all of the family's idiosyncratic approaches to communication. As he puts it, he "leads by following." Another key structural technique is *enactment*. Freud had said that in the final analysis, "Nobody can be hanged in effigy," so that the only way the patient's conflict (illness) can be "executed" is by reviving it in the transference. Minuchin would agree, but he doesn't work with transference. Instead he uses enactments. Having lunch with the anorexic family is a form of enactment, but whatever the conflict, Minuchin tries to bring it into the room.

If I tried to join the family à la Minuchin as a distant uncle, I am sure I would be unwelcome. I would be clumsy and artificial. So I work with more of a sense of separateness and autonomy. Neither do I track or use mimicry like Minuchin, although I do try to find metaphors that will speak to the family, couple, or individual patient. Minuchin himself plays down technique (Minuchin and Fishman

1981) and openly discusses the ad hoc nature of many of his innovations as a sort of fly by the seat of your pants learning experience that he only later somewhat systematized. Like the Zen master, the therapist must master technique only to transcend it. For Minuchin, far more central is the therapist's belief in the growth potential of every family. Minuchin doesn't believe that there are healthy families and pathological families, only families who are stuck in self-defeating, repetitious patterns of interaction. He expresses the hope that we will have a new nosology of family pathology. Of course, Minuchin does have a concept of family health characterized by hierarchy, boundaries, and structure. I think what he wants to convey is that every family has the potential to elaborate toward structure.

Minuchin makes some interesting (and revealing) comments on the differences between himself and family theorists like R. D. Laing, who emphasized liberation from toxic families and pathologized the parents of patients (cf. Laing and Esterson 1964). These theorists themselves came from extremely troubled families, who treated them cruelly or at least insensitively, and they hate their families of origin. In contrast therapists like Minuchin come from loving, albeit neurotic, families whose troubles came from stress and too rapid change, and they see the family, no matter how disturbed—homeostatic, stuck, double-binding—as having intrinsic, inherent strengths and capacities for creative evolution. Accordingly, a thinker like Minuchin aims at strengthening families while a thinker like Laing looks to separate patients from families and to provide alternate networks such as Laing's Kingsley Hall, a therapeutic community for severely disturbed patients. This raises interesting questions when one thinks about adapting Minuchin's approach to the treatment of addicted families. The Haley-Minuchin view that the individual can only get better if the family gets better would leave little hope for many addicts from severely dysfunctional homes. Haley and Minuchin do not seem to be able to recognize that some people and some families are toxic and need to be detached from. Ed Kaufman and Pauline Kaufmann (1992), who wrote the pioneering text on the family therapy of addiction, do not agree with me. They state that the family therapy of addiction is not possible without a strongly Minuchin-type base. They strongly favor bringing the whole family along, rather than helping the addict separate from a toxic family.

Minuchin's equation of structure with family strength, health, and functionality finds an interesting echo and implicit support in the anthropological literature on alcoholism (here defined as frequent drunkenness). Peter Field (1962) presents evidence that there is a correlation between societies (cultures) that lack social structure and those with the highest rates of drunkenness. The less structure the more drunkenness. If one assumes that structure is internalized, this argues that a chaotic inner world predisposes to addiction and that chaos is, in Winnicott's words, an "environmental deficiency disease."

So the structuralist reframes the problem as a systemic one, "joins" the family, takes control, challenges pathological structure, uses directives to establish clear boundaries and hierarchical subsystems, uses mimesis and tracking to understand (and change) the family structure and dysfunction, respectively, and uses enactments to bring the problems into the treatment room. All of this is done with humor, warmth, and authority. Not a bad prescription if one can follow it (I would guess few can) and if one is comfortable with such a high degree of control and manipulation.

EXPERIENTIAL FAMILY THERAPY

If strategic therapy is about strategies of change, and structural therapy about the establishment of firmer structures, then experiential therapy is about *experience*. It is not the therapist as strategist nor the family therapist's manipulation of structure, nor is it interpretation, exploration, or education that cures; rather, it is experience that the family has with the therapist(s) that enables change. What is mutative is felt interaction in the here and now. Change isn't primarily something that occurs as a result of therapy; it is what happens during the therapy. Experiential therapy is clearly allied with both the Gestalt and humanistic schools of psychotherapy. It is the stepchild of Carl Rogers's (1961) belief that the job of the therapist is simply to provide the conditions of growth—given the necessary environmental provisions, the indwelling tendency of every organism (or organization of organisms) is toward self-actualization—and of his belief that interpretation is too intellectual to be mutative; of Abraham Maslow's (1968) phenomenology of self-actualization with its offspring, the human potential movement; of Fritz Perls's (1969) injunction to "lose your mind and come to your senses" and his confrontational ways of engaging people in the here and now, picking up on their gestures, postures, and body language as well as verbal communications; and of existential psychotherapists' [such as Rollo May (1969)] emphasis on patients confronting ultimate issues, especially death, limitation, and meaninglessness.

There is something quintessentially American about experiential family therapy. It is pragmatic, skeptical of theory, and action oriented. Its principal exponent is Carl Whitaker, an aggressively (in the sense of loving to portray himself as a self-defined) Iowa farm boy. My association is to the great American pragmatist John Dewey with his truth as instrumental rather than absolute or doctrinaire. Who but an American pragmatist could have called his book on aesthetics *Art as Experience* (Dewey 1934)? There is a strong antiintellectual bias in experiential therapy, and Whitaker is aggressively antitheoretical. But this is deceptive, and to some degree either disingenuous or self-deluded, for Whitaker has a strongly held belief or set of beliefs about human nature, the influence of unconscious process, transference and countertransference (although he doesn't use those words), and family dynamics that are determinative of his way of working. His nontechnique is nevertheless a technique and his spontaneity the product of much thought. For all his frequent, sometimes snide, almost always critical comments on Freud, he is clearly more indebted to him than he acknowledges. I don't think Whitaker would be much bothered by the paradoxes I see in his approach; nevertheless, they are worth noting.

In discussing experiential therapy, I will concentrate on Whitaker (Whitaker and Bumberry 1988), who calls his method *symbolic-experiential*, with briefer discussions of Walter Kempler's (1981) *gestalt family therapy* and Virginia Satir's (1964, 1972) *humanistic therapy*.

In *The Catcher in the Rye* (Salinger 1951), Holden Caulfield says that he judges a writer by whether or not he wants to call him up. I judge therapists and writers on therapy in much the same way. Would I want to be in therapy with them? Haley doesn't much attract me; I admire the clarity and power of Minuchin's writing but I have no desire to be his patient; not so Whitaker. Reading him, I got a little wet eyed wishing that my parents and I had been in family therapy with Whitaker. What attracts me to Whitaker is his humor, his humanism, his courage, and his way with language. His freedom from jargon and his metaphors, which resonate, make him the best writer of the major family therapists. It also occurs to me that Whitaker reminds me of a beloved supervisor, Claude Miller, another iconoclast who plays the Midwestern rube, and that my transference to Claude has something to do with my admiration for Whitaker. Transference aside, Whitaker has interesting and important things to say about therapy.

Whitaker started out as an obstetrician/gynecologist and one wonders if his emphasis on "emergence," the coming into being of a new experience in the therapy session, is not related to the coming into being of new life in the delivery room. Somehow the obstetrics seems congruent with the farm background, both earthy and elemental. Whitaker, unlike Minuchin and Winnicott, who continued to practice their original specialty, pediatrics, left obstetrics behind when he became a psychiatrist. He came to psychiatry in a unique way that must also have been formative. During World War II, he did a scaled-down psychiatric residency and was assigned to the staff of Oak Ridge Hospital, treating those who were to create the atomic bomb and their families. One wonders if Whitaker's later insistence that there be no secrets in the family or between family and therapist was influenced by the secrecy of wartime Oak Ridge.

Freud tells of a patient whom he could not treat analytically because the patient was a high official who refused to free associate lest he reveal state secrets. Did Whitaker have similar experiences? One also wonders if Whitaker's passionate insistence on the power, immortality, and ubiquity of the unconscious "impulse life" characterized by sexual, dependent, murderous, and suicidal urges and wishes, is not somehow related to his Oak Ridge experience. J. Robert Oppenheimer's comment after Hiroshima that "physicists now know sin" comes to mind. All this is my fantasy, but the influence of one aspect of Whitaker's Oak Ridge experience is not speculative, that being the effect of his inexperience and undertraining. One way he dealt with this was to use cotherapists. Working with schizophrenics, first individually and later in family therapy, Whitaker found that he felt overwhelmed. Their irrationality and craziness was too much for the therapist, and the cotherapist was brought in both for his/her wisdom and as a protective ally.

Whitaker never had a training analysis, but he agrees with Freud that "to be human is to be neurotic," or worse, and that the therapist is as much in need of "treatment" as the patient. Health and illness are not disjunctive; they are extremes in a continuum. We are all "sick" and we are all "well." So far, Whitaker isn't saying anything an analyst wouldn't agree with, but the conclusions he draws, namely that both the patient and the therapist are there because they are both in some way crazy, and that the purpose of their mutual encounter is mutual "cure," goes far beyond the usual analytic stance. Patient and therapist each gain out of their encounter and existentially neither is weller (or sicker) than the other, although their social roles differ.

The idea that we gain through encounter with patients and learn from countertransference is not unique to Whitaker, but he brings it into the therapy in an outspoken and explicit way, telling his families that he is there to meet his needs no less than theirs. One cures in order to be cured and is cured by curing. But the cure is not an enduring one. Again paralleling Freud, Whitaker believes that we struggle with the same issues all of our lives. The best we can do is to be more in contact with our impulse life, and to own our stuff rather than projecting it.

Whitaker soon stopped treating schizophrenia, which he saw as a misdirected creativity, the symptoms being futile attempts at getting "unstuck" and resuming growth, in individual therapy, and started treating schizophrenic families. At Emory University Medical School where he created the Department of Psychiatry, Whitaker started using therapy teams as extrapolations of the cotherapist model to treat

his families in the hope that a team would have strong-enough defenses to avoid being involved in the enmeshed family. The image
that comes to his mind is that of many flies having a better chance to
avoid the spider web than does the single fly. Maybe. In the course
of his work at Emory, Whitaker moved from an intrapsychic to an
interpersonal view of human dynamics in sickness and in health.

> I have finally come to realize that I don't believe in people. There's
> really no such thing as an individual [Cf. Winnicott's, "There is no such
> thing as a baby"]. We're all just fragments of families floating around,
> trying to live life. All of life and all of pathology is interpersonal.
> [Whitaker and Bumberry 1988, p. 36]

An object relations theorist would (almost) agree. But then Whitaker
almost agrees with the object relations theorists because of his focus
on making conscious the unconscious impulse life, which really can
only be understood as an intrapsychic one, no matter what he says.
Perhaps Whitaker exaggerates his position for rhetorical purposes,
but as Emerson said, "A foolish consistency is the hobgoblin of little
minds." Whitaker left Emory to return to his native Midwest, spend-
ing the rest of his career as professor of psychiatry at the University
of Wisconsin.

Whitaker's whole approach is one of engagement, of intense affective interaction. Yet he is much less of a joiner than Minuchin.
He carefully guards and talks about his autonomy and separateness.
As he puts it, "I move to join with them (the family), as well as to
individuate from them. This freedom to move in and out is a basic
task of therapy, of all living. We seek simultaneously deeper levels of
belonging and individuating" (Whitaker and Bumberry 1988, p. 10).
You must belong to differentiate, and to individuate to belong. If life
is a process of ever greater differentiation and integration, as I believe it is, we must first bond with, attach to, Mother; only then can
we separate and individuate. Later we go through the same process
with our families. As is so clear in marital therapy, there can be no
bonding of two into one (assuming for the moment that such a merger
is more than fantasy or at least can be at privileged moments) unless
there are two. The undifferentiated who looks for wholeness in an-

other who is also undifferentiated never finds it; yet if we are whole, why affiliate? Certainly herein lies one of the tragic paradoxes of life. But Whitaker, Minuchin, and Bowen (see below) are surely right when they point out that separateness and togetherness are two poles of being that stand in a yin-yang dialectical relationship and not in stark opposition. For a more philosophical take on the two poles of separation and relatedness consituting the self, see my *Theories of the Self* (1992).

Whitaker is a joiner with reservations. There and not there; in and out. Although he doesn't talk about resistance, he has two key technical means to deal with the resistance inherent in any family system: the struggle for structure and the struggle for initiative. In the *struggle for structure*, the therapist establishes control, but Whitaker's control looks different from Haley's. Haley is obsessed by the power struggle he sees as intrinsic to all human relating and is determined to be the one in control—for benign and therapeutic motives, of course. Whitaker's struggle for structure is part of the "political" aspect of therapy. In a sense, it is a prolegomenon to therapy, although paradoxically, the struggle for structure is profoundly transforming. Its essence is Whitaker's insistence that all members of the family attend the first session. He refuses to deal if the family won't play by his rules.

Whitakerian structure is analogous to the analytic "frame." In the struggle for structure, Whitaker defines himself as parent, not peer. He also reframes the problem as a systemic and interpersonal, not an individual one. He does this not by teaching; "Nothing worth knowing can be taught" (Whitaker and Bumberry 1988, p. 85), but by doing. Of course, this is a form of affective learning. What Whitaker suspects is intellectualization. The family, having learned that the therapist is a parent who imposes the structure, naturally looks to the therapist for answers, which occasions the struggle for initiative. The therapist must firmly put the ball in the family's court. He or she vigorously leaps from the pedestal, saying such things as, "I'm lucky if I can muddle through my own life let alone live yours." He makes it clear that he has no "reality" answers. His function is to enable growth, not to tell anyone how to live.

Whitaker uses all sorts of confrontation, humor, and absurdity to win the battle for initiative. There is a paradox here also. The therapist is demanding that the patient—the family—be free and responsible. "I order you to be free" somehow doesn't work; returning the ball does. Another kind of reframing goes on here: the problem is redefined during the struggle for initiative from symptom removal to growth. The therapist has no interest in symptom removal. Here, too, Whitaker sounds like a nonanalytic analyst. I imagine that the Whitakerian therapist has as much chance to sell no symptom removal to the managed care people as Freud would have had with his insistence that the analyst "should have no therapeutic ambition." Here both Freud and Whitaker are profoundly respectful of human autonomy. Again, the struggle for initiative isn't taught; it is lived in the encounter between therapist and family. That is why it is convincing. The therapist cannot win the struggle for initiative unless he genuinely and passionately believes that the family, like every family, has the resources to find its own way, its unique solutions. It is this passionate conviction conveyed by the refusal to take responsibility for the family that facilitates the family's changing. This cannot be faked. If you think you know more about how to live than the family you are healing, you will lose the struggle for initiative. You can do other kinds of therapy, but not experiential family therapy.

This raises real questions for the substance abuse therapist who does think that he or she knows a better way (sobriety) of living, and wishes to alter the reality situation of patients in a determinate way. Perhaps there is no way out of this dilemma and substance abuse therapy is incompatible with both analytic and experiential therapy.

Whitaker's stance is reminiscent of Fritz Perls's telling patients, "You have to be your own Fritz" and of analysts and Cornell Medical School dean Bob Michaels telling his patients, "I'm a fantasy not a reality doctor." It is also a stance that raises questions about transference. Kohut (1971, 1977a) believes that the establishment of what he variously called narcissistic and selfobject transferences (see below), including the "idealizing transference," are recapitulations of normal developmental stages and that they should be allowed to unfold and only then worked through. For the therapist to not permit the idealization is antitherapeutic and may unintentionally repeat a traumatic disillusionment with the parent who did not allow phase appropriate idealization. Kernberg (1975), on the other hand, sees idealization as a setup to control and ultimately to devalue. In a way, the Kohut-Kernberg debate is a rerun of the old controversy of whether or not to interpret the positive transference, and if so taken, Whitaker is closer to Kernberg here, certainly not agreeing with Kohut, but his tone and emphasis are very different. For him, it is natural and inevitable for the family to look to the therapist for magic. It is the therapist's responsibility to refuse to be a shaman. It is the failure of the therapist to do so, not the pathology of the family looking for answers, that leads to difficulties. Whitaker is absolutely adamant on this point, referring to therapists who pity and direct in order to help as "emotional whores" selling their empathy for money. Caring simply isn't enough. If the therapist is there for his or her own growth, the transaction becomes more real and more honest.

Whitaker's self-revelation is tricky. In some ways, it is similar to the analyst's use of countertransference, but it can easily pass into self-serving and exhibitionism. The therapist reveals himself to model, to enhance authenticity, and to speak in a nonthreatening way of unconscious process. He or she thereby learns and grows, but that growth is a by-product. The therapist is not there to solve his or her problems, but to use his or her experience and being to help all concerned grow. I like what Whitaker tells us about what he does, but I am suspicious of it. For self-revelation to work, the therapist must have worked through much of what he reveals. An example of Whitaker's comes to mind in which he speaks of freeing himself from his mother's sexual attraction to him at age 13 in order to enable the family he is working with to face and talk about their incestuous feelings—for Whitaker, a universal phenomenon. He comments, "This was no longer an issue for me, having long since accepted my mother's sexual feelings" (Whitaker and Bumberry 1988, p. 119). I remember going to a first supervisory session and saying, "I'm very anxious." The supervisor replied, "Better you than me," which is both part of the struggle for initiative, returning the ball to my court, and quite revealing of who the supervisor was.

Whitaker calls the struggle for initiative the *political stage of therapy*. A vital part of this political struggle lies in its spontaneity, a spontaneity that paradoxically flows from its structure.

As part of his insistence on spontaneity and aliveness, Whitaker abhors history taking, calling it voyeuristic "pornography." No psychosocials for him. There is more than a grain of truth in this perception of history taking. For Whitaker, there is also no diagnosis. Again, try selling this one to your friendly managed care company.

The political struggle is over once the family accepts responsibility, and we are in the middle of the "journey of family therapy [which] begins with a blind date and ends with the empty nest" (Whitaker and Bumberry 1988, p. 53). Blind dates engender anxiety, and Whitaker makes it clear that anxiety is the motivating force for change. Accordingly, he does nothing to reduce the anxiety level; on the contrary, he makes moves to heighten it. Once again, he shares assumptions with the analyst and once again, he rejects symptom relief.

Whitaker also relishes his toughness (he tells families how tough he is), comparing therapy to surgery. Like the surgeon, his business is to cut away diseased tissue, not to avoid bloodletting. The bleeding is irrelevant as long as he has his clean field and is able to operate. It is noteworthy that Freud also compared himself to a surgeon, and urged the analyst in his paper "Recommendations to Physicians Practicing Psychoanalysis" (1912) to proceed with the same fearlessness and disregard for the patient's discomfort as the surgeon does. So once again, the vehemently antianalytic experientialist lines up with the father of analysis. Does Whitaker protest too much?

The metaphorical surgeon excising pathogenic tissue is incongruous with Whitaker's dominant metaphor of the coach coaching the family out of an impasse. Although not as opposed to diagnosis as Minuchin, Whitaker clearly sees his job as enabling growth, not healing disease, yet here in the notion of the surgeon excising pathogenic tissue, that is belied. There is a tension within Whitaker between the physician and the existentialist.

Perhaps related to toughness is Whitaker's use of the *bataca* (pillow bat), which he instigates the family members to use on each other. Borrowed from bioenergetics and Gestalt therapies, this more direct variant on pounding the pillow both surfaces suppressed (or repressed) anger and aggression, and demonstrates (gives the experience of) anger not destroying its object.

The middle phase of Whitakerian family therapy is characterized as *symbolic therapy*, which deals with unconscious process. "Just as water flows through pipes under our streets, impulses flow through our unconscious. . . . We all have these emotional infrastructures that ensure the flow of our impulse life" (Whitaker and Bumberry 1988, p. 75). The symbol world is representative of this unconscious impulse life. Freud would call these symbols "derivatives." They are both universal and particular. The themes of loneliness, rage, sexuality, and death are universal; they are particularized among other ways in family rituals. Whitaker does not interpret the unconscious; rather, he *surfaces*, largely through the use of his own associations. Since the themes are universal, the therapist's articulation of his countertransferential thoughts and feelings frees up the family to surface their infrastructure. Whitaker also uses confrontation and reductio-ad-absurdum techniques. "My husband always runs away from me" is answered by, "Why don't you shoot him?" "How could I?" His answer, "With a gun, or you might use a bow and arrow." Before long, the wife's murderous rage surfaces, having been tapped by Whitaker's literalism, which is paradoxically the use of symbolism. Whitaker's whole technique has been called a "theater of the absurd." Particular emphasis is put on death and loss, and here experiential therapy becomes highly existential. Mortality and limitation heighten the value of present experience, or as Freud (1916, p. 305) so beautifully said, "Transience is scarcity value in time."

Another experiential therapy technique is confusion. It is used to break rigid ways of perceiving and being. Confusion breaks up the "blame game," and turns dualistic all-good/all-bad into dialectical contrariety. In analytic terms, it undermines the defense of splitting. It also "surprises them [the family] enough to break [them] free of the family-of-origin hypnosis we are all subject to" (Whitaker and Bumberry 1988, p. 82). Symbol work "seeds the unconscious" and those seeds may sprout in ways beyond the therapist's wildest dreams. Whitaker also advocates starting with the father, since he believes that gender differences are biological and that men are less in contact with feelings, symbols, and impulses. So go after Dad first and hard. Whitaker emphasizes the intergenerational transmission of patterns, shared symbols, and rituals. He believes that at least three generations are germane to the current family functioning, and he includes grandparents, if he possibly can, saying such things as, "We are stuck and need help. Would your parents [the grandparents] come and help us." This intergenerational conceptualization, along with his notion of the hypnotic power of families of origin, makes Whitaker far less ahistorical than Haley, Minuchin, or the Gestaltists. He doesn't interpret the past, but he works with it and tries to bring it into the room.

Whitaker doesn't end therapy. Although his treatments tend to be brief, it is the family that must take the initiative to terminate, leaving the therapist sad (empty nest), relieved, and perhaps joyful.

Pondering on Whitaker's "Nothing worth knowing can be taught," one wonders how much of his experiential therapy is learnable or transferable. Whitaker is definitely one of the charisma boys. His antitheoretical theories and technique-free techniques are not easily integrated into other styles, and his therapy of the absurd becomes demeaning insult in the wrong hands. For all my admiration for him, I wonder how efficacious his therapy is? Do the families really change, or, like an encounter weekend, does the intensity fade and other and older patterns reestablish themselves? I don't know. Of course, an orgasm is no less worthwhile because it doesn't last long; experiential therapy may be like that, wonderful but transitory.

Walter Kempler (1981) is the best-known Gestalt family therapist. Atheoretical, ahistorical, encountering, countertransferential, and emotional, he, like Perls, tries to move the family to be able to experience or experience more deeply the Gestalt quadrilateral orgasm, grief, anger, and joy. Virginia Satir (1964, 1982) is the charismatic gal among all those charismatic guys. Starting as a member of Bateson's communication group, she wound up the heroine of the human potential movement, basing herself at Esalen. I include her here for the sake of completeness, since she is an important name, but I find I have little to say about her. The least theoretical of the "nontheorists," she traveled around the world demonstrating her humanistic approach. Her stock in trade was warmth, optimism, and working at many levels, from the sensory to the emotional to the cognitive, using massage, exhortation, sensory awareness, relaxation, confrontation, bodily awareness, yoga, Zen—you name it. In direct contrast to Whitaker, she presented herself as a teacher who could teach individuals and families better communication. I never saw her work, but those who did were said to have come away deeply moved. I am not sure that I would have been one of the deeply moved, finding her too upbeat for my taste.

Experiential family therapy, along with its sidekicks Gestalt family therapy and humanistic family therapy, would appear to have limited application to the treatment of substance abuse or the actively addicted family. Its stated indifference to symptom removal, its agnostic take on diagnosis, and its focus on the symbolic representation and enactment of the unconscious impulse life seem too akin to analytic neutrality, while the usual stance of substance abuse therapy is that the therapist must take a strong stand for sobriety, which puts the initiative on the therapist, concentrates on removing the symptom, and ignores the unconscious. I am fairly sure that Whitaker would disagree. He says, "Alcoholics drink because they're afraid of being afraid" (Whitaker and Bumberry 1988, p. 86). If that is the case, then experiential therapy would seem to be just the thing with its push toward experiencing the anxiety intrinsic to being fully alive and aware. I am sure that sometimes that would indeed work. The problem is that if you ignore the pharmacological regression concomitant with addiction, you may miss the very thing that makes the experiential approach irrelevant. My association is to Carl Jung's famous treatment of Roland H., an American businessman who had completed a successful analysis with Jung for his alcoholism. When Roland returns to Jung during a disastrous relapse, Jung tells him that his case is hopeless. Roland pleads with Jung for help, and Jung finally says, "Only if you experience a profound psychological reorganization, a 'transvaluation of values,' do you have any chance of recovering." In Whitaker's terms, only if you can experience your fear can you change.

Experiential, Gestalt, and humanistic family therapy would appear to be much more suited for work with the recovering family. The problem I have here is Whitaker's insistence on working with the whole (however that may be defined) family; it ignores (cf. my somewhat similar discussion of the application of Minuchin's approach to addiction) the real toxicity of some families and some family members. As I see it, better to work with the workable than let the fully boarded ship sink.

MULTIGENERATIONAL SYSTEMS FAMILY THERAPY

If Whitaker is an atheoretical theorist, Murray Bowen (1978a) is a theoretical experientialist. There could be no more polar opposites than Bowen and Whitaker. For the cerebral Bowen, theory is the sine qua non of any therapy. Without a theory and its empirical verification, there can be no rational therapy. Ad hoc, fly by the seat of your pants, touchy-feely, and just emote are equally abhorrent to Bowen. Another Midwesterner, Bowen is a physician and psychiatrist who trained as an analyst. His later rejection of analysis seems to be deeply felt. Having evolved a new theory of emotional development that he believes to be scientific, verifiable and indeed verified, he has no doubt whatever that Freud's metapsychologies are simply wrong. Or perhaps *wrong* is the wrong word. In his view, Freud's theory simply lacks conceptual vigor and uses a language that was originally borrowed from prerelativistic physics, explicitly from dynamics. Being antiquated it no longer shares a conceptual base with the rest of science and has long since ceased to be, if it ever was, taken seriously by the mainstream of the scientific community.

Bowen, like the logical positivist, would probably say that Freud's theory is meaningless rather than wrong, meaningless in the sense that it can neither be verified nor falsified. Bowen would not allow that the intrapsychic and the interpersonal, or systems, views of human nature are complementary, two valid perspectives on complex phenomena. On the contrary, he believes that his systems theory is incompatible with intrapsychic formulations and that it gives a veridical and verifiable account of the human situation. All of this makes Bowen sound rigid and dogmatic, yet the tone of his writing is quite different—calm, reasonable, clear, gently persuasive, careful, and strongly argued yet dispassionate and conceptually rigorous. The style is the man; it is also the therapy.

For all of his rejection of the analytic paradigm, Bowen is clearly indebted to analysis, and many of his ideas seem more dynamic than systematic. This is particularly true of his central notions of *differentiation*, *family ego mass*, and *intergenerational projection*. Like Whitaker and Minuchin, he doth protest too much. I found myself wondering about his training analysis. My fantasy is that his analyst pushed him toward affect and he resisted, each interpretation of his intellectualization driving him further from the analytic camp. But who knows? Bowen gives clinical and objective reasons for his metamorphosis. His conceptual scheme was the product of evidentiary, painstaking research. Whatever its emotional antecedents and determinants, Bowen certainly is right in relating his theory to his research and to his attempt to make sense out of schizophrenia.

As we shall see, Bowen experienced himself as caught in what Minuchin would call an enmeshed family, and developed a therapy for disenmeshment. His strongly stated belief that health is only possible by differentiation from one's family of origin is, like the systems of all the great psychodynamic theorists, a generalization from his core personal experience. This in no way denigrates his achievement or denies the reality or saliency of the clinical research approach he used to develop this theory. Bowen would argue that he was only able to deal with his own "system" (family of origin) problems after he had the tools he developed in his work with schizophrenic families. It isn't that his theorizing or his therapy are epiphenomena of his personal situation; on the contrary, it is the universally applicable truths about the human condition and techniques derived from these truths that allowed him to come to terms with his own family. Perhaps so.

Bowen started his professional career at the Menninger Clinic in the late 1940s when it was a bastion of psychoanalytic psychiatry. He developed a special interest in schizophrenia and initially tried to treat it analytically. Like many before and after him, he found it tough sledding. Individual dynamic psychotherapy, at least in Bowen's hands, simply wasn't very effective with schizophrenia. This being the era of the schizophrenogenic mother, Bowen came to understand schizophrenia as a manifestation of an inappropriate symbiotic attachment between mother and patient. The ego psychological perspective later elaborated by Margaret Mahler and colleagues (1975) sees psychosis as failure to differentiate out of symbiosis. In Mahler's well-known developmental scheme, the infant starts in an objectless *autistic stage*, then progresses to an awareness of Mother, and fusion with her. This Mahler calls *symbiosis*, a term she borrowed from biology, where it refers to a mutually beneficial relationship between two mutually dependent organisms, in contrast to parasitic relationships, which work to the benefit of one and the detriment of the other organism. Symbiosis and symbiotic have taken on a pejorative coloration, and one easily forgets their original meanings. For Mahler, the *symbiotic stage* follows the autistic and is a part of normal development. Fixation or regression to either autism or symbiosis results in psychosis.

Mahler calls her next stage *separation-individuation. Separation* refers to the experiencing of oneself as separate from Mother and occurs concomitantly with the acquisition of motor skills that allow physical separation from Mother. *Individuation* refers to the experiencing of oneself as unique and in possession of certain qualities. I am not only separate from Mother, I am *me* with all that entails. There are four substages of separation-individuation: *differentiation*, in which I differentiate, that is, experience myself as separate; *practicing*, in which I use my new locomotive tools to experiment with separateness, that is, to explore the world apart from Mother; *rapprochement*, in which I return to Mother and temporarily symbiose with her once again; and *separation-individuation proper*, both a physical, interpersonal process and an internal psychic representation in which conscious or unconscious self-representations undergo a development from a fused selfobject (me–Mother) representation into one in which self and object representations are sharply differentiated.

Mahler and colleagues (1975), Kernberg (1975), and Masterson (1976) have postulated that borderline personality disorder arises from vicissitudes in the rapprochement subphase of separation-individuation; if Mother either doesn't allow or punishes separation or doesn't allow rapprochement, the seeds of severe problems in relating are planted. We need both the freedom to explore on our own and the security of knowing that we can return "home."

Mahler's interest is in the internal world. Bowen was aware of Mahler's work and cites her. He is going in a different direction, but his schema retains a Mahlerian cast. It is also of some interest that Otto Kernberg, who was to develop an internal self and object representational model of human development that owes much to Mahler, was working at Menninger toward the end of Bowen's stay there. I don't know if they knew or influenced each other.

By the early 1950s, Bowen understood schizophrenia as an interpersonal process. Researchers as diverse as Theodore Litz and his colleagues (1957) at Yale; Bateson and his group (1956) at Stanford, and the analyst Frieda Fromm-Reichmann (1948) at Chestnut Lodge Hospital outside of Washington were pursuing the same idea, an idea whose time had come. Bowen began working with the mother and child together. He then moved the mothers into the hospital, having them live with their schizophrenic children in cottages on the grounds. He carefully observed their interactions, finding the intensity of their involvement with one another far stronger than he had anticipated. Bowen found little support for his work at the then analytically oriented Menninger Clinic and moved to the National Institute of Mental Health (NIMH), where he moved entire families onto the ward, once again meticulously studying their interactions. (Try to get funding for similar research today!)

Bowen's model, in its treatment if not in its research side, of having the entire family, not just the identified patient, become the focus in an inpatient setting has been widely imitated in substance abuse treatment. Many rehabilitation facilities have "family week," in which the entire family lives in and becomes the "patient." Although part of what happens during family week is didactic and educational, it is essentially a systematic treatment. Those who have participated in rehab family weeks inevitably find the experience powerful. How transforming it is, is another question. Like any other therapy, the results are highly variable; however, at the very least, such family weeks plant seeds.

Family week in substance abuse treatment facilities is now becoming extinct. The ravages of managed care, together with other financial constraints, have led to the demise of one program after another. This is a very real loss. I do not believe that a family week experience is always right for either the addict or the rest of the family, but sometimes it is very right, and an opportunity to significantly reduce human suffering is being lost through economic shortsightedness. No money is saved by such false economies; the long-term price of preventable emotional and psychosomatic illness consequent on the chaos of living in an addictive family is far larger than the cost of inpatient treatment to ameliorate that stress. The intensity of a week in rehab is not easily duplicated in subsequent outpatient treatment, even if it occurs. And most families not treated in rehab never go for other treatment.

The most important insight to come out of this research was Bowen's recognition that the *family works as an emotional unit*. The family emotional unit has a reality transcending the reality of the members of the family and their emotions, although this emotional unit is the product of the family relationship system. It wasn't only Mother who was overinvolved (enmeshed) with the patient; the whole family was. The family was a *system*.

Bowen's notion of system is quite different from general systems theory and its family therapy derivatives. It is not system as servomechanism, or nexus of feedback loops, negative and positive. Nor is it primarily homeostatic. Rather it is what Bowen calls a natural system, which, like any other living system, is a product of evolution. In trying to make psychiatry scientific (unlike that unscientific analytic stuff), Bowen looked for an established science to provide a conceptual base. He found it in biology. He places great stress on the necessity for a scientific psychiatry being comprehensible to other scientists; accordingly, he wants a terminology that will be understood by other scientists. But it is more than terminology; it is the concepts themselves that are the most important to Bowen. He chose a biological model because he believed that it was closer to the data of psychiatry than the physical one used by Freud.

So now Bowen has his two key concepts—natural system and family emotional system. The family emotional system is a special case, and its laws are just as immutable and knowable as the laws of any other natural system, be that an organism, a herd, or a solar system. In this connection, Bowen shows himself to be a rationalist to the core.

Leaving the NIMH in 1959, Bowen became a professor at Georgetown University, where he applied his insights into the systemic nature of schizophrenia to the problems of much less impaired families. Now working primarily with outpatients, Bowen generalized his findings on schizophrenic families into an interlocking conceptual vision that he called Bowen theory, a theory he sees as empirically and clinically validated.

The cornerstone of Bowen's theory is *differentiation*, explicitly *differentiation of the self*. This is a direct borrowing from biology. All development entails differentiation. In the embryo, the undifferentiated cells in the blastula and gastrula differentiate into ectoderm, mesoderm, and endoderm cells, which in turn differentiate into even more specialized cells. It is only after differentiation that the integration necessary for the formation of tissues and organs can take place. All development involves differentiation and integration. Without differentiation there can be no integration, and without integration we have a colony instead of an organism. Dedifferentiation is always pathological. The dedifferentiated cell is the malignant one. Bowen doesn't quite see it that way, and he doesn't use the term *integration*, rather he implies it. He sees differentiation as necessary for relationship; without it, there is either submersion in the *undifferentiated family ego mass* (the family emotional system), or defensive isolation.

Differentiation is a universal biological phenomenon (as is exact replication and homogeneity, the two forces being in dynamic equilibrium), which manifests itself in differentiation of the self from the undifferentiated family ego mass (which I tend to misread as "mess"). Differentiation of the self is also a family process of contending symbiotic and individuating forces. For Freud, Eros (libido) unites, while Thanatos (the death instinct) separates; for Bowen Eros ensnares, while some unnamed force individuates. The mature Bowen isn't much of an instinct (drive) theorist, and although he alludes to contending forces that are the product of evolutionary process and that drive the organism—here, the person—this way or that, he looks on Freud's instinct theory as unscientific. That it may well be, yet Bowen's failure to specify the nature of the differentiating force leaves a gap in his conceptual system. Winnicott and other object relations and ego psychological theorists postulate that aggression, which they conceive of as an innate drive, makes separation possible. One could also evoke the third law of thermodynamics, the principle of entropy, in which a closed system moves toward homogeneity. Energy is conserved but differentiation (difference in energy levels) is lost, so that no work can be derived from the system. It is "dead." One must then postulate an antientropy force at work in living systems, including the family. Bowen might go for such a model, or he might reject it as too speculative, too unscientific.

Over and over again, Bowen speaks of the undifferentiated being stuck in the family ego mass. There is a feeling of ensnarement, stickiness, entrapment. Images of flies caught by flypaper or entangled in spider webs come to mind. Another association is to the existential philosopher Jean-Paul Sartre's accounts of the stickiness of being-in-itself, the solid stuff of the universe trapping being-for-itself, consciousness, and self-consciousness. The notion is of consciousness being caught in the stuffness of matter. Sartre's metaphysical categories have been interpreted as femininity and masculinity, respectively, and his ontology interpreted as an intellectual representation of men's fear of entrapment by women. Bowen's notion is less gender-based (if that is really where Sartre is coming from); both men and women get stuck. If you don't fight to separate from that family ego mass, you may never get free. The danger is *fusion*, and the mature Bowen speaks of a dynamic struggle between differentiation and fusion. There is almost a phobic quality to Bowen's fear of fusion, which comes through in both his theory and his account of his own struggle to individuate from his family of origin.

Bowen would be an apt candidate for spiritual grandfather of the codependency movement. To be codependent is to be undifferentiated. Others such as Kohut (see below) and the self psychologists see fusion, which they understand as selfobject relating, as a lifelong need that will find expression in unhealthy ways if healthy ones are unavailable. Whitaker states that differentiation can only take place in relation to, in the face of, the other. He believes that a truly differentiated self is both possible and desirable. That self is not an isolate, nor is it unrelated, but it does not fuse or relate as a selfobject. Bowen and the attachment theorists of various persuasions don't really contradict each other, yet their positions are not reconcilable. They remain differentiated, not fused.

For Bowen, differentiation isn't only between or from people, it is importantly *differentiation of thought and feeling*. Differentiation entails being able to separate thought from feeling, and failure to be able to do so is the mark of ensnarement in the family ego mass. Here too Bowen is reminiscent of Sartre in the primacy of intellectualization. Oddly enough, this also has a very Freudian ring. From his notion of the centrality of insight in the therapeutic process to his discussion of the advance in intellectualization brought about by the development of monotheism in *Moses and Monotheism* (1939), the intellectual is always Freud's highest value. It is also Bowen's. Of course, he is here the heir of the Western philosophical and religious traditions with their suspicion of the emotional and their emphasis on mastery of the passions. Like everyone else in this tradition, Bowen has to make or create a place and role for emotion, and he speaks not of mastery but of differentiation. The Twelve-Step slogan (originally part of the ideology of Abraham Low's (1950) *Recovery Movement* for the severely emotionally ill), "Feelings aren't facts" would meet with his approval. Bowen insists that he is not in any way denigrating the emotional life and indeed is making true emotional relating possible, nor is he encouraging intellectualization as a defense. His is more the notion that the truth (understanding, insight) will make you free. Nevertheless, the contrast with Whitaker and other experiential-humanistic therapists is stark.

Bowen has developed a scale to estimate the degree of differentiation and maintains that the relatively undifferentiated family can function well under conditions of low stress, but falls into dysfunction as stress escalates. This brings us to another key Bowenian con-

cept, *triangulation*. Bowen sees the family and indeed all human relations as systems of interlocking triangles. Triangles are essentially
defenses against twoness, against pairing. Relationships are intrinsically stressful; conflict between people is inevitable, and we flee from
the tension of didactic relationships, of I–thou relating, of two-person
intimacy to triangular relationships. One or both members of the pair
suck in another person to deflect, to support, to ally, to defend, to
dilute. The process of triangulation has two poles, that of the triangu-
lator and that of the triangulated. The least differentiated will feel
the greatest need to triangulate (Bowen doesn't put it this way, but
it may be the case that the non- or underdifferentiated person fears
complete loss of selfhood in a one-to-one relationship and triangulation is a paradoxical and inextricably failed attempt to differentiate),
and the less differentiated will most easily be pulled into the triangle.
The triangulators have an uncanny ability to latch onto the least differentiated family member to fulfill their need for triangulation.
Bowen doesn't say this, but triangulation could be seen as making
biological sense. Pairing is necessary for procreation but the family is
necessarily triangular, so a drive toward triangulation would facilitate child rearing.

The most famous of triangles is the oedipal one. In Bowenian terms,
the child's desire for the opposite sex parent is not so much explicitly sexual as part of the triangulation process. What the boy is looking for in Mother is an ally against Father, not a sex partner. This is
consistent with Bowen's deinstinctualization of motivation as he
moved from analytic to systems conceptualizations. Triangulation is
complex and can lead to varying outcomes. It does not necessarily
reduce tension; it may backfire and exacerbate it. Triangulation has
affiliations with the defenses of splitting into all-good and all-bad. In
the triangle, one side can easily be demonized while the other is idealized with much potential for flip-flopping. With a system of interlocking triangles, the possibilities are infinite. The contrast between
Bowen's and Bion's take on the dynamics of pairing is interesting. For
Bowen, pairing, however intrinsically troubled, seems to be primary,
a given of human existence, while triangulation is a defense against
the anxiety of pairing. For Bion, pairing is one of the basic assump-

tions that work against the completion of the reality task of the group or family. For Bion, pairing is part of individuation and separation from the group; for Bowen, both pairing and triangulations are antithetical to differentiation.

Triangles, inevitable as they are, are the great danger. If the therapist is triangulated into the system, all is lost. The primary task of the therapist is to remain untriangulated so he or she can "coach" the patient, be it family, couple, or individual, on detriangulation. The only way the therapist can avoid countertransferential triangulation is to have worked through differentiation from his or her family of origin. The therapist is a calm, uninvolved, objective teacher explaining the triangulation process in the family and helping develop strategies for detriangulation. Transference is triangulation. It is to be minimized. My association is to Leston Havens's, "If there is one moment without transference, the patient is cured." One could argue that Bowen's view of the role of the therapist is a modified analytic one of the detached interpreter, yet it has a very different flavor. Countertransference is here never a tool but rather always an obstacle to be overcome. That echoes early Freud, not contemporary analytic theory and practice.

Substance abusers are triangulators par excellence and the addictive family is one of triangular entanglements, so Bowen's analysis of triangulation is directly applicable to the treatment of addicted families. If Bowen's fear of being sucked in seems excessive, it is a real danger for the substance abuse family therapist, who needs to be aware of the contending forces trying to enlist him or her as an ally in the family struggle. But this gets tricky when there is an active user, because "joining" the triangle "against" the user is sometimes necessary. Bowen would not agree. He has written on alcoholism (1974) and sees the alcoholic as the least differentiated member of the family system. The "cure" is to enable differentiation rather than focus on the symptom—the drinking. In spite of this difference in approach, Bowen has given us a new way of looking at the multigenerational transmission of addiction. It is a conceptual tool worth having.

Undifferentiation is projected onto the dysfunctional symptomatic family member. The real problem is family fusion. In the fused family, members either have no-selves or pseudo-selves, never real-selves. There is often a pattern of overadequate-underadequate role assignment, the underadequate person being presented as the problem in what is clearly a relationship problem. This has direct relevance to substance abuse treatment. In his paper on alcoholism, Bowen presents the alcoholic as the overadequate partner who is in reality undifferentiated or defending against that undifferentiation by overcompensation. Alcohol provides the fusion that the overadequacy denies. This is a variation on the dependency-conflict theory of addiction. The dependency-conflict theory of addiction states that those who are counterdependent, that is, phobic about intimacy and human relating and hence denying their need for it, covertly meet their dependency needs by the use of substances, particularly alcohol. This is usually a male dynamic but need not be. Thus the drinker/drugger needs no one, is totally independent, and yet of course is totally dependent. Since heavy drinking has, at least until recently, not been seen as dependent behavior, at least by macho men, this is a perfect setup. If carried far enough, the drinker/drugger deteriorates and eventually has to be "nursed," so that the entire drama is lived out by an overt regression to infantile dependency. Returning to the Bowen conceptualization, as the addiction progresses, roles reverse and the drinker becomes underadequate. The possibilities are legion, the point being that it isn't the drinking, it's the fusion and its by-product that need to be addressed.

People tend to select spouses on the same level of differentiation (or undifferentiation) as themselves. They in turn project their undifferentiation onto and triangulate with their offspring, there usually being a favorite target who becomes the most fused family member. Bowen has a complicated theory of birth order and gender (sibling position) to account for who gets the most fused. But it doesn't quite work, since the order is in terms of role, not necessarily chronology. The sibling position aspect of Bowen's theory need not concern us further. But the *family projection process*, meaning the projection of undifferentiation, is of interest and utility. It is a multigenerational transmission process in which the less differentiated marry the undifferentiated who together produce (and create) at least one even less differentiated child who marries the same, so that by the third generation, schizophrenia may appear, although this may take as much as ten generations. What is transmitted is not genetic in the sense of chromosomally encoded, rather it is relational, yet the process seems to be natural selection reversed; it is survival (barely) of the least fit. The application of this to substance abuse makes sense. We frequently see families in which a parent (usually the father) is a "functional alcoholic," or as one of my patients put it, "I want to be a successful alcoholic like my father," while one or more of the children are either dysfunctional, in the sense of not being able to make it in the world, alcoholic, or drug addicted. The process of undifferentiation is here transmitted with exacerbation. For Bowen the only hope lies in one of the family members achieving differentiation and going back into his or her family of origin to differentiate from them, thereby stopping the multigenerational transmission process.

Bowen would certainly agree with James Joyce's (1916) autobiographical protagonist, Stephen Dedalus, when he says, "History is a nightmare from which I am trying to awaken." Another Bowenian concept highly applicable to substance abuse is the *emotional cutoff*, a defensive movement of the pseudo-self that is bound to fail (although it may be better than total submergence in the fused family), since one's fused family remains in one's head awaiting projection and reenactment. An example is moving to northern Alaska and exchanging Christmas cards with the family in lieu of true differentiation. We frequently see this defense enacted in addicts who fuse with their substance of choice instead of with their families. Twelve-Step speaks of this as *isolation*, which it sees as a characteristic character flaw of the addicted. Again the only hope lies in true differentiation and return to the family of origin in a "curative" role. To return to "cure" one's family smacks of hubris, and in the case of some addicted families, is plain insanity. Bowen, like all the family therapists, puts too much emphasis on the need to "fix" the family in order to "cure" oneself.

Being something of a curmudgeon, Bowen has added the notion of *societal regression* to his conceptual scheme. Things are getting worse all the time and the pull toward fusion and dedifferentiation from the culture as a whole have become ever stronger, making the task of self-differentiation all the more difficult. Bowen alludes to the sociologist David Riesman's (1950) distinction between the *inner directed* and *outer directed*. Bowen sees Americans as losing their inner directedness. I think he ignores the counter forces of disintegration at work in America, of the increasing isolation and increasing incidence of divorce and single parenthood. Bowen would reply that these are forms of emotional cutoff and not manifestations of differentiated selves. Be this as it may, few would deny that relatedness between truly differentiated selves is hard to come by and that powerful socioeconomic forces militate against it.

In terms of technique, Bowen went from analysis to systems work, and then from working with the whole family to working with the parents only, and finally to working with individuals from a systems stance in which the therapist-coach prepares the differentiating one to return to his or her family of origin to detriangulate. The patient is to return in a calm, unemotional way and is to enact the strategies worked out with the therapist to disentangle the family. In a sense, what the patient is doing is providing a model of differentiated selfhood and the most significant action that takes place during the return is a dispassionate refusal to be triangulated. Most of the coaching is an instruction and insight into the triangulation process in the patient's family of origin. The patient now realizing his piece of the triangulation action no longer needs to play, and transformation becomes possible.

We often see something very like this when a recovering person returns to his addicted family. With luck, the entire family may move from the fusion implicit in addiction and the games played around it to sobriety and greater differentiation. However, more often than not, that is not the outcome and the recovering person's hurt, disappointment, and rage may endanger that recovery. Bowen would say that the recovering one lacked calm and the ability to differentiate between thought and feeling characteristic of the true self and needed more therapy before attempting further differentiation through differentiation of the family. This seems rather utopian to me, but helping recovering people recognize and avoid enmeshment and triangulation in their still addicted families is highly therapeutic. Some degree of emotional cutoff may be adaptive and indeed necessary to continued recovery. Bowen maintains that the cool refusal to triangulate makes true intimacy possible and actually brings people closer together. That may be true, but it is not easy to come by.

Bowen also developed the technique of *multiple family therapy*, in which a group of families meets at widely spaced (two weeks or a month) intervals with a therapist who is in the coach role. Like the Milan group, Bowen understands time between sessions as a time in which families learn to care for themselves and solve their own dilemmas. Again the therapist creates distance and remains uninvolved. So Bowen has gone in opposite directions, working individually in the systems way, and working with many families simultaneously. Both have been applied to and are highly useful in substance abuse cases. I have no experience with multiple family therapy, but I find a systems conceptualization of individual patient's pathology, particularly those addicted or affiliated with addicts, highly useful. Kaufman and Kaufmann (1992) have successfully applied multiple family therapy to addicted families. Their work is discussed in Chapter 3.

Bowen is greatly interested in genealogy, enjoining his patients to trace their families. He himself has gone back three hundred years. I have trouble connecting with this; genealogy simply doesn't interest me. Clearly related to this is the *genogram*, probably Bowen's best known contribution. All patients, be they individuals, couples, or families, prepare with the aid of the therapist genograms as part of the evaluation process. The *genogram* is a pictorial representation of multigeneration family structures going back at least three generations from the parents. Bowen has a system of symbols for birth, death, divorce, and so forth, but the therapist can use any symbols that vivify relational patterns. The genogram is of particular relevance to substance abuse treatment where the family intergeneration pattern of use and abuse needs to be made manifest. I don't actually draw the genogram, but rather discuss the intergenerational pattern; most of my colleagues would consider this poor technique. The genogram is illustrated in the example of the Baker family in Chapter 4.

Bowen, unlike Whitaker, does address symptoms, which he sees as a source of anxiety. Anxiety makes for fusion, so he tries to reduce anxiety which is congruent with his whole thrust to be less emotional, at least less emotionally reactive. The therapist's calm works toward that end. In the case of the active addict whose behavior causes great anxiety to himself and to the system, one would think that Bowen would intervene and address the symptom—the drinking or drugging—and in the context of discussing anxiety, he suggests that he would do so. But in his paper on alcoholism, he focuses on differentiation rather than on the symptomatic drinking. However, in the case of more severe addiction, this is not possible. The pharmacology of the drugs make differentiation impossible. Bowen apparently has the functional alcoholic in mind in his treatment recommendations.

Bowen wrote a long paper on his personal struggle to differentiate from his family of origin, which he presented at the 1973 Georgetown Family Symposium. In it, he details a complicated series of maneuvers comprising letters and phone calls that created a crisis, which he calls "a tempest in a teapot," in order to convene his family for an exercise in detriangulation. He tells us he could not have done this before he developed the theory outlined above. Reading his paper is like reading an overplotted novel. Bowen's account of the strategy he came up with to detriangulate his family is reminiscent of Haley. Both use highly intellectualized, technique-driven plans to effectuate change. The difference is that Haley is atheoretical while Bowen's strategy is theory driven (or at least so he rationalizes). Neither Haley nor this aspect of Bowen does much for me.

Unlike Haley, Bowen does not talk much about power, and his strategizing to detriangulate and individuate from his family is not couched in terms of power relationships. I am sure that Haley would see this as a blind spot and maintain that Bowen's plan—strategy— to avoid fusion is a power play par excellence. In refusing to play, Bowen dominates and controls. Bowen would probably admit as much without embracing Haley's strategic ideology or his obsession with power. All of these maneuvers, outright lies, and manipulations which Bowen uses to remain unenmeshed from his family are, to say the least, hard to follow both narratively and in terms of their purpose.

Bowen goes so far as not to tell his wife what he is up to in this family visit. He fears being triangulated by her. He goes home and does his number. One of his goals is to reestablish contact with his cutoff brother. He manufactures a conflict in order to get in emotional contact with him, but he is not emotionally involved in the artificial fight. His persistent refusal to triangulate frees the family from their triangulation games, fusions, and emotional cutoffs. He reestablishes intimacy with his brother, and he feels a sense of liberation and selfhood he had never experienced before. The end of his paper is as moving as his beginning is off-putting.

When Bowen presented his paper at Georgetown, Minuchin and Whitaker were among the giants of family therapy present. In the discussion, Whitaker said to Bowen, "I wish that you were my brother." Bowen replied, "I can't be your brother. I am already Ackerman's brother," and comments that Whitaker was trying to triangulate him and that he needs to resist that triangulation. This seems to be mistaken, if not phobic. Whitaker is trying to make emotional contact, to say that Bowen's love for his brother so clearly seen in his effort to bring him back from being cut off and to touch him makes Whitaker want a brother (Bowen) who loves him as much. What is pathological or needs to be fled from in this? I don't see the triangle. Besides, it makes no sense to be able to have only one brother. Bowen sees it as the rejection of pseudo-intimacy; the closeness Whitaker offers him is merely therapeutic. I have my doubts, but Bowen doesn't have his. He writes,

> The end of that Sunday afternoon [of the family visit] was one of the most satisfying periods of my entire life. I had actually participated in the most intense family emotion possible and I had stayed completely out of the "ego mass" of my family! I had gone through the entire visit without being "triangulated" or without being forced into the family system. . . . I had attained the technical excellence to make the theoretical system work. [Bowen 1978b, p. 514]

Bowen makes strong claims for the therapeutic efficacy of both individual systems work, as illustrated by his own case, and multiple family therapy, stating that he has operationalized successful outcomes in such a way that vagueness and subjectivity are eliminated. I find his conceptual scheme more useful in working with addicted families and individuals than I do his techniques, but this is indubitably an artifact of temperament and training.

It is very unfair to Bowen, but my association to the complexities of Bowen's strategy of differentiating himself from his family is to a day treatment program I once directed in a state hospital that was aimed at the higher functioning patients on a chronic care ward. The program was intensive, using as many therapeutic modalities as possible to engage the patients. Among these modalities was problem solving. The problem-solving group was led by an overearnest, humorless young psychologist. Each week he would put his problem-solving flowchart and decision-making tree on the blackboard. It was of such complexity that those without doctorates in information theory could not possibly follow it. Most of the patients humored Richard, the young psychologist, as I tried to come up with a tactful way of telling him that there were at least 14 stages too many in his problem-solving scheme. One week, Mr. Bird, a patient who was apparently either catatonic or in a depressive stupor, who had mistakenly been assigned to the predischarge day program, and who usually spent the entire session slumped over, apparently out of contact, slowly pulled himself out of his catatonic posture and loudly proclaimed, "This shit again," whereupon he slumped back into his catatonia. I can envision myself reacting similarly if I were to be coached into such an elaborate, overly clever plan to return to my family of origin to help it (and me) differentiate.

Bowen reaches very far. He is an extremely ambitious systems builder and he is convinced that his notions of differentiation, fusion, and a quasi-genetic selection process of the least differentiated mating with the same, triangulating the least differentiated child as an object of undifferentiated projection in a kind of natural selection in reverse, is an exhaustive account of the appearance of psychopathology in individuals and systems. Bowen selfconsciously identifies with Darwin. His theoretical ambition is reminiscent of Freud as is his conceptualization of normality and pathology as a continuum. Currently unfashionable, Bowen's and Freud's continuum stands in sharp contrast to the work of thinkers like Hans Eysenck (1957), who claimed factor analysis orthogonality for neurosis and psychosis; that is, using the statistical techniques of factor analysis, they find no correlation between the symptoms of neurosis and those of psychosis. Contemporary biological psychiatrists also believe in disparate disease entities. Like all one-factor theories, and Bowen at base has such a theory, his is unable to account for the complexity of health and illness and is ultimately unconvincing. Yet it has elegance, power, and heuristic force; it is unquestionably the product of a first rate mind.

Bowen's relationship to Freud strongly illustrates his theory. In many of his early and middle-period papers, Bowen sharply differentiates himself from Freud by systematically criticizing him as being too intrapsychic. Bowen's manifest reasons are cogent; nevertheless, something like an oedipal revolt, which is after all a form of differentiation, is implicit here. In his late collaborative work with Michael Kerr (1988), Bowen (or his co-author) is much more appreciative of Freud's work. It is as if having established his own identity, Bowen can now afford to affiliate. This is exactly as his theory would predict. The relatively positive view of analysis may also be related to having claimed another spiritual father in Darwin. Freud ends as a therapeutic pessimist (or realist, depending on one's viewpoint); Bowen continues to make the strongest claims for the therapeutic efficacy of his techniques.

CRITICISMS OF STRATEGIC, STRUCTURAL, AND MULTIGENERATIONAL THERAPY

The "fathers" of family therapy have been taking their lumps lately. They have been criticized for being patriarchal, for putting too much emphasis on power, for constructing hierarchical causal systems that are incongruent with reality, for seeing substance where there is only process, and for losing contemporaneity and emergence in their focus on homeostasis. These criticisms are philosophical (Shotter 1993), social constructionist (Jorgenson 1989), and feminist (Gergen 1989). Their philosophical base is Wittgenstein's late *Philosophical*

Investigations (1953), which constructs "self" out of the language games people play with each other. Most of this work parallels the intersubjectivity school of psychoanalysis. The therapist as objective, having superior wisdom, or needing power to enable change is thoroughly deconstructed. I am sure he is always a male in the minds of these critics.

I don't see much that is useful here. Much of this literature is highly intellectualized, not to say ideological, and its clinical implications are fuzzy. It seems to me that Whitehead (see Chapter 1) gives a better account of the dialectical relationship between status and emergence than Wittgenstein, that reality is lost in the more radical social-constructionist's account of therapy, and that there isn't really much new here. What I do find salient in some of this work is its emphasis on the power of language in shaping our experience, the feminist corrective of an overemphasis on separateness and a corresponding underevaluation of relating, and an increased sensitivity to not blaming the victim, which has sometimes been an unfortunate misapplication of the notion of homeostatic resistance to change.

BEHAVIORAL FAMILY THERAPY

There is no question that classical conditioning, operant conditioning, and social learning make a powerful etiological contribution to addiction. These learning paradigms are operative not only historically but now. Behavioral family therapy works on extinguishing the effects of maladaptive past learning, changing present contingencies, and challenging the attitudinal (cognitive or belief) components of dysfunction. Although most often used in individual therapy, these techniques can be adapted to couple and family work. Behavioral family therapy has many incarnations, but these days is strongly cognitively oriented. I find its literature virtually unreadable, yet I have no doubt that behavioral techniques are useful.

Behavioral family therapy uses homework, for example, "Say something positive to your partner every day"; contingency contracts, for example, "If you do your homework, you can watch TV"; reinforcement; modeling by the therapist; and shaping, that is, reinforcing successive approximations to a desired behavior. Behavior therapy encourages self-monitoring, the keeping of diaries, and training in problem solving. The behavioral approach to family problems is most often used with families with recalcitrant teenagers. Generally speaking, the behaviorists focus on the individual patient, seeing the patient's problems as the cause of the difficulties in the family. This is the direct opposite of the systems approach, although behavioral family therapists recognize that the family members may be unwittingly (never unconsciously) reinforcing the aberrant behavior. Like all therapists, I sometimes use behavioral techniques, especially self-monitoring of drinking and drugging, including the interpersonal triggers if they can be observed, but I have not in general found this approach useful with addicted families and choose to work less directively with recovering families.

Two behavioral approaches that can be extremely helpful with recovering families are parental skills training and conjoint sex therapy. There are several varieties of parental skills training; all are essentially educational and all seek to help reduce family conflict. Parenting sober is very different from parenting while drug-involved, and concrete, didactic training, advice, and guidance can sometimes substantially reduce anxiety and conflict in the recovering parent and his or her family, and promote growth into a new role as responsible, emotionally available father or mother.

Masters and Johnson's (1970) style of behaviorally oriented sex therapy using such techniques as sensate focusing is sometimes used for the newly sober who are having a hard time functioning sexually without their drug(s) of choice. This is not incompatible with psychodynamic work on sexual inhibition.

Timothy O'Farrell (1993) has worked out a behavioral marital therapy for alcoholics and their families. It has a substantial success rate. O'Farrell's protocol is discussed in more detail in Chapter 3.

When I think of behavioral family therapy of addiction, I think of John and Mary. Mary maintained that John was obnoxious when he drank, which was often; John maintained that being with Mary sober was virtually impossible. I soon concluded that they were both right, and suggested that Mary find something positive to say about John next time that he was sober and that John do something other than drink the next time he felt criticized by Mary. Not especially psychologically minded, this couple was delighted with their homework assignment. Each stated that they felt hopeful. They returned a week later furious with each other. After five days of John's being sober, Mary had told John that he was thinking much more clearly now that he was sober so that he would surely agree that the most positive thing he could do for her and their family was to hang himself. John did indeed find a way other than drinking to deal with Mary's critical input. (She maintained that her comment was positive because true.) He went to his favorite bar but didn't drink. Instead he picked up the local sleep-with-anybody, and brought her home to his marital bed. (Mary was in it.) I concluded that I wasn't cut out to be a marital behavioral therapist. Mary called me several years later to say that John's liver had finally failed and that he had stopped drinking, but she wasn't giving him any sex anyway. I have no idea why she called me or why they stayed together, but the satisfactions of marital torture have clearly been underestimated.

PSYCHODYNAMIC FAMILY THERAPY

If strategic family therapy focuses on developing strategies to enable change, structural therapy on modifying structure, experiential therapy on providing alternate experience, Bowenian therapy on differentiation, and behavioral therapy on modifying behavior, then psychodynamic family focuses on fostering insight, insight into overt behavioral patterns and interactions and into unconscious reenactments, projections, and identifications. Psychodynamic family therapy uses all of the knowledge Bateson, Haley, Minuchin, Whitaker, Bowen, and the behaviorists have gleaned about systems, communication, power relations, boundaries, intergenerational transmission, positive and negative feedback loops, double binds, social learning, and contingencies of reinforcement in families, but it does so in a nondirective way in which that knowledge is instrumental, not determinative. What the psychodynamic family therapist is primarily interested in is increasing self-awareness, particularly awareness of unconscious process.

The psychodynamic family therapist's preeminent tools are analysis of transference and creative use of countertransference. This approach borrows from analytic tradition its recognition of the influence of past on present, and of the depth beneath the surface, while borrowing from the family therapy tradition its recognition of the recursive nature of relationships, of the reality of the now, and of the influence of the surface on the depth. As far back as Freud describing the formation of intrapsychic structure (e.g., the superego) as formed through identification, a bridge from the intrapsychic to the interpersonal existed. However, it was a long time before anybody walked across it. Nathan Ackerman (1994) was the first major figure to do so.

Nathan Ackerman

Ackerman started out as a classical analyst, but by the 1940s had moved into family therapy. Working in the child guidance tradition, the idea of working with parents was not unique to Ackerman; what he did differently was to work with the family as a whole rather than using different therapists to see the mother (only rarely would the father be involved) and child. By 1960 Ackerman was primarily a family therapist, institutionalizing his approach by founding the Ackerman Institute for Family Therapy in New York City. Ackerman's major theoretical contribution was to simultaneously understand psychopathology as intrapsychic and systemic (familial). Ackerman characterized family dysfunction as arising from a failure of *complementarity*; that is, instead of family members complementing each other, both in terms of role enactments and overt expression of parts of the self in flexible, mutually interactive flow of roles and enactments of the unconscious, the roles and enactments become fixed, rigid, and dead. Although Ackerman (as far as I know) didn't draw the analogy, it is implicit in his analysis that the mental health field had become stultified through a lack of complementarity; instead of the intrapsychic and interpersonal being mutually interactive modes of understanding and therapeutizing, each perspective ossified and came to stand in rigid and hostile opposition to the other.

Whether in the family or in the larger social system, for example, a branch of professional activity, such a failure of complementarity results in *stalemate*, another key Ackerman concept. The family (or system) then deals with the unresolved conflict manifested in the stalemate by *scapegoating*, the scapegoat most usually being the identified patient. What makes Ackerman a psychodynamic family therapist is the unconscious nature of the unresolved conflict. Most of the failure of complementarity is between the parents. Scapegoating serves as a diversion and defense. This is an extremely common dynamic when the identified patient is an adolescent or young adult substance abuser. On a conscious level, the parents are passionately (and genuinely) invested in halting the adolescent's substance abuse; on an unconscious level they "need" the adolescent to continue to use and to be a problem so he or she can be available for scapegoating, and the parents don't have to look at the disturbance in their own relationship.

Inevitably the scapegoat is only too willing to continue in that role, and the drug use remains unabated. Ackerman would see this as a case of *interlocking pathology*. Although the interlock could be broken by change in any of the parties involved by individual psychotherapy or analysis, Ackerman came to believe that family therapy is generally more efficacious. Ackerman's take on homeostasis is an interesting one; unlike Bateson and the communication theorists, Ackerman understands homeostasis as more than a mental mechanism maintaining the status quo, rather it is a drive toward equilibrium that may use change as well as stasis to maintain the integrity of the system. This is a more dynamic view of homeostasis than the cybernetic one.

Ackerman, like the other founding fathers of family therapy, was charismatic. His style was warm, engaged, highly active, open, and confrontational. Coming from an analytic rather than an experiential stance, he nevertheless shares a great deal with Whitaker. Anything but neutral, he takes sides, "unbalances," particularly with the scapegoat, and is in this way reminiscent of Minuchin. One sees why he moved from analysis to family therapy, the latter being so much more congenial to his personality. Although Ackerman didn't make great use of transference interpretation in his family work, he did rely heavily on therapeutic use of countertransference, openly commenting on his feelings. In part this was modeling, modeling openness about sex, dependence, aggression, and anxiety. Ackerman's aims were always to increase self-awareness of both repressed and projective aspects of self, including the enactment of interacting psychopathologies. Whatever— interpretation, confrontation, or self-disclosure—moves the family toward that awareness is therapeutic. Ackerman's self-image as therapist is that of a catalyst of change, all technique being subordinate to the catalytic role. There is a great deal in Ackerman's approach, particularly his understanding of the mutually interlocking psychopathologies, that readily lends itself to work with addicted and recovering families.

Ivan Boszormenyi-Nagy

Ivan Boszormenyi-Nagy is an analytically oriented family therapist who sounds a lot like Murray Bowen speaking of the intergenerational transmission of psychopathology. Boszormenyi-Nagy's, like so many family therapy pioneers, first interest was in schizophrenia. Initially he looked for a biological etiology; not finding one, he turned his attention to the psychosocial determinants of severe pathology. Heavily influenced by Erik Erikson, Boszormenyi-Nagy put the establishment of basic trust or the failure to do so at the heart of his conceptual system. The vicissitudes of trust are the vicissitudes of normality and pathology.

Erikson (1950, 1968) is a psychosocial theorist, each of his developmental stages being simultaneously intrapsychic and interpersonal. Identity, for example, is a concept that only makes sense in the context of roles available for identification and identity formation. Boszormenyi-Nagy's social context is primarily historical. It is the weight of the past on the present that distorts and undermines trust, the key notions here being *obligation, debt, legacy,* and *loyalty.* He came to see that it was not only schizophrenic families, but every family that has emotional *family ledgers,* and that we attempt to meet our obligations to past generations, in particular but not exclusively to parents, in the present, just as we attempt to repay (or collect) the family debts in the here and now of present relationships. This legacy of obligations, debts, guilt, and expectations importantly includes loyalties. In fact, mental illness may be reframed as being an act of loyalty. The heavy-drinking son may in fact be motivated by a sense of loyalty to a heavy-drinking father. To become abstinent would be an act of betrayal and rejection. This is an exceedingly common dynamic of male addiction.

Boszormenyi-Nagy (1987) calls his style of dynamic family therapy *contextual family therapy.* The intrapsychic world can only be understood in terms of its multigenerational context of obligations, loyalties, and debts. Only then is change possible. In Boszormenyi-Nagy's view, this can only be achieved by making the family ledger conscious and by paying legitimate debts and meeting legitimate obligations, particularly to parents. Only then are they not reenacted in marriages and in parenting the next generation.

This has particular relevance to substance use where the acting out concomitant with such use makes the meeting of legitimate debts and obligations impossible, so that one never becomes free of the irrational obligations and debts passed on multigenerationally. This keeps people stuck in their addictions forever.

The meeting of legitimate debts and obligations can only be accomplished when trust is established. Influenced by Martin Buber's (1937) notion of the I–thou relationship, the relationship in which the other is treated as a person rather than as an object, Boszormenyi-Nagy seeks to move family members in that direction, all of which gives contextual therapy a moral or ethical tone. The danger is that it can become offensively preachy and therefore ineffective.

What happens in contextual therapy is that the ways in which old debts are being paid and collected in present relationships is brought into consciousness, obligations to past generations are met so that they need not be cripplingly enacted, and each member of the current family is now free of the past (or as free as humans get) and capable of being engaged in relationships of mutual trust and I–thou reciprocity. It is another way of going back to one's family of origin to differentiate à la Bowen, so as to be free to engage and relate now.

I have never known a contextual therapist nor seen this approach used in its pure form, and I don't quite see how it would work in practice. I discuss it here for two reasons: it is impossible to read the family therapy literature without encountering the name Boszormenyi-Nagy, so one should at least know who he is, and more important, his approach can be cannibalized—trust is a central issue in all treatment, but nowhere more so than in substance abuse treatment. Pathologies including drugging and drinking can be usefully understood as driven by the desire to pay or be paid, and by loyalty and by obligation either felt or expressed. The nature of relating in the addicted family is the antithesis of a Buber I–thou relationship and often drug use a substitute for it, which can be usefully interpreted as one dynamic of addiction. That is to say, because the addict cannot trust people and the family cannot trust him or her, trust is transferred to the substance, which is then deemed to be trustworthy and the addict is locked into a chemical rather than a human relationship.

My association to Boszormenyi-Nagy's take on pathology is Greek tragedy. The weight of ancient hates and scores haunts succeeding generations. Murder avenges murder in an endless chain, fate playing the same role as Boszormenyi-Nagy's family legacy. In Aeschylus' Orestean trilogy (458 B.C.), the endless chain of blood begetting more blood is finally ended by the establishment of an impartial court of justice, the Aeropagus, by Athena, Goddess of Wisdom. Athena is a fitting representation of insight and the court an institutional representation of the Boszormenyi-Nagy notion of the necessity of repaying legitimate debts rather than giving or paying forever. Reason and measure replace unconscious reenactment exactly as in contextual therapy. It is a model of great appeal, however wanting in practical application.

OBJECT RELATIONS FAMILY THERAPY

Jill Savege Scharff and David Scharff

Object relations family therapy seeks to use the insights of object relations theory in family work. Ackerman certainly has a dynamic approach centered on making the unconscious conscious through interpretation and confrontation, yet reading him or watching tapes of his work leaves one with the feeling that a highly intuitive guy is putting on a good show, and that the analytic trappings and Freudian metapsychology are tangential to what is going on. This is not the case with the object relations family therapy developed by Jill Savege Scharff and David Scharff (1991). Although active, interactive, and engaged, the Scharffs shun directive, manipulative, and symptom-focused interventions. Their approach is analytic in that it puts a premium on understanding. It is object relational in that it understands the basic motivation of human life to be object seeking. The Scharffs would heartily endorse Harry Guntrip's (1971) dictum that "We seek persons, not pleasures." By listening and seeking to understand, they provide a *holding environment* that enables growth. Their therapeutic tools are mostly interpretive, although they occasionally use behavioral techniques. This is mainly true for David Scharff, who is also a sex therapist; he uses a Masters and Johnson–style behavioral approach to sexual problems. However, the sex therapy is always embedded in a dynamic context where unraveling the meaning of the sexual dysfunction plays as large a role as the didactic interventions to teach better sexual functioning. The Scharffs make extensive use of countertransference to understand what is happening in the family and in the session. They may or may not verbalize the insight and the understanding that they gain from being open to their own feelings. Countertransferential feelings often help the therapist to become aware of and make sense of the individual and collective transference emerging in the session.

The therapist must not strain or use any particular technique to get in touch with his or her countertransferential feelings. On the contrary, what is needed is simply receptivity. David Scharff repeatedly emphasizes that his style of object relations family therapy is not a set of techniques nor is it essentially a theory, although theory aids understanding. Rather, it is a way of working, more of a weltanschauung than a school. The route to a noncontrolling receptivity is one's own analysis and family therapy, freeing the therapist to feel whatever emerges without defensive blocking. One is reminded of Freud's (1912a) injunction in his papers on technique that the analyst bring an "evenly hovering attention" to the analytic frame, an attention that is isomorphic with the analysand's free associating. "Even" implies without prejudgment or prejudice as to what is important or what the analysand should be addressing; "hovering" implies watching over, observing without intruding or impinging; "attention" emphasizes engagement. Mutatis mutandis, this is attitudinally and existentially exactly what the Scharffs have in mind by their unstructured openness to emergent countertransference.

Transference interpretation is central to object relations family therapy. The Scharffs draw heavily on the work of Melanie Klein on projective identification and projective counteridentification (see below), and tend to interpret transference as projective identification. They draw equally heavily on the metapsychology of Ronald Fairbairn using his model of the mind rather than Freud's structural model to comprehend the inner world of their patients whether seen in individual, couple, or family therapy. Similarly they see the dynamics of family life as driven by mutual projective identification of the aspects of the ego (self) described by Fairbairn.

The Scharffs were not the first to develop an object relations family therapy. James Framo (1982), who worked with Ivan Boszormenyi-Nagy at the Eastern Pennsylvania Psychiatric Center (which he founded), applied Fairbairn's theorizing about internal objects and their reprojection to work with couples and families. Henry Dicks (1967), working at the Tavistock Clinic in London, developed an object relations method of studying and treating couples, putting an emphasis on the mutual attempt to fulfill unconscious needs in marriage. But the Scharffs are the ones who most fully developed an object relations approach to family therapy. The influence of Dicks is direct, since he was a teacher of David Scharff at Tavistock.

The Scharffs use dreams, drawings, and play as integral parts of their work. They deal equally with the interpersonal surface and the unconscious depth, with the present and the past, with behavior and the internal world. This lends a richness to their approach. I have the highest regard for their work, which is difficult to summarize. They take the stance (which I agree with) that theory is a model that guides us and is subject to revision (cf. Freud's [1914, p. 77] comment in his essay *On Narcissism*, "Theory is the capstone of the pyramid that can be replaced without damage to the structure because the base of the pyramid is observation," and Kohut's [1977, p. 206] observation, "All worthwhile theorizing is tentative, provisional, and has an element of playfulness"), not a description of concrete realities. Their work comes alive in their classical vignettes found in Scharff and Scharff (1991, 1994), and David Scharff (1992), and these works are highly recommended to the reader. The clinical material in Samuel Slipp's (1988) work on object relations family therapy is also valuable.

It is not possible to understand individual object relations theory and practice without some understanding of Melanie Klein and Ronald Fairbairn, to whom we now turn.

Melanie Klein

Melanie Klein, who is generally considered the founder of object relations theory, emigrated from the Continent to England after being analyzed by Freud's disciple, Karl Abraham, and remained influential in the British Psychoanalytic Society throughout a long and bitter rivalry with Anna Freud. Abraham had anticipated Freud's proto–object-relational constructs adumbrated in *Mourning and Melancholia* (1917), where the internalization of the lost object plays a key role. Abraham undoubtedly influenced Klein, an intellectual without a higher education who was attracted to analysis in its early, wide-open days. There was a Mr. Klein somewhere, but he doesn't seem to have played much of a role in her life. Klein worked mostly with children, whom she analyzed exactly as one would analyze an adult, in contrast to her rival, Anna Freud, who pioneered play therapy in the analysis of children. Klein's theories developed out of her clinical work with children and are less in danger of "adultomorphic" distortions of infantile experience, or projecting adult pathological states understood as developmental arrests onto infants, than developmental theories derived from clinical work with adults—at least, one would think that should be the case.

Klein is not a facile or clear writer, and she is difficult to follow. Her collected papers (1921–1945, 1946–1963) are best supplemented by her disciple Hanna Segal's (1973) lucid summary of Klein's theoretical and clinical work.

Melanie Klein and her followers are virtually the only analysts who subscribe to Freud's death instinct. It is her starting point. According to Klein, we come into the world with the death instinct within us, a desire to return to the quietus of the inorganic—a pull toward death—which must be externalized, moved from inside to outside, if it is not to destroy us. There are two ways this can be done: the death instinct can become aggression and attack external objects, an option not readily available to the neonate; or it can be projected onto the environment so that it is experienced as external instead of internal, so that which would kill me if it remained inside me is now able to kill me from its position in the environment. At least that's the way it would be experienced according to Klein. A dubious gain, yet Klein thinks that this projection of the death instinct is a universal developmental phenomenon.

Once the death instinct is projected outside, the environment becomes persecutory. The death instinct, no longer recognized as mine, now hovers over me and characterizes my objects. They become persecutors, and I am in the *paranoid-schizoid position*. The Kleinian positions are developmental stages other than the psychosexual ones described by Freud or the stages in the development of libido also described by Freud. They are also modes of being that persist throughout life. Klein originally called the stage following the projection of Thanatos the paranoid position, but modified its denotation when Ronald Fairbairn pointed out that the response to persecution is defensive withdrawal, hence the paranoid-schizoid position. So far, it sounds like Klein is an instinct theorist, which she really isn't. Once

Thanatos has been projected, it plays no further role in her developmental theory, which becomes an object relations one.

Projected Thanatos adheres in objects, particularly in Mother, the first object, and those objects are now dangerous persecutors, "bad objects." To control them, these bad objects are (re-)introjected, and the persecutors are now, once more, within, but no longer as highly dangerous as the preprojected death instinct; now they are merely *internal bad objects*. These internal bad objects can be (re-)projected onto the environment. Alternately, the goodness within may be projected outward to protect it from the inner badness. The world of the Kleinian paranoid-schizoid position is a ping-pong game with good and bad objects flying across the net, where they change from internal objects to gratifiers and persecutors. Reintrojection propels them back across the net again. Herein lies a problem (as if there were no others) with Kleinian theory. At this stage of development, there is no net, no boundary, because the developmental task of separation from symbiotic union with the environment, chiefly Mother, has not been completed. If the ego psychologists are right about development of the self, this is indeed a strange ping-pong game; not only is there no net, but both players are on the same side of the table. Be that as it may, this is Klein's vision of early life.

You may well imagine that the paranoid-schizoid position is not a comfortable one, and it is, in fact, pervaded by anxiety of psychotic proportions, which engenders all sorts of defensive maneuvers. It is a stage characterized by rage (why not if the world is persecutory?), envy (since my goodness is projected out, I must envy it), and part objects. Part objects are objects like Mother and Father, who are regarded as breasts (only) and penises (only), respectively. Objects are reduced to part objects, in part, to make them manageable, but they also exist because integration into whole objects has not yet taken place. Now my internal bad objects, which were created by my internalizing the objects "spoiled" by my original projection of the death instinct, are reprojected onto that part object, Mother's breast, which becomes the "bad breast." Similarly, my good internal objects are projected to protect them from my internal badness onto Mother's breast, creating a second part object, the "good breast." But I envy the good breast, so I must spoil it, destroy it with my envy, greed, and rage, turning it into a bad breast. The splitting of the breast into the good breast and the bad breast is reinforced by the ineluctable frustration of the infant's needs. No mother is always there. Interpersonally, the good breast feeds, while the bad breast refuses to gratify. Although Klein realizes that environmental provocation makes matters worse, she doesn't much pursue the role of the environment.

If Freud is notorious for his concept of penis envy, Klein is equally notorious for her concept of *breast envy*. Her whole theory is a theory about the child's aggressiveness toward the mother, and she sees normal biological functions such as feeding and excretion as acts of aggression: "I want to bite, piss on, shit on the good breast because I envy it." In real life, Klein had exceptionally awful relations with her own children, and I don't know what impact, if any, this had on her theorizing.

If things weren't bad enough in the paranoid-schizoid position, they are about to get worse. At some point in development, I (the infant) realize two things: first, that the good breast and the bad breast are one; and second, that I have created the bad breast by aggressing against the good breast out of envy and hatred. These realizations move me into the *depressive position*, at about age 2. I defend against this realization by using the psychological defense of *splitting* to keep good and bad (part) objects separate. When ego psychologists talk about the achievement of *object constancy*, when good and bad self- and object representations coalesce into one complex self- or object representation, they are talking about the same phenomenon that Klein denotes as the depressive position. The depressive position is the developmental stage in which good and bad internal and external objects become just objects, with all of the ambiguity of reality, and in which part objects become whole objects.

The depressive position is depressing because I feel guilty about spoiling the good breast, and the way I deal with my guilt is by making *reparation* for my aggression. The notion of reparation is central to Kleinian theory and practice. What happens to my innate envy that has been causing all this difficulty? I overcome it with *gratitude*, another key Kleinian notion. Instead of envying, I feel grateful for the good breast and its successors, and I more or less spend the rest of my life working through the depressive position. Klein goes no further in her developmental scheme. The task of working through the depressive position is the task of integration and of owning that which is being projected.

One response to the depressive position and its guilt-induced pain is to institute a *manic defense*. The notion of mania and its derivatives as a defense against underlying depression is a Kleinian contribution. Klein puts great emphasis on early fantasy, moving the Oedipus complex back into the first six months of life. She claims to have found support for her entire schema in the fantasies of her child patients.

Is Klein's theory a fantastic fairy tale that, far more than Freud's placing sexual fantasies within the mind of the child, makes children monstrous? Thinkers as diverse as Saint Augustine (397) and Freud have emphasized the innateness of aggression, but nobody but Klein has developed this aspect of the self to this extent. In a way, you can see her theory as the psychoanalytic version of the doctrine of original sin, with the death instinct and its derivatives playing the role of original sin. Perhaps, and I certainly find Klein less than persuasive. Yet history is one long record of bloody and barbaric aggression and man's inhumanity to man seems to know no bounds, so we cannot rule out Klein's understanding of the death instinct and its vicissitudes. Further, Klein adumbrated the defenses of splitting, projection, and introjection as universal, playing a central role in human behavior, not only in infancy and in psychopathological states, but in all human interactions.

What about the self in Kleinian theory? There is no self. There are only instincts and their projection to create objects. Presumably the self is built up out of the internalized reintrojected objects, and this is part of the working through of the depressive position. However, Klein doesn't discuss this. The Kleinian notions of reparation and gratitude have both developmental and therapeutic relevance. The Kleinian (non)self is fragmented by its biological givens, and the only way it can be reintegrated, both its goodness and badness made once more part of the self, is through reparation for damage unwittingly caused by projection. Gratitude reduces the need to attack and to project, which facilitates the integration of internalized objects into a self.

The Kleinian positions are not merely developmental stages, they are states of being that recur throughout life. Thomas Ogden (1986) adds a third even more primitive position the *autistic/contiguous position*, which is the existential stance in which we struggle to evolve and maintain a self. There is no self without an object and there are no objects that are not in part constituted by projective aspects of self. In Donald Winnicott's famous phrase, "There is no such thing as a baby"; that is, there are no babies without a mother or a mother substitute. But there are no mothers without babies, so we are constantly defined by our reciprocal relationships. We literally come into being through relationships, and all our lives require affirmation from others even as we affirm them. We are always coming into being (that is, working through the autistic/contiguous position); always splitting, repressing, and projecting, thereby creating persecutory objects that we fear and flee (that is, we are always working through the paranoid/schizoid position); and struggling to re-own our projections, to integrate our split selves and objects and to come to care about those objects, or as Winnicott put it, to develop the "capacity for concern" (that is, we are working through the depressive position). Nevertheless, in healthy maturity our existential stance is predominantly that of the depressive position.

Kleinian developmental theory has particular relevance for understanding the phenomenology of addiction and the twelve-step movement can be understood as a kind of Kleinian therapy in which the addict works through the depressive position by making reparations (see AA's ninth step, "making amends"). The twelve–step programs put tremendous emphasis on gratitude, gratitude being seen as an antidote for resentments. AA's resentments are Klein's rage and envy. Reparation for aggression against the bad breast (which is really the good breast or rather the only breast) makes sense for those who split the world into the good breast (alcohol, coke, or whatever) and the bad breast (all the rest), and aggress against whatever separated them from their good breast. Gratitude makes integration possible, envy manageable, and rage controllable and tolerable.

Ronald Fairbairn

The Scharffs are great admirers of Ronald Fairbairn, and rely heavily on Fairbairn's (1952) model of the mind (self) to understand the intrapsychic and interpersonal worlds of their patients. Their comprehension and interpretation of family dynamics and of transference is essentially Fairbairnian.

Fairbairn, who persuaded Klein to relabel her paranoid position the paranoid-schizoid position, was a Kleinian who went his own way. A Scot who practiced in Edinburgh and who had a phobia about urinating in public that restricted his travel, he was isolated physically and intellectually from the mainstream of British analytic thought. Not surprisingly, his clinical interest was in schizoid phenomena. He alone among psychoanalytic thinkers believes that the self, which he calls the ego, is primordially integral. Only later, and for defensive reasons, is it "split" into a central ego, a libidinal ego, and an antilibidinal ego. The *central ego* is the relatively rational residue of the originally integral ego; the *libidinal ego* is the yearning, longing, exciting, perhaps tantalizing part of that ego; and the *antilibidinal ego* is the angry, aggressive, self-critical part of that ego that cannot let go of the rejecting bad object. Fairbairn originally called it the *internal saboteur*. Fairbairn's self has its own energy. It is a self that represses and splits because it cannot stand the pain of frustration, abandonment, and rejection. Since frustration is inevitable, we all repress and split; however, the severity of the rigidity of the repression and splitting depends on the environment.

Fairbairn objected to the dichotomizing of structure and energy in Freudian theory, where the drives are energetic and the ego without power. Hence Fairbairn's ego, or self, has power and need not borrow it through such dubious theoretical constructs as neutralization. The Fairbairnian self in its three aspects relates to three objects: the ideal object, the exciting object, and the rejecting object. The primordially integral self is only split in this way because the environment is not sufficiently, or consistently, supportive. This is the exact opposite of Klein's vision; it isn't badness but goodness that is primordial for Fairbairn. The task of Fairbairn's psychotherapy is the healing of the split self.

In David Scharff's view, there is a further secondary repression of the libidinal ego by the antilibidinal ego so that the longing part of us becomes inaccessible. This is illustrated in Figure 2–1.

Thus the internal world consists of repressed aspects of the self, the objects these aspects of the self relate to, and the affects engendered by those relationships. This internal world is the repressed part of the self, and *internal objects* are then projected (or reprojected) onto external objects, which are colored and distorted by these projections. Yet somehow we find ourselves and our lost objects in the external

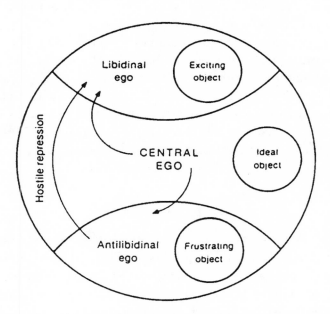

FIGURE 2–1. Fairbairn's model of psychic organization, by David E. Scharff, from *Refinding the Object and Reclaiming the Self.* The central ego in relation to the ideal object is in conscious interaction with the caretaker. The central ego represses the split-off libidinal and antilibidinal aspects of its experience along with corresponding parts of the ego that remain unconscious. The libidinal system is further repressed by the antilibidinal system. Reprinted courtesy of David E. Scharff.

world, which we hold and which holds us. The notion here is that interpersonal relations are inextricably rendered problematic by our projection of our internal objects, yet only in relationship is there hope.

The notion of *holding*, which the Scharffs borrow from Winnicott, has great saliency in their theorizing and their practice. It is the holding function of the mother, of the family, and of the therapist that provides the matrix and nexus that enable growth and differentiation. It is the failure of holding on the part of parent, spouse, family, or therapist that engenders regression, splitting, and projection of the exciting and rejecting internal objects. Holding need not be perfect, only *good enough*, another Winnicottian concept. In fact, Winnicott says that we succeed by failing, as parents and as therapists; that is, if we are good enough, our failures to empathize, be there, and provide support also enable growth and differentiation. Addictive families are almost always inadequate holders. Holding is first physical, bodily holding, only later becoming symbolic and relational, yet all our lives we crave and need physicality, actually being held as we hold.

Although the Scharffs acknowledge their indebtedness to Klein and even more especially to Fairbairn as their spiritual and intellectual parents, tending to mention Winnicott in passing, he is such a fine thinker that he deserves more of our attention.

D. W. Winnicott

Donald W. Winnicott is not a systematic thinker. In some ways more of a poet than a scientist, his insights are diffused throughout his deceptively simple papers. A pediatrician who later became a psychiatrist and psychoanalyst, he never ceased practicing pediatrics. From the beginning, he was concerned with mothers and babies and their interaction. The Winnicottian self emerges from that interaction. Winnicott's thinking encompasses a developmental scheme, a notion of self pathology, and an object relational notion of self. Developmentally, Winnicott postulates three stages of ego development: integration, personalization, and object relating. To steal a phrase from the title of one of Winnicott's books, ego development comes about through the interaction of *The Maturational Processes and the Facili-*

tating Environment (1965). Winnicott's notions of ego and self are object relational; they come into being only in the presence of and through interaction with others. Self is defined in relation to others from the outset. The first stage of ego development is *integration*, the process by which the paradoxically undifferentiated and unintegrated infant begins to differentiate from the experience of merger into separateness. This "me" is fragmented, consisting of isolated "me" experiences, which begin to cohere or integrate into an "I." During integration, and indeed during all of Winnicott's developmental stages, the experience of continuity and going-on-being is vital to the establishment of a healthy self. Going-on-being is threatened by *impingement*, traumatic disruptions that fragment self-experience. Many substance abusers suffered traumatic impingement. Adequate (good-enough) maternal care minimizes impingement and establishes going-on-being. Self-cohesion comes from continuity of care.

Winnicott's notion of good-enough parenting is reassuring to anxious parents and therapists. Since frustration is necessary for development, "We succeed by failing."

Personalization is the achievement of psychosomatic collusion, of living in the body rather than in fantasy. What Winnicott calls the *holding environment*—initially literal holding, later symbolic holding—enables the infant to feel whole. The establishment of psychosomatic collusion, the sense of being one with my body, is vital for mental health; failure to succeed in doing so leaves one prone to experiences of depersonalization, which are often self-medicated. In this stage, the body comes to be experienced as a "limiting membrane," as a boundary, further establishing the distinction between me and not-me. The move from integration to personalization is a move from "I" to "I am." When a person says at a twelve–step meeting, "My name is John and I am an alcoholic," the affirmation that "I am" is just as curative as admitting the addiction.

In the third stage of ego development, *object relating*, separateness is consolidated and ambivalence accepted, moving the infant into the depressive position. Winnicott's depressive stage is much less depressing than Klein's. Rather than emphasizing guilt, he focuses on what he calls the acquisition of the "capacity for concern."

The child's experience is now "I am alone," but "there are others I can relate to and make part of me" (as internal objects), so that being alone is tolerable, even enjoyable. In one of his most beautiful papers, "The Capacity to Be Alone" (1958), Winnicott tells us that the acquisition of the capacity to be alone, which is an achievement and not a native endowment, is a paradox. It arises out of the experience of being alone with another, another who is not impinging. If we are fortunate enough to have spent sufficient time as toddlers "alone" with Mother, Father, Grandfather, or Grandmother while Mother, Father, Grandfather, or Grandmother "let us be," we internalized that loving caregiver and acquired the capacity to be alone, because now when we are alone, we are not alone because whoever spent that time with us is now a part of us. The Winnicottian capacity to be alone has nothing to do with schizoid defensive isolation; it is its opposite, and it is a prerequisite to mental health and to creativity. Many addictions are driven by a failure to acquire the capacity to be alone, the substance serving as companion.

The achievement of identity through separation is facilitated by the use of *transitional objects*. Linus's blanket in the comic strip "Peanuts" is the quintessential transitional object. Fantasy turns the inanimate, a teddy bear or a blanket, into a substitute for Mother, and permits me to separate from her. It isn't the teddy bear, per se, but the teddy bear suffused with meaning that constitutes the transitional object. In Winnicott's view, all of culture is a transitional phenomenon derivative from that blanket or stuffed animal. Winnicott emphasizes playfulness, and the creation of transitional objects is play; so is therapy, and so is creativity. Therapy provides a *transitional space*, in which transitional objects can be created as the patient struggles to proceed with his or her development.

This brings us to a final Winnicottian (1960) concept, that of the true self and the false self. The *true self* is the self with all of its feelings, drives, and id-derived instincts striving for expression. The true self is messy, egocentric, unsocialized, and filled with hate and envy and destructiveness, but it is also the repository of love, gratitude, and creativity, as well as the repository of yearning and the desire to be loved. The true self is not the id, but includes id as owned, as personalized. It is "it" become "I" without being deinstinctualized. If the true self is unduly threatened by a nonfacilitating environment, particularly one that cannot accept its aggression, it goes into hiding deep within the recesses of being to be replaced (as far as social reality is concerned), by a *false self*, a compliant, "people-pleasing" self that looks for approval at all cost. The twelve-step movement sees the people-pleasing false self as vulnerable to relapse. The false self organization often leads to outward success, especially in intellectual pursuits, but at the cost of vitality and feelings of aliveness and genuineness. The experience is of hollowness, an absence of deep satisfaction. However, the true self has not been destroyed; it is merely in hiding. The true self contains within it, and protects, all that is felt to be threatened by destruction. It is consistent with this notion of the need to protect that which is valued from harm that Winnicott defines God as the repository of the good aspects of the self, which we need to project outward to protect them from our inner badness. Successful therapeutic intervention surfaces the true self, establishing experiences of wholeness, aliveness, genuineness, and worth.

Projective Identification and Projective Counteridentification

Klein, Fairbairn, and later object relations theorists developed the concept of *projective identification*. In Klein's original conception, projective identification is the notion that infants project unacceptable aspects of themselves onto the environment in order to protect their inner goodness from their inner badness; essentially it is projection of the death instinct and its derivatives. Once the projection is in the environment, it takes on an object characterization and becomes a persecutory object. The persecutory object is then reintrojected because it is too dangerous in the environment, and a whole sequence of introjection and projection ensues.

More contemporary understandings (Ogden 1982, 1986) view projective identification as a process in which a child or an adult rids himself of unacceptable feelings, aspects of self, or states of being by engaging in behaviors that induce the very same feeling or state of being in someone else. Not only small children and sick adults, but all human beings engage in projective identification. In therapy, the projection is processed; that is, the projected affect or state of being is contained and tamed. Projected, not now by Klein's mysterious fantasizing process but rather through a behavioral inducement, the affect state is now present in the therapist, who has more mature resources to handle the feeling, and in that sense, processes it in such a way that it is tamed. The projector, in this case the patient, is now able to identify with that which he or she has projected, which is now in a more benign state, so it's his stuff, but his stuff in a more manageable form, and now through identification, he is able to take it back in, where it will now be more easily managed, assimilated, and owned. In this version, there is nothing mysterious about projective identification. It's about behavior-induced affective states in both the projector and the recipient of the projection. The recipient of the projection does something with it, which the projector was unable to do, and this something induces a behavioral state in the one who originally projected it, so he or she can more easily identify and own it.

Object relations family therapy makes extensive use of the notion of projective identification. It sees the family as a nexus of projective identifications and projective counteridentifications, and uses the feelings engendered in the therapist by the family's projective identifications, that is, the therapist's countertransferential feelings (or the part of them coming from the patient) to understand, identify with, and empathize with the family and its members. The therapist containing the projections constitutes holding, and as such facilitates integration and development. The therapist may also choose to interpret the feeling or state of being induced by the projective identification, but only does so if such a communication is judged to be facilitative.

Introjective identification is the taking in of something (feeling, value, object, part object, state of being) from the environment; *projection* is the displacement onto the environment of unacceptable or unsafe aspects of the self including affective states and self evaluations; *projective identification* is an interpersonal process in which self modifies object in order to safely store a part of that self and then recognizes itself in the other, perhaps now introjectively identifying with its own projection. David Scharff's illustration of these processes is shown in Figure 2–2.

The Scharffs speak of the contextual transference and the focal transference. The *contextual transference* is the holding; it is both the relatively rational aspect of the therapeutic relationship and a reliving of early and satisfying maternal holding. The contextual transference has also been called the working alliance (Greenson 1965) and the therapeutic alliance (Zetzel 1956). The *focal transference*, the reliving of early conflicts, particularly oedipal ones, in the relationship with the therapist, is weak and tends to play a minor role in psychotherapy, while in psychoanalysis, a powerful, interpretable, focal transference sometimes called the transference neurosis develops and is exploited therapeutically. David Scharff believes that in the first year or two of therapy, there is very little focal transference, which can only develop in the security of the contextual transference. Object relations family therapy makes use of both the contextual and the focal transference, while recognizing that nothing is going to happen until the contextual transference develops. You have to build a trampoline before you can jump on it.

Of the nonanalytic family therapists, the Scharffs consider themselves closest to the structuralists, sharing with Minuchin activity, albeit in a muted form; joining, albeit in a much lower, nonexhibitionistic key; tracking, using the family's language and style to better communicate and to build an alliance; and in the use of the therapist's feelings.

Object relations family therapy thus is a family therapy that seeks to make conscious the inner world of internal objects and fragments of self and their projection onto external objects through the use of dreams, fantasies, drawings, play, and the transference, relying heavily on countertransferential interpretation of projective identification. It is nondirective and non–symptom oriented. It aims at insight, integration, and strengthening of mutual holding. It draws heavily on the theorizing of Klein, Fairbairn, Winnicott, Guntrip, and others, yet holds that theory is metaphor and model and is not to be taken too concretely. It is masterfully practiced by the Scharffs, who beautifully describe it in the clinical vignettes in their books.

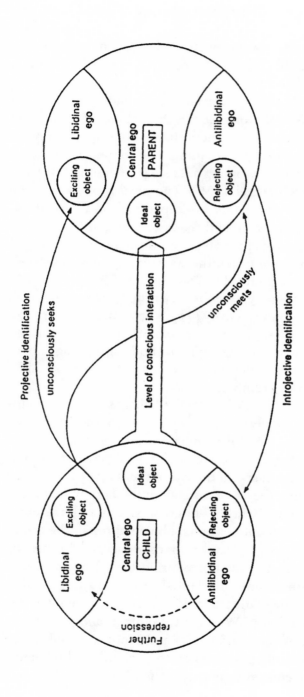

FIGURE 2–2. The action of projective and introjective identification, by David E. Scharff, from *Refinding the Object and Reclaiming the Self.* The mechanism here is the interaction of the child's projective and introjective identifications with the parent as the child meets frustration, unrequited yearning, or trauma. The diagram depicts the child longing to have his needs met and identifying with similar trends in the parent via projective identification. The child meeting with rejection identifies with the frustration of the parent's own antilibidinal system via introjective identification. In an internal reaction to the frustration, the libidinal system is further repressed by the renewed force of the child's antilibidinal system. (Reprinted courtesy of David E. Scharff.)

Object relations family therapy has multiple applications to work with addicted families. On the theoretical side, it helps us understand the addictive process and its interpersonal, familial dynamics. On the therapeutic side, it is a powerful way of working with recovering families and can be modified by the incorporation of confrontational and directive elements for use with actively addicted families.

The Scharffs' reliance on Fairbairn's model of the mind is not merely theoretical and heuristic; it serves not only to enable understanding, but rather it lies at the heart of their interpretive activities. Object relations family therapy understands human life as an open-ended process of holding and being held, or failure to hold or be held (the contextual transference), commencing at birth (or before birth in fantasy about the fetus) and ending only in death (and not then for the survivors), and of projection, projective identification, and introjective identification of the aspects of the defensively split and repressed ego (self), that is, of the libidinal ego, the antilibidinal ego, and to a lesser extent, of the central ego and their internal objects, the exciting object, the rejecting object, and the ideal object.

Transference (here the focal transference) is not something that only happens in therapy, although various therapeutic techniques contrive to maximize transference; it is *life*. All of our relationships are transferential or, more accurately, to a greater or lesser degree, a mix of the realistic and the needfully projected. As Wordsworth said, "The world is half created and half perceived." The object relations family therapist interprets (perhaps silently to him- or herself to augment understanding and empathy or perhaps verbally) the interactions within the family, the family members' relationship to the therapist (the contextual and focus transference), his or her own feelings (the countertransference), as well as dreams, drawings, and play in terms of Fairbairn's model. In fact, the therapy itself is seen as a form of play in what Winnicott calls the "transitional space," that is, in a realm between fantasy and reality. Freud too spoke of the transference as play insofar as it has no reality consequences and consequently is a "safe place," as Leston Havens (1989) calls the therapeutic space. The self itself comes into being and exists only in relationship to its objects; Freud (1923) had something similar in mind in his notion that the ego (self) is the precipitate of abandoned object cathexes, but here Freud seems to concretize process and put it in the past, while Fairbairn and the object relations theorists, although well aware of the precipitates of the past, are focused on the living here-and-now process of the transference. Freud of course knew this too, and elsewhere, writing of the transference, said that "When all is said and done, it is impossible to destroy anyone *in absentia* or *in effigie*" (1912b, p. 108); that is, the demons—the conflicts—of the unconscious can only be slain (come to terms with) by their transferential reincarnation, which makes them available to be worked through.

As applied to the treatment of addicted families, object relations family therapy sees the abused substances as disavowed parts of the self and its projected internal objects, particularly as exciting and rejecting objects. As in all object relations work, the focal transference is interpreted both genetically, that is, in terms of its historical antecedents and precipitants (the early experiences that lay down the intrapsychic structure) and as a here-and-now process with a life of its own, whatever its origins may be. The substance use can also be usefully understood in terms of the contextual transference as an attempt to get from a chemical what was unavailable from persons, or is phobically avoided from persons, or both. The withdrawal of one or more family members from the mutual holding of healthy interdependence to relationships with substances, or compulsive activity, in turn distorts and diminishes the holding function and relationship in the entire family, and those distortions too may be usefully interpreted by the object relations family therapist.

SELF PSYCHOLOGICAL FAMILY THERAPY

Heinz Kohut

The self psychology of Heinz Kohut has many overlaps with object relations theory, yet it has its own contribution to make. Although there is no self psychological family therapy, Kohut's notion of the selfobject and his discussion of the relationship between self and selfobject provide a bridge between the intrapsychic and the interpersonal and readily lend themselves to understanding family dynamics. From there it is a short way to a self psychological family therapy.

Kohut was not primarily a theorist; he was a clinician. His theory of self arose from his work with a group of patients he called narcissistic personality disorders, and out of his observation of how they related to him as extensions of themselves. His theory is an inference from clinical data.

Kohut (1971, 1977a) defines the self as a unit, both cohesive in space and enduring in time, that is a center of initiative and a recipient of impressions. It can be regarded either as a mental structure superordinate to the agencies of the mind (id, ego, and superego) or as a subordinate content of those agencies. Although Kohut believed these conceptions were complementary rather than mutually exclusive, he emphasized the self as a central or superordinate principle. Kohut borrowed the notion of complementarity from physics, where electromagnetic phenomena are understood as both waves and particles, and saw the same complementarity as pertaining to the self as an overarching, central psychological construct and as a representation in the agencies of Freud's structural model. Some phenomena are best understood as waves (superordinate self) and some as particles (subordinate self).

The self as superordinate is, so to speak, the organized and organizing center of human experience, which is itself experienced as cohesive and enduring. According to Kohut, the infant develops a primitive (fragmented) sense of self very early. That is, each body part, each sensation, and each mental content is experienced as belonging to a self, to a "me," as "mine"; however, there is no synthesis of these experiences as yet. There are selves, but no unitary self. Nor are there clear boundaries between self and world. Kohut designates this stage as the stage of the *fragmented self*; it is the developmental stage at which psychotic persons are fixated or to which they regress. Kohut also observed regressive, temporary fragmentation in his narcissistic patients when they became highly anxious. We frequently see this in substance abusers. His reasoning went from clinical data to metapsychology. He cites such evidence as hypochondriasis, in which the integrity of the self fails and isolated body parts become the focus of self-experience, as evidence for the existence of a stage of fragmentation in self-development. Although there are important differences, Kohut's stage of the fragmented self corresponds to Freud's stage of autoeroticism; it is another way of understanding the stage of human development that precedes the integration of the infant's experienced world.

According to Kohut, at the next stage of development an *archaic nuclear bipolar self* arises from the infant's experience of being related to as a self rather than as a collection of parts and sensations. This self is cohesive and enduring, but it is not yet securely established. Hence it is prone to regressive fragmentation, to "going to pieces" or "falling apart." It is nuclear in the sense of having a center, or nucleus, and it is archaic in the sense of being a primitive precursor of the mature self.

The development of the nuclear self from the fragmented self brings to mind the story of the man who goes to the doctor and says, "Doctor, my feet hurt, I have a dreadful headache, my throat is sore, my bowels are about to burst, and to tell the truth, I myself don't feel so well either." The "I myself" is the nuclear self, while the aching feet, head, throat, and bowels are the fragmented self.

The archaic nuclear self is bipolar in that it contains two structures, the *grandiose self* and the *idealized parental imago*, the internal representation of the idealized parent as part of the self. In this stage, there is a differentiated self, which is experienced as omnipotent, but there are no truly differentiated objects. The omnipotence comes from the grandiose self and the undifferentiation from fusion with the idealized and internalized parents. Objects are still experienced as extensions of the self, as what Kohut calls *selfobjects*. Selfobjects are representations in the same sense as self-representations and object representations, except in this case the representation is that of a fused, undifferentiated amalgamation of self and object. The child's grandiose self attempts to exercise omnipotent control over his selfobjects, and indeed our knowledge of it is an inference from such behavior.

Kohut's notion of the selfobject is confused. Sometimes he uses the term to denote the internal representation of nondifferentiation, but more often he seems to use selfobject to mean person, the people who provide what he calls selfobject functions, that is, who meet my needs, particularly my needs for self-esteem regulation, modulation of anxiety, soothing, and self-cohesion. It is as if they were extensions of me or were totally under my omnipotent control. In selfobject relating, I either treat you as part of me, so of course you will (should) be perfectly under my control, or I merge with you and participate in the omnipotence I endow you with through *idealization*. These forms of relating are universal, but particularly characterize the addict's relationship to his substance and the addicted family's interactions.

Idealization is an important Kohutian concept; he regards the need for idealization as both stage-specific and an enduring need throughout life. Kohut arrived at his concept of the bipolar archaic nuclear self by examining the transferences of his narcissistic patients to him. They either treated him as an extension of themselves whose function was to perfectly mirror them, to reflect back their glory, which he called the *mirror transference*, or they merged with him, conceived of as an all-perfect, all-powerful ideal object. This way of relating he called the *idealizing transference*. Thus, the bipolarity of the nuclear self is an inference from the behavior of adult patients.

What Kohut calls *psychic structure* is built through the process of *transmuting internalization*, the piecemeal, grain-at-a-time internalization of not objects, but the functions performed by (self)objects, through optimal or nontraumatic failure of the selfobject to perform its functions. The notion is that if my needs are perfectly met, then I have no reason to acquire the means of meeting them through internalization, nor would I have any sense of separateness. If, on the other hand, my needs are so poorly met that it is traumatic, I have little to internalize and am too anxious to do so. In either case, that which was originally outside fails to get inside and become part of me, and a self-deficit results. Concretely this means that I am unable to do certain things, such as soothe myself, maintain my self-esteem, or experience myself as cohesive, that is, as a healthy mature self. If I fail to acquire the capacity, through transmuting internalization, to provide myself with a sense of cohesion, continuity, and stable self-esteem, I must look to the outside and find people to provide them. The addict looks to substances to fulfill selfobject functions. When

Kohut is talking about structure, he is really talking about capacity, the ability to do certain things, experience certain things, and carry out certain tasks, particularly those tasks having to do with the self.

The internalization of psychic structure is codeterminous with the formation of the archaic, nuclear, bipolar self. As Kohut puts it, "The rudiments of the nuclear self are laid down by simultaneously or consecutively occurring processes of selective inclusion and exclusion of psychic structure" (1977a, p. 183), so it would appear that the archaic nuclear self with its bipolar structure comes from both inside and outside, is maturational in the sense of being a development out of the stage of the fragmented self, and yet is also the product of internalization, the transmuting internalization of psychic structure, and the internalization of the idealized parent. The grandiosity that is a manifestation of the grandiose self seems to be maturational and inborn. That is, it doesn't seem to depend on environment, but universally comes into being at a certain stage of development. In maturity, the grandiose self develops into realistic ambitions, while the idealized parental imago, now depersonalized, develops into ideals and values. This transformation into mature structure is often deficient in the addicted, and twelve–step programs intuitively address themselves to amelioration of these developmental deficits. Maturation of self is a process of depersonalization in the sense that attributes and functional capacities that were acquired from others take on an autonomy and become integrated into us in such a way that they are no longer identified with those from whom they were acquired. This is important to a healthy sense of selfhood. I need to feel I can soothe myself, maintain my self-esteem, modulate my anxiety, and maintain my sense of ongoingness, initiative, and boundaries even in the face of great stress. If I cannot do these things, as many addicts cannot, I am subject to regression to the stage of the fragmented self.

According to Kohut, I do not lose or outgrow my need for selfobjects (here meaning persons who relate to me in a certain way) in maturity. However, the mode of my selfobject relating does change and take on mature forms. *Pathological narcissism* is the regression-fixation to the stage of the archaic nuclear, bipolar self. It is characterized by the presence of a cohesive, but insecure self, which is threatened by regressive fragmentation; grandiosity of less than psychotic proportions that manifests itself in the form of arrogance, isolation, and unrealistic goals; feelings of entitlement; the need for omnipotent control; poor differentiation of self and object; and deficits in the self-regulating capacities of the self. Furthermore, affect tolerance, the ability to experience and stay with feelings, is poor. The tenuousness in the cohesion of the self makes narcissistically regressed individuals subject to massive anxiety that is, in reality, fear of annihilation.

Kohut emphasizes the normality of our narcissistic needs and the deleterious consequences of repression or disavowal of those needs. For him, a healthy narcissism is a vital component of mental health, and it is at least as important as object relating or the ability to achieve instinctual gratification. Kohut is highly critical of what he calls the "maturity morality" implicit in much of psychoanalysis, which he views as unaccepting of the narcissistic needs of the self. He is equally critical of the denial of the legitimacy of our need for self-affirmation by the Judeo-Christian religious tradition that condemns self-centeredness. He sees many factors working to deny or disapprove of the fulfillment of narcissistic needs and believes, as with any repression, it will fail and the repressed will return. If narcissistic needs are not met in healthy ways, they will certainly be met in unhealthy ways, including the expression of *narcissistic rage*, the response to narcissistic injury, with its unquenchable desire for revenge; and the idealization of demonic leaders such as Hitler and the Reverend Jim Jones. In addicted families, narcissistic needs are not met in healthy ways and narcissistic rage is rampant.

Kohut states that early analytic patients were what he calls *guilty man*. They were primarily suffering from conflict between desire and conscience. They were caught between the pressures of the id and the prohibitions of the superego. The central issue in their treatment was making their desire and their guilt conscious, so they could find a way to live with them. The contemporary patient, in contrast, is what Kohut calls *tragic man*. Tragic man is not suffering from internal conflict; rather, he is suffering from narcissistic injury, from lack of a cohesive self, from lack of fulfillment and inability to feel whole, integral, or securely there. Kohut (1977a) quotes with approval the alcoholic Eugene O'Neill's lines in *The Great God Brown*, "Man is born broken. He lives by mending. The grace of God is glue" (O'Neill 1929, IV, 1).

I have developed a theory of the psychodynamic correlative of addiction being pathological narcissism, as defined by Kohut, that is, regression/fixation to the stage of the archaic nuclear self (see Levin 1987). This model well accounts for the empirical psychological data on the clinical addictive personality and provides a common explanatory hypothesis that reconciles competing psychodynamic theories of the etiology of addiction. The addict's relationship to the substance or impulsive activity is a combined mirror and idealizing transference. Kohut sees the addiction as a futile attempt to build psychic structure, but like the sufferer from gastric fistula who tries to cure it by eating, the stuff just runs through. Psychic structure can only be built from relationships, as Kohut (1977b) puts it.

> The narcissistically disturbed individual yearns for praise and approval or for a merger with an idealized supportive other because he cannot sufficiently supply himself with self-approval or with a sense of strength through his own inner resources. . . . The addict craves the drug because the drug seems to him to be capable of curing the central defect in his self. It becomes for him the substitute for a selfobject which failed him traumatically at a time when he should still have had the feeling of omnipotently controlling its responses in accordance with his needs as if it were a part of himself. By ingesting the drug, he symbolically compels the mirroring self-object to soothe him, to accept him. Or he symbolically compels the idealized self-object to submit to his merging into it and thus to his partaking in its magical power. In either case, the ingestion of the drug provides him with the self-esteem which he does not possess. Through the incorporation of the drug he supplies for himself the feeling of being accepted and thus of being self-confident; or he creates the experience of being merged with a source of power that gives him the feeling of being strong and worthwhile. And all these effects of the drug tend to increase his feeling of being alive, tend to increase his certainty that he exists in this world.

It is the tragedy of these attempts at self-cure that the solutions which they provide are impermanent, that in essence they cannot succeed. . . . They are repeated again and again without producing the cure of the basic psychological malady. And the calming or the stimulating effect which the addict obtains from the drug is impermanent. Whatever the chemical nature of the substance that is employed, however frequently repeated its consumption, however cleverly rationalized or mythologized its ingestion with the support from others similarly afflicted—no psychic structure is built, the defect in the self remains. [pp. vii–viii]

In family therapy, relationships can be viewed in terms of their selfobject functions and the mirror and idealizing transferences both to the therapist and within the family used to understand the dynamics of the family. The addict's (and frequently family members') relationship to the drug can also be understood as mirror and idealizing transferences. If it appears to be useful, they can be interpreted.

In the addicted family or early recovery family, the developmental level of the addict and his or her enabler is generally that of the archaic, grandiose self, and the therapist may anticipate boundary problems, the centrality of control issues, narcissistic rage, and compensatory grandiosity covering abysmally low self-esteem. The work itself is not too different from other dynamic family therapy, but Kohut's understanding of the inner emptiness of the addict, and the developmental level and style of relating, is used by the therapist to increase his or her empathy and to make sense of the "games" the family plays. As in object relations family therapy, mutual holding, understood by the Scharffs as a contextual transference—the selfobject relationship—and its failures hold center stage. It is the focus of the work. Transmuting internalization of the therapist and the internalization of structure is much the same as the dynamics of the contextual transference. Like all forms of holding, it facilitates growth.

Just as the object relations family therapist understands and interprets relationships between family members, relationships with the therapist, relations with the abused substance, and fantasy, play, art (drawings), and dreams in terms of internal objects and ego aspects and their projection, projective identification, and introjection, the self psychological family therapist understands and interprets the same phenomena in terms of self–selfobject relationships, activation and projection of the grandiose self and the idealized parental imago, defenses against regressive fragmentation and its concomitant panic terror, mirror and idealizing transferences, and compensatory grandiosity defending against awareness of the paucity of psychic structure consequent upon failures of internalization. Such interpretation can be and usually is both here and now and genetic.

The dynamics of the addicted family can be usefully understood as a failure of self–selfobject relating resulting in developmental arrest (cf. Winnicott's "personality disorders are environmental deficiency diseases") and absorption in transferences to substances and compulsive activities. We also frequently see an endless cycle of narcissistic injury followed by narcissistic rage, which in turn inflicts yet more narcissistic injury in these families. Therapy seeks to help family members experience rather than act out or anesthetize the pain of the injuries—present and past—and to contain the narcissistic rage so the cycle stops being self-perpetuating. The strengthening of the self through transmuting internalization of therapist and family members reduces vulnerability, perceived injury, and retaliatory rage.

The object relational and self psychological approaches are not mutually exclusive, and, contrary to what their respective purists, that is, ideologues, say, can be fruitfully integrated. Aspects of classical analytic theory, the sort of approach Ackerman uses, can also be worked in. The rage of the superego against the ego and its projection have special application to work with addicted families. This will be illustrated in later chapters.

Dynamic family therapy uses drive, ego, object, and self models of the psyche to enable insight. It focuses on transference and countertransference. Interpretation of defense and projection as manifested in family interactions and relationships with the therapist is at the very center of its thinking and working. It uses tracking to establish and maintain communication with the family. It understands that this work can only proceed in the context of a therapeutic alliance, and seeks to bring this about by a stance of nonjudgmental, unconditional positive regard. It seeks to understand, not to judge. It believes that all this takes time, that trust is never instantaneous, and the very condition—the holding—necessary to do the work evolves. You have to build the trampoline before you can jump on it.

Dynamic family therapy, at least the object relations and self psychology versions of it, is conceived to be approximately a two-year process, although its conceptualizations can be drawn upon in briefer therapies. It is essentially nondirective, although it sometimes confronts and sometimes advises. It is not symptom oriented, although in its application to addicts and addicted families it recognizes that the emotional and pharmacological regression consequent upon substance abuse may make dynamic work impossible until that use is brought under control, yet even there the goal is the same—the creation or re-creation of a matrix that makes growth possible for each member of the family.

The Addicted Family: Addiction-Specific Family Therapies

There is a considerable literature on the addicted family. Some of this is empirical research, some of it is clinical generalization, and some of it is popular. There is a parallel literature on children of alcoholics (COAs) and adult children of alcoholics (ACOAs.) All of these have obvious relevance for a rational family therapy of addiction. Unfortunately, there is a radical inconsistency, even contradiction, between the findings of the researchers and the findings of the clinicians. Roughly speaking, the researchers find much less pathology than do the clinicians; incidentally this is also true of the research on the "addictive personality," if there be one. There's also a number of addiction-specific family therapy treatment models more or less closely related to the empirical psychological and clinical theoretical constructs.

For our purposes, it is worthwhile to look at the evidence for a genetic or constitutional factor in addiction, at the research on COAs, and at the family studies. Of particular interest are the work of Steinglass and colleagues (1987), and the work of John Bradshaw (1988a,b). The first is rigorously empirical while the latter is a brilliant if oversimplified synthesis of the psychodynamic and systems insights into addiction. Stanton and Todd (1982), Kaufman and

Kaufmann (1992), McCrady (1992), and O'Farrell (1993) have developed addictive-specific couple and family therapies that are worth our attention. The vast majority of the empirical work on heritability and family dynamics is on alcoholism, which accordingly must of necessity serve as our model addiction.

In looking at the alcoholic family literature we will start by reviewing the evidence for a genetic factor. There is no doubt that alcoholism at least must have some form of familial transmission. However, the nature of that transmission is multifactoral: neurochemical genetically controlled vulnerability; assortative mating, that is, the well-established tendency of COAs, especially daughters, to marry alcoholics; modeling; identification; identification with the aggressor; and reaction to the experience of being raised in an addictive home. The interaction of heredity and environment must also be factored into any etiological theory of the familial transmission of alcoholism. As the statisticians say, we must consider the "main effects," that is the effects of heredity and environment acting alone as orthogonal independent variables and the "interaction effects" of heredity and environment in dialectical interaction.

EVIDENCE FOR A GENETIC FACTOR IN ALCOHOLISM

Evidence for a genetic factor in alcoholism comes from several sources: animal studies, family studies, twin studies, biological marker research, and adoption studies.

Animal Studies

Animal studies are generally aimed at demonstrating the hereditability of appetite for alcohol and preference for alcohol. Since people are among the very few animals that naturally drink ethanol in more than minimal quantities, finding animal models for alcoholism is difficult. Elephants are apparently an exception, getting smashed on fermented palms and going on rampages, but it is not clear that it is the alcohol rather than the palms that attract them, nor are we certain whether alcoholic elephants see pink elephants. In any case a laboratory of inebriated elephants would be difficult to staff, so rodents are generally used.

Alcohol does not appear to be strongly reinforcing for most animals. A *reinforcer* is something that increases the frequency of a behavior; if alcohol is reinforcing, drinking it should increase the frequency of drinking it. Animals generally do not want more alcohol to drink after drinking some; that is, they don't find it reinforcing. This is strikingly different from the animal response to cocaine. If a rodent is given a choice of pushing a lever that delivers cocaine and one that delivers food, he or she will choose the cocaine, continuing to do so until he or she collapses.

Appetite for alcohol and *preference for alcohol* are traits that occur in some, but not all, rodent individuals and strains. Strains of mice and rats have been bred to drink alcohol, and some in fact prefer it to water. There are even rodents that will voluntarily drink enough alcohol to have withdrawal symptoms when they stop. The mouse souse is not found in nature; neither is the heavy-hitting rat. These anomalies are created by breeding with each other those animals that show some appetite for alcohol and in turn selecting those of their offspring with the greatest appetite for alcohol to mate with those of the offsprings' generation that are similarly inclined. The process of selective breeding is continued over the generations until a strain of rodents with a distinct appetite for alcohol emerges. Surprisingly, Martini Mickey can be bred in as little as ten generations. With some such strains, continued selective breeding results in animals that prefer alcohol and even in animals that show a physical dependence. These results argue strongly for the existence of a genetically transmitted appetite for alcohol in rodents. Although extrapolating from animal models to humans is inferential and it is not certain that similar propensities are inherited by humans, the heritability of an appetite for alcohol in rodents is a striking find that strongly suggests similar mechanisms exist in humans. Additionally, the heritability of a tolerance for alcohol, as measured by the *righting response* (the ability to remain on or regain one's paws after a heavy dose of ethanol), has been demonstrated in rodents.

One ingenious, if highly speculative, hypothesis to account for the relatively low rate of alcoholism in Jews is as follows. Jews once had rates of drunkenness, problem drinking, and alcoholism as high as any other group. However, living as a persecuted minority in constant danger, the Jews who liked to drink were more vulnerable and more likely to be killed before reproducing than Jews who did not. Over the centuries the genes that mediate a high appetite for alcohol diminished and became infrequent in Jews. For other peoples who did not share the special vulnerability of the Jews, drinking alcohol was safer than drinking the often contaminated water and had survival value, so these heavy drinkers reproduced, while the Jews who were heavy drinkers were less likely to reproduce. An ingenious hypothesis indeed, but the time scale—a mere few hundred years—seems too short.

There are rodents that like to drink and rodents that do not, and the ones that do are the descendants of many generations of rodents with similar inclinations. One wonders about environmental effects. Do heavy drinking rodents mother differently? Are there intrauterine influences? Those who do the mouse work do not believe so, regarding the selective breeding result as entirely genetic.

Biological Marker Studies

Research on biological markers is "hot." Researchers are intrigued by the search for metabolic, neurophysiological, and other biological correlatives of alcoholism. If alcoholism is associated with a biological trait known to be heritable, then that association can be interpreted as evidence for the heritability of alcoholism. As in all research on addictions, it is often difficult to tell what is the chicken and what is the egg, what is causative of and what is resultant from drug abuse. For example, if high levels of enzyme X are found in alcoholics, is the high level caused by the drinking itself? Or is it etiological? Or is the elevation of enzyme X a genetically transmitted trait that shares a chromosome with a gene that transmits a trait that increases the susceptibility to alcoholism? These are difficult questions to answer.

Color Blindness

The first biological marker discovered for alcoholism was thought to be color blindness (Cruz-Coke and Varela 1966). However, Varela and colleagues (1969) later demonstrated that the color blindness in the Cruz-Coke and Varela study was the result of severe alcohol abuse.

Platelet Enzymes

Researchers study the levels of various enzymes in blood platelets because they are easily assessable and because platelet levels are assumed to reflect brain levels. The base levels of these enzymes are known to be under genetic control.

The two platelet enzymes that have received the most attention are monoamine oxidase (MAO) and dopamine B-hydroxylase (DBH). Tabakoff and colleagues (1988) found significant differences between alcoholics and nonalcoholics in the degree of MAO depression following drinking. Alexopoulos and colleagues (1983) found depressed levels of platelet MAO in alcoholics and their relatives.

Studies on platelet DBH are conflicting. However, there is considerable evidence that plasma, spinal fluid, and platelet levels of DBH are significantly depressed in alcoholics. This may be caused by the subjects' alcoholism. Depressed levels of DBH may contribute to the relatively poor reality testing characteristic of active alcoholism and the early stages of recovery from it. Paradoxically, there are studies (Schuckit and Gold 1988) that show significantly higher DBH levels in high-risk (FHP) than in low-risk (FHN) groups of young men. High levels of DBH are associated with less subjective feelings of intoxication after alcohol consumption. This could contribute to heavy drinking by the high-risk group.

Tabakoff (1988) also found abnormalities in the stimulation of the enzyme called platelet adenylate cyclase by various metabolites in alcoholics and thought this might be a biological marker of alcoholism. The depression of platelet MAO, DBH, and adenylate cyclase activity persists into abstinence in recovering alcoholics and is postulated to contribute to the prolonged withdrawal syndrome; that is, behavioral, emotional, and intrapsychic effects of the drug endure long into sobriety.

High-Risk Studies

Schuckit and Gold (1988) studied the difference between high-risk college students (those who had a family history of alcoholism) and those who had an average risk (they were free of a family history of alcoholism) on a number of biological markers including platelet MAO levels. Schuckit and Gold found no significant difference at baseline (that is, before drinking).

Challenge doses equivalent to three to five drinks of ethanol (ETOH) increased the difference between the family history positive (FHP) and family history negative (FHN) groups on levels of platelet MAO. The research on platelet MAO in abstinent alcoholics is inconsistent, but depressed levels persist for a long time. Some studies show no change in this trait with sobriety. It is likely that lower platelet MAO is a biological marker for alcoholism. The persistence of biochemical abnormalities long into sobriety, whether such abnormalities be antecedent or consequent to the addiction, has important implications for treatment. Such phenomena as postcocaine anxiety syndrome will strongly affect the recovering person's behavior and reverberate throughout the family system.

Blood Levels of Acetaldehyde

Schuckit and Gold (1988) also found significantly higher levels of acetaldehyde, the first breakdown product (metabolite) of alcohol in FHP students after drinking. This finding is intriguing since high levels of acetaldehyde are aversive and presumably would discourage drinking, yet apparently such is not the case in high-risk subjects. It is possible that high levels of acetaldehyde are implicated in addiction to alcohol.

Static Ataxia

Also known as upper-body sway, static ataxia is a measure of unsteadiness that presumably is related to underlying neurological status. To what degree such unsteadiness is genetically controlled or environmentally determined is unknown. Ataxia is the medical term for staggering; static ataxia is staggering while standing still. Some degree of body sway is found in everyone and each of us has a baseline measure of it. Schuckit and Gold (1988) found no difference in baseline measurements of body sway between FHPs and FHNs. They did find a significant difference in the effect of alcohol on body sway in FHPs and FHNs. The high-risk subjects showed significantly less increase in static ataxia after a challenge dose of ETOH. Other research (National Institute on Alcohol Abuse and Alcoholism 1988) has demonstrated significantly higher baseline body sway in children of alcoholics, and it has been suggested that static ataxia is a biological marker for alcoholism.

Serum Hormone Levels

Schuckit and Gold (1988) also found significantly lower blood plasma levels of the hormones prolactin and cortisol after challenge doses of ETOH in FHP subjects. Persistently low levels of serum prolactin and serum cortisol are found in abstinent alcoholics and may play a part in the protracted withdrawal syndrome.

Subjective Experience and Objective Measures of Effects of Drinking

There is a set of research findings that suggests that those who are at high risk for alcoholism have a "hollow leg" (that is, they experience fewer adverse effects than do other drinkers from the same dose of ETOH). They also feel less drunk. Here science supports the folk wisdom of AA, most of whose members report that they could really "sock it away," early in their drinking careers. It makes sense that someone who can easily drink a lot of an addictive drug will be more likely to become addicted to it. Schuckit and Gold's (1988) research supports this. The FHPs reported feeling not only less impaired but also better. That is to say, alcohol is highly reinforcing for these subjects.

Surprisingly, Schuckit and Gold found objective correlates for these subjective reports. The FHPs either suffered less impairment or improved on a variety of objective tests of cognitive functioning and motor performance. This may be because alcohol is highly anxiety reducing for high-risk subjects. If so, this is at variance with the research of Mello and Mendelson (1970) showing that alcoholics are more, not less, anxious on objective measures of anxiety after drinking, although the alcoholics themselves report the opposite. Apparently, alcoholics react differently to alcohol after they develop their addiction than they did before. This may explain one mechanism of addiction. If those who "benefit" most from drinking drink more to obtain those benefits but lose them in the process, they may nevertheless continue to search for the old rewarding experience by continuing to drink long after such reinforcement is obtainable. This is congruent with AA folk wisdom that points to the already mentioned high capacity for drink—the hollow leg—and the futile search for the old magic as antecedents of alcoholism.

Electroencephalograph Studies

The electroencephalograph (EEG) records brain waves. There are two main EEG findings about alcoholics: the first concerns alpha waves and the second event-related or evoked potentials.

It has been shown (Pollack et al. 1983, Propping et al. 1981) that Cloninger's type 1, milieu-limited alcoholics (see Adoption Studies, below) have low rates of slow alpha waves, high rates of fast alpha waves, and poor synchrony of those waves when they are abstinent. This may be true of other addicts as well. Minimal poorly synchronized slow alpha activity and excessive poorly synchronized fast alpha activity are experienced as dysphoric. Such a pattern is a neuro-electrical correlative of tension. Type 1 alcoholics show a marked increase in slow alpha activity, which also becomes better synchronized, and a marked decrease in fast alpha activity when they drink

ETOH. Subjectively, these changes are experienced as calm alertness and relief of tension. In other words, their anxiety levels drop when they drink. Cloninger (1983) calls this type of anxiety *cognitive anxiety*, which is characterized by anticipatory worry and guilt. This suggests that for some alcoholics excessively high levels of anxiety are antecedent to their alcoholism and that alcohol was a particularly effective antianxiety drug for them. Nonalcoholic FHP subjects have a greater increase in slow alpha tracings and a greater decrease in fast alpha tracings when they drink than do controls (that is, alcohol is more reinforcing for them). Women FHPs were found to have minimal slow alpha activity, suggesting that they would be more subject to type 1 alcoholism, which is exactly what epidemiological research shows.

Evoked (or event-related) potentials are spikes in the EEG that reflect brain activity in response to a visual or auditory stimulus that is either unpredictable or task relevant but not usual. Porjesz and Begleiter (1983) found that both sons and daughters of alcoholic fathers have significantly higher amplitudes of event-related potentials. They are *stimulus augmenters*—those who experience stimuli with particular intensity. Cloninger type 2 (male limited) alcoholics are stimulus augmenters in terms of the amplitude of their evoked potentials when abstinent. Alcohol either decreases their augmentation or changes it to *stimulus attenuation*, a decrease in *stimulus reactance* that is assumed to be pleasurable and reinforcing. Cloninger (1983) speaks of his type 2 alcoholics as suffering from *somatic anxiety* (bodily tension) in contrast to the cognitive anxiety of type 1 alcoholics. In both cases, alcohol consumption reduces anxiety, in the first by reducing stimulus augmentation (amplitude of the evoked potential) and in the second by reducing fast alpha brain activity and synchronizing it.

An evoked potential known as the P3 (or P300) wave has received special attention. There have been several important findings, including the nonreversible flattening in the amplitude of P3 in alcoholics and decreased P3 in the sons of alcoholics (Begleiter et al. 1984). Since P3 is an orienting response, this may correlate with findings (Tarter 1981) of attention-deficit disorder (ADD) in alcoholics shown to have been hyperactive in childhood. Hyperactivity is believed to be ante-cedent to alcoholism in a considerable number of male alcoholics.

The National Institute on Alcohol Abuse and Alcoholism (NIAAA) (1988) found cognitive deficits of various sorts (for instance, impaired problem-solving ability) in nonalcoholic sons of alcoholics. It is hy-pothesized that these deficits may be manifestations of the same underlying factor that manifests itself in hyperactivity and abnormal P3 waves. It is not known if the deficits found are the result of envi-ronmental or genetic factors or an interaction of the two.

The biological marker research, especially the studies of children of alcoholics, strongly suggests that biological vulnerability plays a role in the etiology of addiction. This research also has an important clinical implication, namely that when users maintain that their use is beneficial, they are speaking the truth, at least about the early stages of that use, and therapists need to acknowledge this.

Family Studies

There is long-standing evidence that alcoholism runs in families. As long ago as 1820, Thomas Trotter (Jellinek 1994), taking note of al-coholism running in families, wrote that alcoholism is caused by heredity and premature weaning (not a bad guess). Since then, there have been numerous empirical studies confirming Trotter's generali-zation and a long tradition of folk wisdom on the subject.

Family studies (Amark 1951, Bleuler 1955, Pitts and Winokur 1966) have consistently shown an increased incidence of alcoholism in relatives (parents and siblings) of alcoholics compared with various control groups or the general population. These findings are robust as well as consistent. Studies show a greater risk for male relatives (fathers and brothers) than for female relatives (mothers and sisters), and a higher risk for both male and female relatives than for control groups. These findings do not shed light on how alcoholism is trans-mitted, whether by culture, learning, or genetic factors. Correlation does not demonstrate causality. An important clinical and educational implication of these studies is that (particularly male) children of alcoholics are at high risk of themselves becoming alcoholics.

Twin Studies

Since family correlation studies can only suggest heritability, scientists look for ways to tease out the relative effects of constitution and environment. One way they have done this is to study the differential rates of concordance between fraternal and identical twins for alcoholism. That is, are the odds of a fraternal twin of an alcoholic also being alcoholic lower than the odds for an identical twin? This turns out to be the case, and studies of twins have contributed evidence for a genetic factor in alcoholism. Such studies are conducted by calculating the concordance between identical (monozygotic) and fraternal (dizygotic) twins for alcoholism; the *concordance rate* is the percentage of twins sharing a given trait or condition. In this case, the percentage of alcoholic twins with an alcoholic twin is calculated for populations of identical and fraternal twins. Since identical twins are the product of the same fertilized egg, or zygote, and fraternal twins are the product of different fertilized eggs, a higher concordance between identical than fraternal twins is taken as evidence of a genetic factor in the transmission of the trait or condition. The results consistently show that identical twins of alcoholics have a statistically significantly higher incidence of alcoholism than do fraternal twins of alcoholics. In a typical study, Kaij (1960), using male twins, found a concordance of 53.5 percent in identical twins and a concordance of 28.3 percent in fraternal twins. However, too much should not be made of this evidence for a genetic factor. Environmental factors, including the fact that identical twins are more likely to be treated alike, confound such studies.

Adoption Studies

The most powerful, albeit flawed, family studies are what is called population genetic studies in which the rates of alcoholism in children of alcoholics who have been adopted by nonalcoholics are compared with control groups.

This promising research design studies children of alcoholics who were adopted very early in life by nonalcoholic adoptive parents, following them into adulthood and determining their rates of alcoholism and comparing those rates to their generational peers. The first of these adoption studies was conducted by Goodwin and colleagues (1973) in Denmark. They followed children of alcoholics who were adopted at or shortly after birth and raised by nonalcoholic parents. An early study (Roe 1945) found almost no alcoholism in children of alcoholics who were raised by nonalcoholic adoptive parents. This result may be confounded by the disproportionate number of girls in the study. Goodwin and colleagues' results were the opposite. Chronic alcoholism was four times more common in fifty-five adopted-out sons of alcoholic fathers than among seventy-eight adopted-out sons of nonalcoholics. The sons of alcoholics had a 25 percent rate of alcoholism, higher than the 17 percent rate Goodwin found for male children of alcoholics raised by those alcoholics. This, of course, means that 75 percent of the sons of alcoholics raised by nonalcoholic adoptive parents did not become alcoholic; therefore, simple Mendelian inheritance of alcoholism is not the case. Alcoholism was not found to be significantly more prevalent in adopted-out daughters of alcoholics raised by nonalcoholics.

It is of considerable interest that Goodwin and colleagues' adopted-out male children of alcoholics had significantly higher rates of hyperactivity, shyness, sensitivity, and aggression than adopted-out male children of nonalcoholics. Adoptees whose biological parents were not alcoholics but who were raised by alcoholic parents did not have significantly higher rates of alcoholism. In contrast to their findings on alcoholism, Goodwin and colleagues found no correlation between problem drinking (alcohol abuse that did not qualify as alcoholism as they defined it) and alcohol abuse in biological parents. This study has been criticized for small sample size, lack of later follow-up, and the fact that if the heavy drinking and alcoholic groups are combined, no effect of heredity can be demonstrated.

A Swedish study conducted by Bohman (1978) and reported by Cloninger (1983) extended and confirmed Goodwin and colleagues' findings. It was based on a much larger sample (862 men and 913 women) of known paternity born to single women between 1930 and 1949. Cloninger found a high correlation between what he called male-limited or type 2 alcoholism in biological fathers and type 2 alcoholism in adopted-out sons of these fathers, who were raised by nonalcoholic adoptive parents. Male-limited (type 2) alcoholism is early-onset severe alcoholism associated with antisocial and even overtly criminal behavior. It was found only in males. The sons of type 2 fathers raised in nonalcoholic families had nine times the rate of alcoholism of the sons of all other fathers in the study. However, these sons tended to have "moderate" alcoholism as measured by Bohman, while the model suggests transmission of severe alcoholism. Approximately half of the adopted-out sons of type 2 alcoholics became alcoholic, but half did not, so once again the evidence does not support direct Mendelian inheritability but, rather, indicates that in one form of alcoholism biological vulnerability to alcoholism is inherited.

Goodwin (1988) speculates that what makes for the vulnerability may be low levels of the neurotransmitter serotonin, citing evidence that alcoholic rats have low levels of serotonin in certain parts of their brains, and that serotonin reuptake blockers like Prozac decrease appetite for alcohol in these rodents. Since alcohol increases serotonergic activity initially, it might be highly appealing to a person with a serotonergic activity deficit, while its biphasic impact on serotonin levels results in its ultimately decreasing serotonergic activity, setting up a vicious cycle resulting in addiction. Goodwin acknowledges the highly speculative nature of this theory of what is inherited. None of the environmental variables measured by the researchers significantly influenced the appearance of this type of alcoholism, increasing the likelihood that it is highly heritable. The Swedish data also indicated that type 2 alcoholism is extremely treatment resistant. An American longitudinal study (Vaillant 1983) did not find any worse outcome for what it defined as sociopathic alcoholics than for its nonsociopathic alcoholics. This is puzzling, since Cloninger's type 2's are presumably similar to Vaillant's sociopaths.

Adopted-out sons and daughters of what Cloninger called type 1 or milieu-limited alcoholics, who are characterized by late onset, treatability, absence of antisocial behavior, and worry and guilt and who are approval seeking were also significantly more likely to develop alcoholism. The type of alcoholism they developed was the same as that of their biological parents. However, this occurred only if they were reared in adoptive homes where heavy drinking was the norm. The actual environmental variable measured was working-class, lower socioeconomic status, which the researchers argued went with a heavy drinking lifestyle or at least with approval of intoxication as recreation and relaxation in Sweden at that time. This type of alcoholism was called *milieu-limited susceptibility* and was far less heritable. A reanalysis of the Swedish data (Cloninger et al. 1981) indicated a strong correlation between type 1 alcoholism in the mothers and type 1 alcoholism in the adopted-out daughters. There was, however, no control for intrauterine effects of maternal drinking, so this correlation may have nongenetic determinants.

Like Goodwin, the Swedish investigators found that children whose biological parents were not alcoholic, but whose adoptive parents were, did not develop alcoholism at rates significantly higher than children of nonalcoholics raised by nonalcoholics. They concluded that alcoholism in children of alcoholics is not transmitted by learning, modeling, or unconscious identification, let alone by the maladaptive use of alcohol to ameliorate the pain of being raised in an alcoholic home, although environmental provocation is necessary for milieu-limited alcoholism to occur. However, there may be a confounding variable here. It is known that many children of alcoholics become teetotalers, and it may be that the environmental, emotional, and interpersonal, as opposed to the genetic, influences of parental alcoholism may be to increase the likelihood of either alcoholism or total abstinence, while decreasing the likelihood of becoming a social drinker. This hypothesis was not tested in either the Danish or the Swedish studies. A more recent American study (Cadoret et al. 1984) using the same design found that adopted-out sons of alcoholics were three times as likely to develop alcoholism as adopted-out sons of nonalcoholics. An important additional finding was that these Iowa children of alcoholics had a significantly higher rate of conduct disorder than their peers, a finding congruent with the high rates of hyperactivity in the Danish study and with retrospective evidence (Tartar 1981) of childhood hyperactivity in clinical alcoholic populations.

Goodwin's isn't the only theory of biological vulnerability, and alcohologists have argued about what, if anything, is inherited in alcoholism. A variety of suggestions have been made. Winokur (1974) has argued that there is a genetically transmitted depressive-spectrum illness in which women are at risk for unipolar depression and men are at risk for alcoholism or sociopathy. He argues that a common mechanism predisposes them to these diseases, but he does not specify what that mechanism might be. Others have pointed to the association of childhood hyperactivity and adult alcoholism found in the Danish study and elsewhere as a clue to what might be transmitted. However, hyperactivity has not been consistently found in the childhoods of alcoholics.

Critics have pointed to methodological flaws in these adoption studies and they are there. What conclusion can be drawn from all this? The best evidence we have, which is fragmentary and based on small samples, shows that a predisposition to some forms of alcoholism is inherited. Alcoholisms can probably be arranged in a continuum ranging from those in which constitutional factors play little or no role to those in which constitutional factors play a major role. One-third of alcoholics report no family history of alcoholism. From a clinical standpoint, the most important finding of these studies is that children of alcoholics are at high risk for alcoholism, even if this predisposition is not exclusively genetic. Familial alcoholism, particularly if it is early onset, increases the odds that one cannot drink "safely."

CHILDREN OF ALCOHOLICS (COAs)

The literature on COAs is contradictory. There is a vast and best-selling popular literature addressed to adult children of alcoholics (ACOAs). It purports to find a personality disorder characterized by relationship problems, fears of intimacy, low self esteem, and an inability to find satisfaction in achievement. Each author has (usually) her "shopping list." Critics point out that the items on these lists are so broadly defined and refer to such universal human problems that

almost anyone could qualify. Like the fortune teller, the reading always applies. Other critics are less harsh, yet maintain that no unique
ACOA syndrome has emerged. Donald Goodwin, author of the
Danish adoption study (Silford 1989), has been a particularly vehe-
ment critic of the ACOA movement, calling it a hoax, since children
of alcoholics are like adult children of everyone else with a problem
(and that's practically everybody). He further maintains that therapists invented the ACOA profile to create a patient population with
a problem that they could allegedly cure. In short, it was a way for
therapists to make money. This is a strange position to be taken by a
researcher who believes that he has established the heritability of
alcoholism. Apparently he believes that COAs either have a biological disease—alcoholism—or they don't have it and are more or less
like everyone else.

In her best-selling book, *I'm Dysfunctional; You're Dysfunctional*,
Wendy Kaminer (1993), coming from a very different perspective
than Goodwin, attacks the ACOA movement as institutionalizing
self-pity, lack of responsibility for one's actions, a belief that the pain
inherent in the human condition is pathological, and a culture of vic-
timization. A lawyer by training and a public policy analyst, Kaminer
is particularly distressed by what she sees as the focus on private pain
to the exclusion of serious attention to the public realm or to the
issues of inequitable economic distribution, injustice, prejudice, and
power differentiation between classes, genders, and races. This sounds
like the Marxist critique of psychoanalysis updated by a liberal and
applied to a social movement rather than to a therapeutic procedure.
Kaminer sees the twelve–step movement and its "spirituality" as engendering political passivity on the part of those she sees as potential
recruits to her political agenda.

The ACOA movement is primarily a female one, and it is indeed
difficult to demonstrate a pathological, or pathognomic personality
profile in this group. It has also been pointed out that the ACOA
movement consists of white, middle class, highly educated female
children of alcoholics, and tells us nothing about the effects of parental drug use in poor minority males and females, which may be
quite different. It is probable that being the son of two street crack

addicts has consequences that being the daughter of an excessive martini drinking physician does not.

There has also been a difficulty in demonstrating psychopathology in the younger children of alcoholics. In an exhaustive review of the literature, Seilhamer and Jacob (1990) conclude that COAs are amazingly resilient and on average do as well as or better than other children. Similarly it has been difficult to establish higher rates of anxiety, depression, and other psychopathology in ACOA populations, although the literature is inconsistent, and some researchers do report significant differences. The positive findings we do have are not robust. What we do find in ACOAs are elevated rates of alcoholism and other addictions and codependence manifest in relationships with or marriage to an alcoholic or addict. What are we to make of this? Is it all what a cynical colleague called the "kvetch factor" when he said, "Thank God for the kvetch factor among ACOAs; it keeps my treatment hours full"? Not exactly Mr. Empathy, this colleague shares and confirms from within a clinical context Goodwin's acerbic take on ACOAs. I am not sure, but I simply do not find it believable that it is possible to grow up without scars and developmental deficits in a home where one or both parents are seriously addicted. I realize that the counterintuitive can be true, yet my clinical experience is all to the contrary. Several factors help account for this research/clinical conflict.

A distinction has been made between families with alcoholism and alcoholic families. It is an unusually heuristic differential. To grow up in a family that has strengths in the capacity to love and to function reasonably well and in which a parent is alcoholic is a very different experience than to grow up in a family which is (dis)organized around the behavior of the drinker. When we are talking about COAs and ACOAs, we are talking about millions of people whose experience growing up with alcoholic parents is enormously variable, so it is not surprising that when they are lumped together for research purposes clear trends do not emerge. The contrast between "family with an alcoholic" and "alcoholic family" begins to address this heterogeneity. Presumably those growing up in alcoholic families are far more damaged than those growing up in families with an alcoholic.

So a subset of ACOAs may very well manifest elevated levels of anxiety, depression, and personality disorder.

I would hypothesize that another intervening variable is the high proportion of narcissistic pathology in the subset of ACOAs that is seriously impaired. I am using narcissistic in Kohut's sense (Levin 1987, 1991; see also Chapter 2) of regression/fixation to the stage of the archaic bipolar nuclear self experienced as a sense of inner emptiness, futility, meaninglessness, rage often turned against the self, and deficits in the capacities to self-soothe, to modulate anxiety, to maintain a reasonably constant and satisfactory level of self-esteem, and to be alone. Being narcissistic in this sense leaves one vulnerable to the primitive idealizations characteristic of this developmental stage manifesting themselves in what in these days is called codependency or in schizoid defenses against such idealizations, resulting in isolation and pervasive feelings of loneliness. (Sorry, Dr. Goodwin, but here is a shopping list that just might make sense.) This population of mostly female ACOAs often includes high or even overachievers and this often masks deep pain and emotional disaffectment. These are what the alcoholic family literature calls "heroes," parentified children who were early called upon to "rescue" their alcoholic and codependent parents. So a self-psychological, that is, Kohutian, understanding of the ACOA paradox makes sense of the conflicting findings. I elaborate a self-psychological model of addiction in my 1987 book, *Treatment of Alcoholism and Other Addictions: A Self-Psychology Approach*.

If the impact of familial alcoholism on adult women is equivocal, the effects of parental alcoholism on sons is far clearer. This is particularly so for sons of type 2 alcoholics. Elevated rates of undercontrol, undersocialization, hyperactivity, ADD, other cognitive and learning deficits, and conduct disorder are found in some studies of COAs (Searles and Windle 1990). Once again, these findings are not consistent or robust, yet reappear with a compelling suggestiveness. Antisocial personality disorder, particularly when manifested in overt criminality comorbid with alcoholism in fathers, strongly predicts conduct disorder and ADD in sons. In turn, conduct disorder and ADD in boyhood are strongly correlated with adult alcoholism.

Longitudinal studies by McCord and McCord (1960), Robins and colleagues (1962), Loper and colleagues (1973), and Vaillant (1983) clearly demonstrate externalizing defenses, undercontrol, and rebelliousness in childhood as increasing susceptibility to alcoholism. (For a fuller discussion of these findings, see Levin [1995].) Although the empirical evidence is weaker, it is likely that daughters of such fathers are prone to depression. Winokur (1974) has described a depressive-spectrum disorder that manifests itself as alcoholism and antisocial behavior in men and depression in women. He makes a distinction between primary alcoholics whose depression or sociopathy is secondary to their drinking and secondary alcoholics who are self-medicating depression or manifesting antisocial trends. The contradictory data starts to make sense taking Winokur's theory into account. The male ACOAs suffer masked depression, but display externalizing defenses that include substance use, conduct disorder, and perhaps ADD, which may or may not have a neurological substrate, while the female ACOAs either suffer overt depression or mask their depression with perfectionism and compulsive striving. The family hero looks great and feels like hell.

There is also a fascinating set of studies discussed as evidence for a genetic factor earlier in this chapter, contrasting college-age children from families with alcoholism (FHP) with those who have no alcoholism in their families (FHN). FHP students have less upper-body sway (static ataxia) after drinking a "challenge dose" (three to five drinks) of ethanol than FHN students, and both report and objectively measure less impairment or even improvement on a variety of cognitive and motor tasks. All of which can be interpreted as alcohol being highly reinforcing for FHP subjects. These studies also support the "hollow leg" hypothesis of susceptibility to alcoholism. Although usually taken as evidence for a biological etiology of alcoholism, environmental factors may very well contribute to these findings. Some EEG studies show sons of type 2 alcoholics to have abnormal P300 waves, an orienting response that may be a neurological correlative of ADD and elevated P300 is associated with what Cloninger calls somatic anxiety—bodily tension. Drinking reduces the P300 response, and once again we have evidence that alcohol would be highly rein-forcing for these children of type 2 alcoholics.

Both sons and daughters of type 1 alcoholics have abnormalities in their alpha waves (well-synchronized slow alpha waves are cor-relative with "serenity") and what Cloninger calls cognitive anxiety—worry, and drinking acts as a corrective, again being highly reinforc-ing. Of course, to say sons and daughters of type 1 alcoholics have abnormalities in their alpha waves is to state a statistical average in a few studies with very small populations, and it would be a question-able generalization. Further, there have been difficulties replicating these studies. Nevertheless, it is a highly suggestive finding. (See Levin [1995] for a more detailed discussion.)

Cox (1987), reviewing the empirical psychological findings and the longitudinal studies, concludes that there is compelling evidence of a prealcoholic (male) personality characterized by nonconformity, im-pulsivity, and reward-seeking characteristics. There is even more com-pelling evidence that clinical alcoholics are characterized by negative affect (depression and anxiety) and low self-esteem, as well as by a cognitive perceptual style that includes field dependence, external locus of control, and stimulus augmentation—that is, relying on en-vironmental rather than internal cues, feeling controlled by "fate," and experiencing stimuli as powerfully impinging, respectively. (A de-tailed discussion of the pre- and postaddictive personalities can be found in Levin [1995].) The negative affect and low self-esteem are characteristic of secondary alcoholics, that is, those who drink to relieve emotional or psychiatric problems, for whom they are ante-cedent. Cox points out that the proportion of male and female alco-holics in secondary alcoholics is quite different than their proportions in primary alcoholics, with many more females being secondary alco-holics. He argues that negative affect and low self-esteem are conse-quences in primary alcoholics, although they may be antecedents in secondary alcoholics. Citing Tarter and Alterman's (1988) studies, he speculates that the alcoholic perceptual style may be largely ante-cedent and a manifestation of a specific inherited neural dysfunction. Other investigators see the alcoholic perceptual style as either a con-sequence or as environmentally determined.

My model (Levin 1987) of regression/fixation to pathological narcissism as the psychodynamic correlative of addiction accounts for these characteristics of the addictive personality.

What all this means for the family therapist is that the male children of some alcoholics are likely to have difficulties around bodily tension, ADD, hyperactivity, and possible conduct disorder, while both male and female children of type 2 alcoholics are at elevated risk of suffering from high levels of anxiety. Family members who are actively addicted frequently suffer from and manifest angry acting out and not infrequently antisocial behavior, field dependence, stimulus augmentation, and ego weakness: impulsivity; lack of affect tolerance; low self-esteem; the use of primitive defenses, including denial, projection, and splitting; as well as anxiety and depression. Externalizing defenses against the anxiety and depression as well as reactive grandiosity may more characterize the clinical presentation than the underlying character structure and psychopathology.

The addictions family therapist, even while working from a systems perspective, needs to understand the intrapsychic world of the addicted family member(s) and the behavioral impact of their inner worlds on the rest of the family. The following section surveys major psychodynamic theories of addiction.

PSYCHODYNAMIC THEORIES OF THE ETIOLOGY OF ADDICTION

Sigmund Freud

The earliest psychoanalytic insight into addiction is contained in a letter from Sigmund Freud (1897) to his friend Wilhelm Fliess. Freud wrote, "It has occurred to me that masturbation is the one great habit that is a 'primary addiction,' and that the other addictions, for alcohol, morphine, etc., only enter into life as a substitute and replacement for it" (p. 287). Thus, in Freud's view, masturbation is the "model" addiction. All later additions are modeled after it. They are substitutes for and reenactments of the addiction to masturbation. According to Freud, infantile masturbation is both compelling and guilt inducing. Often it is forbidden by parents or other caregivers, and the child comes to internalize the prohibition. A struggle ensues between a wish for instinctual gratification and the internalized prohibition. The struggle not to masturbate is almost always lost; the pleasures of genital, or pregenital (oral and anal) masturbation are too great. However, the return to masturbation is accompanied by guilt and the fall in self-esteem that accompanies the failure to carry through a resolution. Masturbation can then be used as a way of assuaging the anxiety, and a vicious cycle is set up. This certainly sounds familiar and is indeed the pattern of much addictive behavior. From this point of view, later addictions are not only displacements and reenactments of the original addiction to masturbation but also attempts to master, through repetition, the traumatic loss of self-esteem that followed the failure to live up to the resolution not to masturbate.

Freud returned to this theory of addiction many years later in *Dostoevsky and Parricide* (1928). There he analyzed the great Russian novelist's compulsive (addictive) gambling. Playing on the word *play* Freud traced Dostoevsky's compulsion back to an addiction to masturbation, but he added the insight that the addiction also served as a means of *self-punishment* for the original forbidden wish. The "payoff," for Dostoevsky, his conscious wishes notwithstanding, was losing at the gaming table. There can be a condensation of guilts: masturbatory, oedipal (for incestuous wishes toward parents), and for the addiction itself, all of which are "punished" by the negative consequences of the addiction.

Freud's insight into the self-punishing potential of addiction has more than a little validity. Freud's theory has the additional merit of highlighting the narcissistic nature of addiction. In masturbation, one's love object is oneself, one's genitals, or at best one's fantasy of another object, but it is not another person. Similarly, in addictions, there is a regression (or fixation) to a state in which there is no human object. The love object of the addict becomes the abused substance itself, which is experienced as either an extension of the self or as an omnipotent substance with which the addict merges.

Freud's theory also highlights another aspect of the narcissistic pathology inherent in addictions: the loss of self-esteem that the masturbator or addict experiences when he or she gives in to the addiction. This loss of self-esteem in turn requires more of the addictive substance or activity to attempt to raise the lowered self-esteem, and an addictive cycle is established. Freud's (1920) late theory of the *repetition compulsion* also sheds light on addictions. In this theory he postulates the existence of an innate "death instinct" which drives all organic being to seek the quietus of the inorganic. Life is a struggle between Eros, the force that makes for integration, union, and growth, and Thanatos, the force that makes for dissolution, disassociation, and regression. Comparing his vision to that of the Greek pre-Socratic philosopher Empedocles, who wrote of the eternal war between Love and Strife, Freud thought that some sort of innate destructive drive had to exist to account for such phenomena as self-mutilation, suicide, and addiction. He also cited the *negative therapeutic reaction*, in which the better the therapy patient does in treatment, the worse he or she feels, and the compulsive reenactment of destructive relationships as evidence for the innateness of Thanatos. Most analysts have rejected Freud's theory of the indwellingness of a self-destructive drive, but they have thought him correct descriptively; that is, human beings do hold on to and repeat the familiar no matter how pernicious the experience, and this built-in conservatism—resistance to change—is a factor with which the addiction therapist must contend.

Karl Abraham

Karl Abraham, one of Freud's early students, published the first psychoanalytic paper on alcoholism in 1908. In it he stated that "alcoholism is a nervous and sexual perversion" (p. 87). By perversion he meant oral regressive and homoerotic tendencies. Abraham based his theory on an analysis of male alcoholics and on his observation that homophobic men become openly physically affectionate in the camaraderie of the beer hall. He inferred that heavy drinking allows the expression of forbidden homosexual wishes and postulated that addicts have especially intense conflicts about repressed homosexuality. In emphasizing the regression to orality in alcoholism, he not only calls attention to the oral ingestion of the drink but also points out the parallel between drunken stupor and the warmth and security felt by the satiated infant. It is this state of satiation that the addict craves. Abraham highlights the psychological and emotional regression brought about by the drinking itself, irrespective of the underlying developmental fixation.

Edward Glover

Edward Glover (1928), an English analyst, emphasized the *aggression* in addiction. Writing from the viewpoint of classical analysis, he spoke of "oral rage" and "anal sadism," by which he meant drinking or drugging *at* somebody, using one's addiction as a weapon to hurt others. Addictive rage is partly in defense of the addiction, partly self-hatred projected outward, partly a response to narcissistic vulnerability (that is, ego weakness that sets one up to be easily hurt), partly pharmacologically induced, and partly Glover's regressive oral and anal fury. In any case the management of anger is crucial in addiction therapy. Most "slips" are rage responses. Glover also cites alcohol's antianxiety properties, in particular its use to quell *castration anxiety*, that is, fear of retaliation by the father for murderous wishes toward him.

Sandor Rado

Sandor Rado (1933) was the first to point to the similarity between addiction and manic-depressive psychosis, with the cycle of elation during the alcohol/drug high and depression during the hangover paralleling the manic-depressive cycle. Rado related both the mood alterations of manic-depressive illness and the addictive pattern of highs and lows to the cycle of infantile hunger and satiation. He movingly captures the addict's futile attempt to chemically relieve "tense depression" and turn it into elation, only to fall into an even deeper depression, necessitating more intake. As the addiction proceeds the periods of elation become briefer and briefer and in the end there is nothing but unrelieved depression. Much alcoholic drinking and addictive drugging is just such self-medication. It is an important dynamic in addiction even when the dysphoria being medicated is caused by the drug itself. Rado saw the key issue in addictions as a disturbance in the regulation in self-esteem.

Robert Knight

Robert Knight (1937) emphasized the depressive aspects of the alcoholic personality. Frustrated orality results in repressed rage and hence in depression. Knight was the first to highlight the severity of alcoholic psychopathology. The depression he spoke of is both an "empty" depression and an "angry" depression with rage turned against the self.

Otto Fenichel

Otto Fenichel (1945) also thought that oral dependence and frustration result in chronic depression in the alcoholic. He saw alcoholism as a maladaptive defense mechanism used to resolve neurotic conflicts, especially conflict between dependence and the expression of anger. It is to Fenichel that we owe the observation that "the superego has been defined as that part of the mind which is soluble in alcohol" (p. 379), making it possible for the drinker to use alcohol to indulge in forbidden impulses and resolve id-superego conflicts.

Karl Menninger

Karl Menninger (1938) was one of the few American analysts who subscribed to Freud's theory of a death instinct. He called alcoholism a form of *chronic suicide*. It is a destructive aggression against the self as punishment for hostile, aggressive feelings that are unacceptable to the self. Alcohol makes manageable the conflict between passive erotic dependence on and resentment of the father, who the drinker experiences ambivalently.

There is no question that alcoholics engage in self-destructive behavior. Their addiction costs them dearly in terms of health, career success, relationships, emotional tranquility, and sometimes life itself.

The question is, Is that self-destruction sought on if not a conscious then an unconscious level? Analytic writers like Menninger cite clinical material as evidence that alcoholics do deliberately seek self-destruction, whether they realize it or not, while researchers and behaviorally oriented clinicians believe that alcoholics initially sought "positive affect" (elation) and only later, after alcohol itself had produced dysphoria, drank to alleviate "negative affect" (tense depression), and that in both cases the self-destruction is a side effect, not a desired outcome at any level. The analysts, with their notion of a dynamic unconscious, ask why was the elation sought in the first place if there wasn't an underlying depression to start with. I cannot help but observe that drinking and drugging can simultaneously serve as an act of forbidden aggression and as a punishment for that aggression, a "double hook" that is indeed powerful.

EGO PSYCHOLOGY AND SELF PSYCHOLOGY APPROACHES TO ADDICTION

Many recent psychoanalytic theorists, including Fromm (1941), Szasz (1958), Hartocollis (1968), Krystal and Raskin (1970), Kernberg (1975), Wurmser (1978), Khantzian (1981), and Levin (1987), emphasize impairments in ego functioning, lack of affect tolerance, and the use of primitive ("borderline") defense mechanisms, including "splitting" into all good and all bad and denial. These theorists stress the adaptive function of the addiction—what drugs do for the person or what the person believes they do. The psychological dimension of addiction is a futile attempt to remediate deficits in the self. Drugs are experienced as an all-powerful mother with whom the user merges in order to raise self-esteem, quell anxiety, feel soothed, feel cohesive or whole, feel full as opposed to empty, feel companioned as opposed to alone, and feel safe. Since drugs cannot do any of these things for very long and in fact exacerbate the very deficits they are used to ameliorate, an addictive cycle is set up. The theories of Szasz, Krystal and Raskin, Khantzian, Wurmser, Hartocollis, Kernberg, and Fromm are summarized below.

Thomas Szasz

Thomas Szasz (1958) views addictions as *counterphobic* activities. The user uses to confront and master intolerable fears, including the fear of being addicted. The drinker's basic motivation is to prove that he or she is in control, that he or she has ego mastery. A defiance of fate is implicit in this counterphobic behavior. Szasz's theory is insightful. In my view, the phobia is a fear of psychic annihilation and oblivion, of both regressive fragmentation of the self and engulfment of the self by the symbiotic mother. Experientially, both outcomes are death. Addicts therefore self-inflict death in order to master their fear of death. Seen in this way, addicts are mythic heroes who descend to the underworld and emerge intact—at least that is their hope. Defensive grandiosity is fed by participation in this unconscious drama.

Henry Krystal and Herbert Raskin

Henry Krystal and Herbert Raskin (1970) offer a theory of affect development in which the infant starts out with global, undifferentiated feelings, including a kind of *ur*-affect (primitive undifferentiated emotion) of dysphoria, which will later differentiate into anxiety, tension, and depression in many gradations and with many fine discriminations. They postulate that addicts suffer *affect regression* to a stage in which affects are massive, primitive, and overwhelming. Affect regression is characterized by dedifferentiation, deverbalization, resomatization, and sexualization. Such regression may be pharmacological or it may be psychodynamic, particularly if the addict has been deprived of the kind of early experience, the *labeling of affects* by loving parents, that facilitates affect development, a deprivation resulting in a fixation to an early stage of affect development. In either case, the addict literally doesn't know what he or she is feeling. Krystal and Raskin's global dysphoria is reminiscent of Rado's tense depression.

Krystal and Raskin's theory has important clinical implications. Verbalization is a crucial developmental task involving both maturation and object relations. Whatever the original socialization experience of the addict, the therapist must facilitate affect progression by giving the addict words for what he or she is feeling. This affect labeling provides cognitive structure, starts the process of affect (re)differentiation, and reduces the terror of the experientially primitive, unfamiliar, and chaotic emerging feelings. Affect labeling is a way station on the road from feelings experienced as mysterious happenings, as lightning bolts from above, to feelings experienced as consciously owned aspects of the self.

Edward Khantzian

Edward Khantzian (1981) emphasizes ego and self deficits in the areas of self-care and regulation of feelings. Khantzian, unlike Menninger, sees alcoholic self-destruction as resulting from a deficit rather than as a self-punishment. The addict is unable to take better care of him- or herself because something is missing inside. There is a "basic fault" (Balint 1969). This deficit also precludes normal affect regulation and tolerance, resulting in maladaptive defenses including drug use. Khantzian reinterprets addictive dependency not as a form of orality, but rather as a necessary consequence of deficiency. This has been called the "self-medication" hypothesis of the etiology of addiction.

Leon Wurmser

Leon Wurmser (1978) sees the addict as caught in a seven-stage vicious cycle. In stage 1, there is a sudden plummeting of already tenuous self-esteem, usually following a disappointment in reality or in fantasy, which leads to a narcissistic crisis (stage 2). This crisis leads to a breakdown of affect defense (stage 3) in which feelings become overwhelming, global, generalized, archaic, and incapable of being expressed in words. This experience is intolerable and leads to repression and denial of inner reality, leaving only a vague tension and restlessness (stage 4). In the process, the self is split and depersonalized. The addict experiences an urgent need to act; since the inner world is denied and externalized, it is logical to look for the answer externally and concretely in the drug. At this point aggression is mobilized, and it may be turned against the self (stage 5). In stage 6, the super-ego is split so that it won't be an impediment to action, and feelings of entitlement and grandiosity lead to a consummation in the binge. The narcissistic crisis ends in pleasure, but it isn't quite successful. Wurmser quotes Rado (1933): "The elation had augmented the ego (self) to gigantic dimensions and had almost eliminated reality; now just the reverse state appears, sharpened by the contrast. The ego (self) is shrunken and reality appears exaggerated in its dimensions" (p. 10). The user is in worse shape than ever, with even lower self-esteem (stage 7).

Wurmser emphasizes maladaptive defenses, particularly splitting of self, superego, and reality into incommunicable parts; denial not only of the addiction but of the inner world of fantasy and feelings; and externalization of inner deficit, conflict, and possibility of resolution.

Peter Hartocollis

Peter Hartocollis (1968) stresses the use of alcohol to bolster defenses. The defense most in need of bolstering is denial, which Hartocollis sees as repudiation of the need for help. His formulation is thus a variation on the counterdependency hypothesis of the dynamics of alcoholism. In a later paper (Hartocollis and Hartocollis 1980), he presents evidence that this denial originates in a disturbed mother–infant relationship, postulating that the difficulty frequently starts in the rapprochement substage of the separation-individuation process (Mahler et al. 1975). Hartocollis hypothesizes that not only do these developmental vicissitudes predispose people to borderline and nar-cissistic personality disorders but that these disorders in turn predis-pose people to addiction. To account for the research evidence of lack of psychopathology in prealcoholics, he points to the relatively smooth surface functioning of narcissists who compensate for their inner emptiness and emotional shallowness by acting "as if." He further suggests that as their compensation falters, they turn to drugs to maintain their "as if" personality (Deutsch 1965).

Erich Fromm

Fromm's interest was only tangentially in addiction, yet he elucidated one of the most powerful dynamics driving addictive behavior, "escape from freedom." In his 1941 book of that title, Fromm convincingly demonstrated that one of the social dynamics behind the rise of totalitarianism is a desire to escape from what the Danish philosopher Søren Kierkegaard (1849) called the "dizziness of freedom," the anxiety ineluctably concomitant with the realization that I am responsible for—indeed in a sense I *am*—my choices.

Fromm saw not only social but individual psychopathology as derivative from a desire to flee the anxiety of being free. A neurosis, a psychosis, or an addiction is a constriction, a narrowing of possibility. The history of any addiction is a history of progressive enslavement. Seen from this point of view, addiction with its progressive impoverishment of the self and loss of potentiality is clearly an escape from freedom. The achievement of sobriety is a reclamation of freedom. Fear is always concomitant with this newfound freedom, with its choices, decisions, and responsibilities. The result is a sort of ontological agoraphobia, which can arouse such intense anxiety that sobriety is jeopardized. The dizziness of freedom has caused many a slip and affects not only the recovering addict but the entire family, which is also suddenly "free."

Fromm's existential understanding of the dynamics of addiction has great clinical utility, particularly in family therapy. An exploration of the choices the addict and the family needed to flee often opens unexpected vistas that provide insight and strengthen sobriety.

Otto Kernberg

Otto Kernberg sees addiction as a symptom of underlying personality disorder. He stresses disturbed object relations, by which he means abnormalities in the inner, representational world. The internal world is initially undifferentiated. There is nothing but a global, undifferentiated representation that does not distinguish between self and other. Kernberg calls this a *selfobject representation*. In response to experiences of gratification and frustration, this global representation is split into good and bad selfobjects. If development goes no further, reality testing is never developed since self and world are confused. At the next stage, good and bad selfobjects are differentiated into good self, bad self, good object, and bad object representations. This is the inner reality of the borderline who oscillates wildly in terms of self-evaluation and relations to others. In twelve–step language, this is the world of "the great I Am and Poor Me." In a healthy maturity, the good and bad self and object representations are integrated, with goodness predominating over badness, and the internal world becomes one of complex, differentiated, more or less realistic self and object representations. Kernberg theorizes that the inner world of the addict lacks such integration. His treatment is aimed at modification of this internal world.

ADDICTIVE RAGE

The Kohutian notion of narcissistic rage illuminates much addictive behavior. Narcissistic rage, unlike mature aggression, is not instrumental in the service of a reality-based goal; rather, it is the response of the unmirrored self to narcissistic injury, injury to the core of self (Levin 1993), which is characterized by deep pain, intense feelings of shame, a precipitous fall in self-esteem, and an unquenchable desire for revenge. It is the response of the offended monarch, "Off with their heads."

Narcissistic rage turned against the self can result in suicide. Addictive rage is multidetermined: part of it is pharmacological, the result of the drug's effect on central nervous system tissue; part of it is in defense of the addiction; part of it comes from the accumulation of unexpressed anger (addicts have a lot of bluster, but rarely are effectively communicative or assertive); part of it is self-hatred projected outward; part of it is historical (that is, unconscious rage over childhood injury); and part of it is narcissistic rage as a consequence of narcissistic vulnerability (that is, lack of the resources to process the "slings and arrows of outrageous fortune," not to mention everyday disappointments and slights), and feelings of entitle-ment of the archaic grandiose self.

CARL JUNG: ADDICTION AND SPIRITUALITY

Carl Jung had an important, albeit indirect, role in the foundation of Alcoholics Anonymous (AA) and a strong influence on one of its founders, Bill Wilson. It seems highly improbably that Jung, a Swiss psychiatrist whose writings are often obscure, would have influenced an American self-help organization, but he did. It is an interesting story, already referred to in Chapter 2, that has become part of the AA mythology. At the risk of redundancy, I would like to retell it in more depth here.

Jung had treated a patient known in AA literature as Roland H. He was a successful American businessman who had come to Jung for help with alcoholism. He had undergone a seemingly successful analysis with the master himself and left Zurich certain that he had been cured. Roland believed that he had such a deep self-understanding that he would never have trouble with alcohol again. In a short time, however, he returned to Jung drunk and in despair. Jung told him that there was no hope. Roland asked if there really was none at all, and Jung replied that only a major personality reorganization driven by a powerful emotion, in essence a "conversion experience," could save him. Roland left in deep despair, but Jung's words touched some-thing deep inside him and he did what AA would later call "hitting bottom." In his despair he reached out for help and did indeed have a conversion experience, joining the Oxford Movement, which was an upper-middle-class revival movement popular in the 1920s and 1930s. He became and remained sober.

The Oxford Movement had a set of spiritual steps that their mem-bers followed. These steps became the basis of the famous twelve steps of Alcoholics Anonymous. Roland spread the good word to his friend and fellow drunk Ebby Thacker, who also became sober. Ebby in turn went to visit his buddy, Bill Wilson, who was drunk. Ebby told Bill the story of his meeting Roland and joining the Oxford Movement.

Bill entered a hospital to dry out. There he experienced some sort of "peak" or mystical experience. When he left the hospital, he too joined the Oxford Movement, and he borrowed a great deal from it. He began to work with drunks on his own. Shortly thereafter, he joined with another drunk, Bob Smith, whom he helped to get sober, and thus Alcoholics Anonymous was born. Ebby did not make it; he died in Rockland State Hospital of alcoholism. Many years later, Bill Wilson wrote to Jung to tell him the story, and Jung (1961) replied,

> [Roland's] craving for alcohol was the equivalent on a low level of the spiritual thirst of our being for wholeness, expression in medieval language: the union with God. . . . You see, "alcohol" in Latin is "spiritus" and you use the same word for the highest religious experience as well as for the most depraving poison. The helpful formula therefore is: *spiritus contra spiritum.* [p. 625]

THE ADDICTED FAMILY

The addicted family has been described in the most variegated, indeed contradictory, ways. Some of these ways have an empirical basis; others are more intuitive, having been inspired by clinical work. Virginia Satir (1972) and Sharon Wegschieder-Cruse (1985) have described a set of roles played by children in addicted homes. Wolin and colleagues (1979) have studied the transmission of alcoholism, Peter Steinglass (1987) has looked at how alcoholic families actually work, and the charismatic John Bradshaw (1988a,b) has elaborated a view of the dysfunctional family driven by addiction to drugs, power, and control.

The following roles have been described in the addicted family: the Hero or *parentified child*, the Lost Child, the Mascot, and the Scapegoat. The Hero early learns that Mom and/or Dad is incompetent and takes over. In the process, the Hero is deprived of a childhood. Heroes grow up to be angry controllers who know somewhere that they have been deeply cheated. They tend to be perfectionistic, high achievers. The Lost Child suffers emotional and sometimes physical neglect, and grows up feeling lost, unloved, and directionless. He or she may also have learned all too well how to get lost, to hide, and may have terrible difficulty integrating into any group. The Mascot, sometimes called the Clown, has learned how to cheer up the addicted and/or depressed grownups as well as him- or herself. The Mascot may or may not consciously feel the despair beneath this manic defense. The Scapegoat is the kid who gets the physical and/or emotional beatings and often grows up rageful and looking for somebody, who usually turns out to be spouse or child, to beat in turn. There is also the Rebel who is probably the healthiest if the rebellion stops short of overt criminality. The Rebel is most likely to be the addict of the following generation.

There is a whole library of books on these roles and one certainly sees people who enact them, yet the entire notion lacks empirical support. Most COAs manifest more than one role incarnation, the Hero most often being seen as a pure type. I have never found the addictive family role stuff particularly useful, although it is occasionally handy as a didactic tool to help patients make sense of their experience. I sometimes tell patients or families about the roles that clinicians have described in addictive families and suggest that one or more of them fit the patient or are being enacted by the family. This provides cognitive structure, reduces anxiety, and makes sense of what is experienced as chaos. There is also a danger in using this shortcut, cookie-cutter set of categories in that they may close down process and exploration in both individual and family. To learn that you were or are the Scapegoat may be helpful, but not nearly as helpful as feeling your scapegoatedness in all of its nuances and intricacies. Like all abstractions, the addictive family roles oversimplify, and like all abstractions, they help organize experience.

There are essentially two views of the alcoholic (addictive) family: the first elaborated by Peter Steinglass sees the addictive family as a problem-solving organism adapting to an illness and at times using that illness to solve impasses in the family life cycle; the second elaborated by John Bradshaw sees the addictive family as dysfunctional and as inflicting deep wounds on its children. The first looks for empirical support in elaborate and ingenious research paradigms; the second also looks for empirical support but is driven by a view of health and deeply held convictions that the roots of addiction are to be found in childhood injury and deficit. It is possible that these authors are talking about different populations, different types of families. Steinglass looks at functional families with a problem, while Bradshaw looks at more chaotic families disorganized by addiction. They cite different data. For example, Bradshaw holds that over 50 percent of ACOAs have been sexually abused, while Steinglass explicitly says that he is describing "stable," far less chaotic or violent alcoholic families. Bradshaw is strongly normative; he knows what a healthy family should be and measures actual families against his standard, while Steinglass sees all families as struggling through their life cycles, dealing with illnesses including addiction as best they can. The first looks toward spiritual and emotional redemption, the second toward making do.

Steinglass and colleagues (1987) start with two "case histories." Noah, whose son Ham, looked upon his nakedness while he was drunk "and incurred his wrath," and Lot's daughters, who got him drunk so he would impregnate them. For Noah's youngest son, the sequence of events initiated by his father's intoxication proved devastating. For Lot and his daughters, otherwise forbidden behavior became socially acceptable, at least partially because it was carried out under the influence of alcohol. Alcohol permitted this family to solve a major dilemma (a threat to family continuity) in an inventive fashion. The family survived, and succeeding generations were guaranteed, presumably because the family was able to act during periods of intoxication in ways that otherwise would have been unacceptable. The significant point of Lot's story is that "intoxication is used to solve a family problem" (p. 6). So alcohol may be divisive (Noah and his sons) or cohesive (Lot and his daughters) for the family.

Steinglass makes a distinction between alcoholic (addictive) families, families organized by the alcoholism and reaction to it, and families with alcoholism, which have a "sick" member whose illness causes distortions but does not dominate family life. The former is of course more problem ridden than the latter, but Steinglass is not into pathology; his stance as researcher and clinician is empathic and nonjudgmental, and his interest is in how both types of families manage to perform the life tasks that even the most disorganized, enmeshed, or unrelated family must perform.

Steinglass reports that the alcoholic families he studied were far more stable (in fact, all too stable), far less chaotic, and far less characterized by the violence, physical abuse, sexual abuse, incest, and storminess generally held to be highly correlated with parental addiction and the addictive family as reported in the clinical and popular literature. (There is some, albeit inconsistent, empirical evidence for these correlations.) In short, addictive families are not necessarily sociopathic families; in fact, in Steinglass's estimation, most are not. The story comes to mind of the newly discovered Tennessee Williams play manuscript in which the hero has sex with his mother in Act One, sex with his father in Act Two, and kills himself in Act Three after having discovered that he is adopted. In effect, the more rabid ACOA movement gurus feel that Steinglass has told them that they were adopted; however, they seem to feel more murderous than suicidal.

Steinglass points out that in addiction cycles no one drinks or drugs all the time, so that the family dynamic is biphasic. His families adjusted to this biphasic characteristic. In effect, the COAs have two mothers (or fathers), which confuses and reinforces the psychological defense of splitting. But splitting can be adaptive, allowing the child to feel loved in spite of the unloving behavior of the intoxicated parent. Steinglass's drunken parents rarely engage in the grosser behavior described in the ACOA literature and were more of an embarrassment when they acted "like assholes." Certainly this is damaging, but not in the same way as being raped or beaten. One wonders how much Steinglass's picture of the alcoholic family is skewed by denial, disavowal, repression, and defensive idealization. The clinician simply has a different database derived from the transference and therapeutic derepression than the researcher, and this partly accounts for the disparate pictures they paint.

Steinglass is particularly interested in the effects of alcoholism in the family on daily routines, family rituals, and problem-solving family episodes and techniques throughout the family life cycle. Those families that were able to maintain their daily routines and rituals and who had a family identity broader than or different from that of the addictive family suffered the least from the invasive effects of the drinking. Steven Wolin and Leonard Bennett (1984), two of Steinglass's collaborators, believe that the preservation of family rituals and their protection from contamination by the effects of drunkenness is the key variable distinguishing "healthy" and "unhealthy" (relatively speaking) alcoholic families. This is interesting in light of the overwhelming clinical evidence that holidays and vacations were hellish and dreaded in the memories of COAs. Possibly Wolin and Bennett are right and the COAs whose families preserved their rituals intact don't come for treatment. The familial transmission of alcoholism is a life cycle phenomenon, the key phase of which is the establishment of the new family. If the COAs forming this family can establish rituals in which alcohol is peripheral or absent, then the generational transmission is likely to come to an end, and this is most likely to happen if the routines and rituals of their families of origin are relatively uncontaminated by the familial alcoholism. Having a strong identity as a new family also reduces generational transmission. Another way of understanding this is that the COAs of the less enmeshed families have the best chance of establishing nonalcoholic families of their own.

In the clinical section of their book, Steinglass and colleagues emphasize the need for the clinician to see the family as it is, with its strengths and weaknesses, and not to countertransferentially discredit it under the rubric of dysfunctional family. Steinglass and colleagues would certainly agree that the phrase *dysfunctional family*, like the phrase *neurotic person*, is redundant. For this individuation of the family to be possible, it is particularly vital that the therapist be cognizant of the life cycle stage, and addictive family stage the family is struggling through (or is stuck in). Yes there is stultifying homeostatic stuckness in addictive families, but they too change as they must and perhaps even grow. As in all family therapies, Steinglass attempts to enable that growth through a combination of insight and direction.

Therapy is conceptualized as a four-stage process: (1) diagnosing alcoholism and labeling it a family problem; (2) removing alcohol from the family system (easier said than done—Steinglass uses behavioral contracting, a technique he borrowed from Haley, and makes this issue the sole issue of the therapy until it is resolved); (3) helping the family pass through the "emotional desert," that is, the emptiness and confusion and loss of alcoholic problem-solving techniques in early sobriety; and (4) family restabilization versus family reorganization (the first essentially perpetuates the routines, rituals, and problem-solving techniques in the context of dryness, while the second leads to something like a psychological remarriage). Bradshaw and the twelve–step people would say that the first is not possible, since the alcoholism was a response to familial and intrapsychic disturbance. They believe sobriety is only possible through growth. Steinglass on the other hand finds that family reorganization is by far the most common outcome of sobriety and that the inherent inertia in these families may make for a highly stable sobriety.

JOHN BRADSHAW:
TREATMENT OF SHAME-BASED BEHAVIOR

John Bradshaw, charismatic and projecting passionate conviction, is a former theologian who planned to become a priest. He is a recovering alcoholic who has had tremendous impact on the community of recovering persons. He writes for the general public, and his popular books and seminars have had wide influence. A systems theorist who draws on much of the work we have already discussed, he is difficult to summarize. Although a "pop" psychologist and intensely evangelical, he has something important to say. His basic position is that addiction is a family disease that perpetuates itself through *poisonous pedagogy*, that is, the idea that children's spirit must be "broken" for them to be under social control, which reduces children to objects, and manifests itself as physical, sexual, and emotional abuse resulting in shame and its repression (Bradshaw 1988b). He calls this *toxic shame*. Bradshaw is not referring here to the shame that comes from or with addiction; rather, he is talking about the kind of shame that comes from having been abused as a child or from growing up in an addictive home particularly if the shame is anesthetized, denied, repressed, or acted out. One suspects that Bradshaw is primarily speaking to and about those alcoholics whose parents were alcoholic.

Like all single-factor theories, Bradshaw's is overly simplistic and his writings tend to be repetitious. They do however have the virtue of highlighting the centrality of shame in the dynamics of addiction. His treatment recommendations are a synthesis of the psychodynamic (such as recovery of repressed memories and dream work) and the cognitive behavioral (such as cognitive restructuring and self-efficacy training). He stresses work with the "inner child." In many ways still the theologian, Bradshaw sees addiction—which he conceives extremely broadly to encompass chemical addictions; eating disorders; addiction to fame, achievement, money, and status; addiction to people (co-dependency); addiction to control; and addiction to rage, obsessions, and compulsive behavior of all types, including political and religious fanaticism—as being the equivalent of original sin. The Bradshawian addictive family is characterized by violence, rage, incest, and abuse of all kinds. Strongly influenced by Alice Miller (1981) and her notions of the cataclysmic consequences, under which she includes Nazism and the Holocaust, of the way humans have treated their children, Bradshaw sees the roots of addiction, that is, sin in the family, as based in pathologial childrearing practices.

All addictions are "mood changers," ways of not feeling genuinely. What the addict doesn't want to feel is shame, pain, guilt, rejection, loss, grief, mourning, mortality, separateness, and aloneness. Bradshaw puts great emphasis on individuation. Healthy relating is only possible for those who are whole and complete in themselves, and therefore capable of affiliating out of love rather than out of need. This seems too idealistic to me.

Perhaps Plato (385 B.C.) was nearer the mark in the *Symposium* when he has Aristophanes tell the myth of the split halves. Humans were once "whole" creatures who rebelled against Zeus who punished them by splitting them down the middle. So we spend our lives looking for our missing (better?) halves. As Plato put it, "Love is child of Plenty and Poverty." If I don't have something to give (Plenty) I can't love, and if I am not in some way impoverished so I need someone to give to me, I have no reason to love. Plato is here more tolerant of human frailty, while Bradshaw insists that only by experiencing and accepting separateness is relationship possible, and only by feeling my pain, including the pain of knowing that I will die, is such relatedness possible.

Bradshaw not only has his version of original sin, the sins of the fathers passed on even unto the fourth generation, he also has his version of salvation. Salvation involves renunciation of *fantasy bonds*, that is, symbiotic ties with parents, renunciation of the gains and avoidances that are our addictions, and coming into contact with the "inner child." If Bradshaw is too evangelical for my taste and promises too much, he is nonetheless convincing when he is talking about addiction as a futile attempt to remediate narcissistic deficit. Here he is right on the money. It is surprising that he nowhere mentions Kohut, for their understandings of addiction are strikingly similar, albeit Bradshaw speaks from a systems stance, while Kohut speaks from an intrapsychic one. Renunciation, acceptance of existential aloneness, and contact with the inner child bring about a "spiritual awakening," and it is easy to see how Bradshaw grows out of and speaks to the twelve–step movement. Bradshaw's view of the addicted family enjoys far wider acceptance than Steinglass's both in the therapeutic and recovering communities.

Bradshaw's therapeutic formats of workshops and video presentations make for high states of emotional arousal and sometimes for intense feelings of connectedness. Like the marathon therapy groups of the 1960s and 1970s, people leave feeling good; however, the degree to which they enable change and maintenance of that change is uncertain. Of course, a great meal or an orgasm does not last forever either, yet are intrinsically positive experiences. Perhaps that is also the case with participation in Bradshaw or Bradshaw-style workshops.

ADDICTION-SPECIFIC FAMILY THERAPIES

There are few addiction-specific family therapies, although I anticipate a spate of publications in this area. Four worthy of our attention are Todd and Stanton's strategic-systems approach, Edward Kaufman and Pauline Kaufmann's multidimensional approach, Timothy O'Farrell's behavioral approach, and Marc Galanter's network approach.

Stanton and Todd

Duncan Stanton and Thomas Todd (1982) worked with Minuchin and Haley at the Philadelphia Child Guidance Center, and under their tutelage developed what they call a strategic-structural family therapy for heroin addicts. They claim great success with their approach with a primarily working-class minority population. Their therapy is "rational" in that it is carefully designed to interpret the potentially fatal dynamics of the addictive cycle.

What they observed in their addictive families was that addiction developed at precisely the moment in the life cycle of the family when the addict was separating from his family of origin and that recovery proceeded more or less smoothly until separation threatened. This suggested to Stanton and Todd that the family needed the addict addicted because the addiction kept him at home, either literally or emotionally, or, as frequently was the case, both. Recovery—stable sobriety—meant individuation and the family unable to negotiate the next stage in its life cycle had to create a crisis that led to relapse. The addict was simply unable to fight against the family pressure to return to enmeshment-symbiosis. Stanton and Todd didn't base this on theory, but rather on a careful analysis of relapse; they also noted evidence for exceptionally close bonds between these heroin-using sons and their mothers. (Lenny Bruce comes to mind.) The whole subjective experience of shooting up is strikingly symbiotic, a feeling of fusion and warmth; it is also a sexual substitute and a sexual tranquilizer (at least for some addicts) so that the importance of heterosexual sex is diminished and the addict remains "faithful" to Mother.

In the case of married addicts, Stanton and Todd noted that the addicted husbands easily, and frequently in the face of crisis or tension, abandoned their families of procreation to return to their families of origin. These researchers also noted the unusually high frequency of sudden, often violent, premature deaths in these families, and speculated that one reason these families were stuck and unable to progress through the family life cycle was their failure to mourn. Paradoxically, they behaved in ways that increased the risk of death of their sons through, say, overdose, in their unconscious maneuvers to keep them bound to the family through their perpetuation of their sons' addictions.

Stanton and Todd thought they had reason to believe that these families found separation through death more acceptable than separation through moving on. Death is involuntary, not usually experienced as betrayal. Stanton and Todd also took note of the extraordinary high rates of addiction in their first-generation immigrant families and postulated that these immigrant families unconsciously feared their children's assimilation and covertly supported and encouraged their addiction to prevent that loss. It is of some interest that the Yiddish version of *King Lear* ("How sharper than a serpent's tooth it is/to have a thankless child!" [IV, i, 33–34]) was one of the most popular plays on the Lower East Side. That generation of immigrants, guilty over "abandoning" their own parents, feared above all else being scorned and rejected by their assimilating children. The addicts display a great deal of pseudo–self sufficiency and counterdependence, which Stanton and Todd call *pseudo-individuation*, but it was all a ruse. The truth was that they had never reached adulthood. Although they studied and treated male heroin addicts, Stanton and Todd state that they have reason to believe that the dynamics of female addicts are not very different.

The therapy that Stanton and Todd devised and elaborated after developing such an intensely psychodynamic model of the cycle of addiction, recovery, and relapse may surprise you. It works entirely by indirection and seeks to increase insight neither in the addict nor in the family. In fact, they carefully avoid it. The setting is a veterans' hospital drug program affiliated with the University of Pennsylvania's psychiatry department. When a patient presented for treatment of relapse usually involving detoxification, the therapist insisted on involving the family. Although the families were contacted with the identified patient's permission, the therapist kept repeating, "You failed again," "You simply can't make it without the help of your family," and so forth until the addict gave in. All excuses were parried and the family contacted there and then. The family was told that Junior was in trouble again, and the therapist needed their help. The therapist was maddeningly optimistic, "This time will be different. If I have your help, this will be John's last detox."

There was a high rate of compliance. In the original research, some families were paid to attend sessions. There was no difference in outcome between the paid and unpaid families. The parents were never shamed, although the therapist understood the identified patient's relapse as a consequence of signals that individuation would destroy the family. (Minuchin regards such "slips" as "noble sacrifices.") Rather, the therapist did everything possible to establish an alliance with the parents who were made to feel that they were the key to success (and indeed they are, in Stanton and Todd's view). The structure of parental authority and generational boundaries is (re)established. The very act of involving the parents in the therapy, in telling them that success depends on their participation, moves them into a new existential stance, one supporting individuation and recovery. In effect the therapist speaks to and forms an alliance with the healthier part of the parents—the part that genuinely wants the child to succeed. I suspect that this happens because the strategic-structural therapist provides such a strong holding environment that the contextual transference provides the security to let the kid go.

Another way of looking at this process is that the parent(s) form a symbiotic transference to the son who serves in lieu of a symbiotic relationship with their own mothers, and that the transference to the therapist serves the same purpose so they can support the child's moves toward health. The parents are never criticized, the underlying dynamics never mentioned, and the pressure on the identified patient to go clean comes from both therapist and parents. This is a short-term therapy in which the therapist offers the parents support without insight and thereby undermines the regressive pull of enmeshment. Stanton and Todd report strikingly positive results with the families in their research project. They allow room for the creativity of the therapist in working with the family, and such interpersonal issues as death and loss are dealt with, and mourning is somehow encouraged, but the thrust is on restructuring. Although I am sure that

Stanton and Todd's outcomes are as good as they claim, I am suspicious that such an essentially manipulated therapy without insight can bring about sustained and profound changes in family dynamics, and I wonder about its generalizability to other populations.

Kaufman and Kaufmann

Edward Kaufman and Pauline Kaufmann pioneered family theories of the addictions, publishing the first edition of their text on the subject in 1979. They too use a strategic-structural approach, but are far more psychodynamically oriented than the Philadelphia Group. Edward Kaufman has also written about individual therapy of addiction, integrating cognitive-behavioral and dynamic approaches. He uses them sequentially, moving from the cognitive to the dynamic in the second year of therapy. Kaufman and Kaufmann use Minuchin's structural techniques, but they are not really structural in Minuchin's sense because they are also interested in promoting insight. Their therapy follows from their understanding of addiction and the addicted family. They see addicts as sharing the following common traits (Kaufman and Kaufmann 1992, pp. 35–36):

1. Drugs are used to facilitate or obliterate concern with sexual performance, communication, and assertion. In neurotics they are used to alleviate symptoms and in psychotics to provide an internal homeostasis.

2. Social factors are important in all classes and ethnic groups. In ghettos and other areas where poverty is concentrated, drugs may be the only available means to an exciting and seemingly fulfilling life. In the middle and upper classes, use of drugs represents an attempt to deal with a lack of meaning in one's life, emotional sterility, and the absence of intimate relationships.

3. The more out of keeping from an individual's social background and cultural norms a pattern of drug abuse is, the more likely it is that the user is suffering from severe underlying mental illness.

4. There is no orderly progression from dependence to independence, and pseudoadult stances are common.

5. Identification with quasi-parenting older delinquents, peers, and siblings is common.
6. Addicts are deficient in self-care with impaired self-regulation, self-soothing, and self-regulation.

The authors also see families with an addicted member as having certain common traits:

1. The drug addict is often the symptom carrier of the family dysfunction.
2. The addict helps to maintain family homeostasis.
3. The addicted member reinforces the parental need to control and continue parenting, yet finds such parenting inadequate for his or her needs.
4. The addict provides a displaced battlefield so that implicit and explicit parental strife can continue to be denied.
5. Parental drug and alcohol abuse is common and is directly transmitted to the addict or results in inadequate parenting.
6. The addict forms cross-generational alliances that separate parents from each other. The closest alliance is between mother and addict and precedes the addiction.
7. Parental death, divorce, or abandonment is common in the addict's early years (before drug use). Early sibling and paternal grandparent death is quite common.
8. Generational boundaries are diffuse—there is frequent competition between parents. Frequently the crisis created by the drug-dependent member is the only way the family gets together and attempts some problem solving, or is the only opportunity for a "dead" family to experience emotions.
9. Addicts form unstable pseudofamilies of procreation.

The Kaufman and Kaufmann therapy is strategic in the sense of being carefully planned and controlled, and structural in the sense that it aims at establishing intergenerational boundaries and hierarchies. These methods and techniques address the dysfunction the traits listed above describe. Their style is warm, involved, active, and not infrequently interpretive in a way Minuchin's would not be.

Kaufman and Kaufmann's interpretations include countertrans-ferential ones, and they make extensive use of countertransference. They also espouse the need to work through, so for all of the strategic-structural borrowings in their technique, this is essentially a dynamic therapy.

Interestingly, they comment that their successes are almost always with enmeshed families, which are primarily Italian and Jewish, and that they have much less success with disengaged families and with blacks. They found this to be true even when a black therapist was available. Kaufman and Kaufmann find the mother–son relationship to be at the heart of the matter, and most resistant to change in His-panic and black families. This contrasts with Stanton and Todd's positive results with a 60 percent black population. I suspect that Stanton and Todd were more insistent, even strident, in their demand for family participation as the only route to cure. They made these parents feel important. Kaufman and Kaufmann are less directive, more structural, and less strategic, and do better with a more middle-class population. Of course enmeshed families are simply easier to bring into and hold in treatment than disengaged ones. Kaufman and Kaufmann's highlighting the effects of ethnicity and their saliency for the therapist puts a focus on a facet of family work not often enough mentioned. Working with an enmeshed Italian family is strik-ingly different than working with a disengaged English one, although both are addicted, and the therapist needs both to "track" and to be aware of the cultural determinants of the family style.

Kaufman and Kaufmann also pioneered a multifamily therapy (MFT) for addiction. MFT is an amalgamation of group and family therapy. Essentially families with a common problem, here an ad-dicted member, are given a chance to meet together. Ten to fifteen families meet weekly with a cotherapist.

As therapy progresses, the role of the family in producing and perpetu-ating the addicts' abuse of drugs is identified. Patterns of mutual ma-nipulation and coercion are identified and negated. The families' need to perpetuate the addict's dependent behavior through scapegoating, distancing, protection or infantilization is discouraged, and new methods of relating are tried and encouraged. [Kaufman and Kaufmann 1992, p. 77]

The coleaders are active, confrontive, and supportive, but most of the work is done by the families. The addict who is in treatment, usually residential treatment, is part of the group, and has the opportunity to confront his or her family. Most families (as well as addicts) are guilt ridden, and the MFT provides a format for deliquescing guilt. Kaufman and Kaufmann report excellent results with MFT, and given its potential for sharing, support, and confrontation, this is not surprising.

Kaufman and Kaufmann call their approach an integrated one, and they advocate a combination of individual, group, family, multiple family, and milieu therapy with appropriate use of medication. This makes sense. We already do well in treating addiction, but our "dosages" of therapy are often inadequate. It is as if we were to try to cure pneumonia with aspirin. Kaufman and Kaufmann know this and wisely advocate the use of heavy artillery.

Timothy O'Farrell

Timothy O'Farrell (1993) has developed a behavioral marital therapy couples group program for alcoholics and their spouses. Again the setting is a VA hospital, this time in Boston with a Harvard Medical School affiliation. The couples are recruited from patients admitted for detoxification. To take part in the program, the alcoholic must agree to take Antabuse (disulfiram, an antioxidant that inhibits the oxidation of the acetaldehyde metabolized from alcohol, producing uncomfortable symptoms when alcohol is ingested), and the spouse supervises the taking of it. The alcoholic is to say, "Thank you for watching me take my Antabuse" to the spouse, and the spouse is to say, "Thank you for taking it" to the alcoholic. In the group sessions, the therapist exercises strong control and gives homework assignments aimed at initiating new behavior and improving communication. All of the usual behavior techniques are employed here in a group setting. Barbara McCrady (1992) has developed a similar therapeutic for use with couples not seen in groups.

The couples are encouraged to talk about their treatment in the group and receive feedback from other group members. The expression of feelings is encouraged in the group, and angry exchanges between spouses are common. This is seen as therapeutic. O'Farrell reports that participants in his couples group did better on both measures of marital satisfaction and sobriety than those alcoholics who were treated with individual therapy alone, this result being attained at a two-year follow-up. He also reported that the improvement in marital satisfaction tended to wane with time and suggested that his short-term, time-limited format might achieve better results if some sort of periodic reinforcement was available.

O'Farrell probably didn't plan it that way, but his couple therapy encourages and institutionalizes a kind of splitting. In the couples group, the alcoholic and his (usually) or her spouse are encouraged to let it all hang out. This is the place for the spouse to vent anger, even rage (the anger and rage ineluctably induced by the aggression, volitional and intended, unconsciously motivated, or incidental to the addictive obsession, discharged upon that spouse by the drinker), and for the drinker to express his anger often long repressed or acted out without being fully experienced, or anesthetized toward the spouse. The recovering drinker's anger is vastly overdetermined, but frequently most salient in early recovery, triggered by the nondrinking spouse's failure to be utterly and uncritically wildly enthusiastic about and appreciative of the drinker's newfound sobriety. Not infrequently, the recovering spouse is paradoxically angry over his (her) growing awareness of how the spouse enabled. All of this is a witch's brew that threatens to blast the cauldron to kingdom come. O'Farrell accordingly tries to restrict the expression of these volatile and potentially violent emotions to the couple sessions, where they can be contained, pacified, interpreted, and worked through. They are also importantly deliquesced by being shared in the group. O'Farrell, coming from a behavioral stance, would not describe what he does in these terms, but as I read him, that is what he does.

"Homework," on the other hand, is traditionally behavioral: self-observation, recording behaviors and feelings, communication exercises, and the directed expression of positive affect and action. "Commit a random act of kindness toward your spouse this week" is very much in the spirit of O'Farrell's instructions, although not literally part of the homework. My association is to Henry James, the convoluted novelist. At the end of his life, having written the incredibly nuanced and complex psychological novels of his last creative phase, he was asked what he had learned during his long life. He replied, "Be kind." That is the essence of O'Farrell's homework assignments. So the split allows for the exploration and expression of ambivalence in the relationship between alcoholic and spouse in such a way that the negative side of the ambivalence doesn't destroy the relationship. Like any couples therapy, this one is only going to work if there is love and commitment lurking somewhere in the chaos and hatred of the active alcoholism.

Network Therapy

Marc Galanter (1993) of New York University Medical School has developed an intriguing treatment modality called network therapy. Since it is a recent development, there is no outcome study as yet (although there is a grant proposal for such a study); nevertheless, Galanter reports encouraging results. An outgrowth in some ways of family therapy, there are important differences. In family therapy, the family system and all of its members are the targets of intervention. Not so in network therapy, where the entire system (family or otherwise) is involved in the treatment, but the alcoholic or substance abuser is the only patient. In family therapy, the identified patient is seen as the repository of all of the pathology in the system, and family therapy seeks to elucidate and make manifest the multifaceted ways in which the system and its members project their dysfunctionality onto the patient. In network therapy, the dysfunction—pathology in the system—is ignored and the network is exclusively used to assist the identified patient, the user or drinker, in achieving and maintaining sobriety. This has some parallels to Stanton and Todd's approach.

This modality is most effectively used with patients who are motivated, however ambivalently, to stop drinking, but who have difficulties resisting cravings. They might be said to be the motivated impulse ridden. In that way, they resemble the population that benefits the most from disulfiram therapy; in fact, network therapy might be seen as interpersonal Antabuse. There is, however, an important difference. Antabuse patients have often destroyed their social networks or been affiliated with highly pathological ones, while the network candidate must either have an intact network or be able to create one that is sufficiently healthy and able to support and not undermine the patient from a stance of nonjudgmental positive regard. This is not easy to come by, so network therapy candidates, in spite of their ego and self deficits, may be assumed to have at least a modicum of ego strength.

In network therapy the therapist is quite directive. Network is an abstinence therapy; no attempt is made to construct or evoke a network until the client has made a commitment to sobriety. At that point, the therapist explores whether the patient can achieve sobriety on his or her own, even with AA or Narcotics Anonymous (NA) support (if the patient is willing to affiliate with a twelve–step group). If the answer is no, the therapist suggests eliciting the help of family, friends, teachers, bosses, and clergy to create a support network. Explicit danger points or situations are probed for and the therapist suggests ways in which the network can be used to get by these rough spots. For example, Bill always got drunk Friday night and gets very strong drink signals on Friday afternoons. He arranges with Uncle Henry to meet Fridays after work to play basketball, which he enjoys. Sally always drank when she felt sad. She arranges with her friend Joan to call her whenever she feels sad and with Aunt Sadie, to go shopping, which cheers her up when she's down.

The therapist meets regularly with the network, although less frequently than with the patient. There are no secrets or privileged communications and everything pertaining to the patient's sobriety is discussed. Galanter recommends that network therapy be used as one component of a multimodal comprehensive treatment program.

Interventions

In counseling and therapy, an intervention is usually something—silent acceptance, reflection, clarification, interpretation, enactment, instruction, and so forth—that the counselor/therapist does to help the patient, be that patient a person, couple, family, or a larger system. Not so in addiction counseling, where *intervention* has a special meaning: the planned confrontation (although some interventionists would object to the use of the term *confrontation* to describe what they do) of the active addict by family, friends, and sometimes physician, pastor, or employer of that addict with his addiction and its consequences, with the purpose of having the addict enter an inpatient detoxification and rehabilitation program. Interventions are usually orchestrated and directed by an addictions counselor or therapist. Interventionists, as those who specialize in this work are usually called, are almost always recovering alcoholics/addicts, although I can see no necessity that this be so.

The secret of a successful intervention is planning and rehearsal. An intervention usually starts with a family member deciding that "we," whoever that might be, "have to do something about Jim (or Sally)," and having heard of interventions, seeks help in arranging one. Not infrequently, the suggestion for an intervention comes from the therapist who is working with a family member, usually but by no means always the spouse. The interventionist carefully explores the motivation of the person proposing the intervention, looking for two things: (1) seriousness and commitment, including a willingness to carry through on whatever consequences the interventionist and the interventors decide will follow from noncompliance on the part of the intervenee; and (2) a possible thirst for vengeance, domination, punishment, or humiliation, which may have more to do with the needs of the intervenor than the needs of the intervenee. If the former is present and the latter absent (or containable in the judgment of the interventionist) and there is an objective need for the intervention irrespective of the motives of the intervenor, the intervention can proceed. If that is the case, the interventionist then works with the intervenor to come up with a list of potential participants in the intervention. What is looked for are people who care enough about and are sufficiently aware of the intervenee's problem and who matter to the intervenee. They must be people who have salience and influence with the intervenee. Their approval and support or their

withdrawal of it become part of the *therapeutic leverage*, more collo-
quially known as having them by the short hairs, brought to bear on
the intervenee.

There are two schools of intervention, the first holding that intervention doesn't work without therapeutic leverage, and the second
holding that the use of therapeutic leverage is blackmail, demeaning
to all concerned and not necessary. The vast majority of interventionists belong to the first school.

After the list is made up, typically consisting of three to seven or
so people—spouse, children, parents, and friends being the usual
cast—each potential intervenor is approached and an attempt is made
to enlist his or her participation. The interventionist screens the people
on the list, eliminating those whose commitment is too tepid or whose
follow-through is too much in doubt, as well as those whose anger,
hostility, rage, jealousy, or envy toward the intervenee is both strong
and not containable. If these so-called "negative" emotions can be
contained during the intervention, they do not necessarily preclude
participation in the intervention.

The next step is to construct the therapeutic leverage. Each participant is asked to state what they would do if the intervenee is
noncompliant. Such consequences as "not give you any more money,"
"not have sex with you," "not let you live here," "not speak to you
until you are ready to go into rehab" are common. If the employer is
involved, and this an intervention of the Employee Assistance Program (EAP) counselor, then loss of job is the therapeutic leverage.

Now the rehearsals begin. Ideally there is nothing spontaneous
about an intervention. Each participant knows exactly what he or she
is going to say and do. The idea behind this is that feelings run too
high to just let it happen, and that intervention is not the place to
deal with family issues. The time and place for the *event*, as the intervention itself is called, is set and the plan for luring the intervenee to
the event spelled out. The interventionist arranges or sees that the
family arranges a bed in a detox or rehab and that financial/insur-
ance arrangements and preapprovals are in place. Since the desired
outcome is that the intervenee go immediately to the inpatient facility, transportation, packing, and such considerations as leave from job

or school are also planned. These days insurance companies are reluctant to approve inpatient stays unless outpatient treatment has failed. This may be an impediment to the intervention, or the goal may have to be changed to participation in an outpatient program, usually a four-nights-a-week group.

Then the event takes place. The interventionist explains why we are all here, and that we are here because we love and care about you. Skilled interventionists protect, insofar as that is possible given the circumstances, the intervenee from shame and humiliation, and they are highly adept at parrying excuses and delays. Good interventionists are usually somewhat histrionic, having something of the actor as well as the director in them. The only acceptable outcome of an intervention is entry into the program proposed by the intervention. There is no negotiating at an intervention.

I have mixed feelings about interventions. I have seen them save lives, and I have seen them destroy families. They are intrinsically coercive and their desirability or lack of it depends on the values of the therapist considering recommending intervention. When they work, they can have an almost miraculous impact on the active user and on the family; when they don't work, they can leave a legacy of bitterness that never heals. They are definitely high-power and high-risk tools that should not be used without the most careful consideration by all involved. I have treated a number of people who were intervened on and never forgave those who did the intervening. Even those who are "grateful" for having been intervened on are ambivalent and their therapists need to help them get in contact with the flip side of their gratitude. Having said this, it should also be pointed out that addiction kills, and that, like radical surgery, a risky treatment may be the treatment of choice.

CONCLUSION

It seems that alcohol and drug-specific family therapies come from two diametrically opposed directions and take two diametrically opposed stances. Behavioral, network, intervention, and the Stanton and Todd variety of structural-strategic family therapies see the user as the identified patient and the family as desiring his or her recovery but not knowing how to bring it about. The family is seen as the therapist's ally in moving the user toward sobriety. These approaches either assume that the family is working toward health or ignore the regressive and pathological side of the family while enlisting their "help." Kaufman and Kaufmann share some of this, but are much more focused on treating the enmeshing dynamic that sets up the addict as the "noble" rescuer of the family, his nobility consisting in a sacrifice of health and perhaps life to maintain the family's symbiosis and homeostasis. This is a more traditional family therapy approach. The therapy in this camp implicitly maintains that the pathology in the system must be addressed before recovery is possible. Even in the Stanton and Todd and structural rather than dynamic side of the Kaufman and Kaufmann approach, there is an implicit attention to pathology in the system.

In the alliance that is sought with the parents, the transference of the parents to the addict, which in many ways uses him as a kind of selfobject to maintain their stability as well as a deflector of their conflicts, is replaced by a transference to the therapist who then provides the holding, the contextual support, and the selfobject functions previously performed by the nobly sacrificing addict, and this transference permits them to let the addict "go," even to actually assist in bringing this about. Here the pathology is treated without being interpreted and without insight. This approach would say that an insight approach would only arouse such strong resistance as to destroy the treatment, while those who are more dynamically oriented would say that such cures without insight are bogus and bound to be short-lived. The reply to this is that the change induced by the structural-strategic therapy sets in motion a dynamic that irreversibly alters the homeostasis and that once freed from the stalemate, the addict and the family become capable of establishing healthy modes of relating. I would say that we need to do both: the strategic-structural approach does indeed lower resistance and makes movement possible, but without interpretation, insight, and working through, the inertial forces in the system will cause it to regress, the dynamic work being temporally subsequent to the strategic-structural work.

There is yet another way of looking at the seeming contradictions between the schools. Each points to something real and how to work with it. Every family has to some degree a rational, health-promoting side, and every family has to some degree a hidden agenda of enmeshment, scapegoating, symbiosis, maintenance of homeostasis, avoidance, and a bewildering complexity of unconscious transferential elements in its relating. My association is to Bion (1961) and his analysis of the group as always simultaneously working as a task group and as a basic assumption group. In working with addicted families, sometimes we need to join and strengthen the task group side of the family, and sometimes we need to make conscious the basic assumption side of the family. Families differ; in most, the desire to move the addict toward health predominates, whatever the regressive forces at work. These families are the ones that form networks and conduct interventions. Then there are those families whose unconscious needs are so great that they will literally destroy the addict to meet those needs. The addictive family therapist works with both types of families and adjusts his or her therapeutic technique accordingly.

PART II

❖

Clinical Practice

❖ ❖ ❖

The Schools Illustrated—
The Baker Family

In this chapter, we take a look at how family therapists taking a communications approach, a strategic approach, a structural approach, an intergenerational systems approach, an object relations approach, an experiential approach, a behavioral approach, and a substance abuse approach might work with the Baker family. The first five therapists have been influenced by Bateson, Haley, Minuchin, Bowen, and the Scharffs, respectively. The experiential, behavioral, and substance abuse therapists have no one model, although Whitaker has clearly influenced our experientialist. The substance abuse therapist most clearly reflects the approach I used in treating the family that inspired these vignettes, although my usual approach would be more psychodynamic.

We see the Bakers in an opening session, greatly distressed by the return of their oldest son who has recently left a therapeutic community (TC) and returned to daily marijuana smoking. Tom is 16; his younger brother, Sam, is 12, almost 13. The parents, Rob and Harriet, are fortyish. They are neatly albeit informally dressed, the boys in age-appropriate jeans and T-shirts, Father in hard-pressed work pants and a short sleeve shirt, Mother in a bright, not quite loud cotton dress and heels. She wears slightly too much makeup (for my taste). Father is a muscular, powerful-looking man. Mother is plump, not quite fat.

The family enters the consulting room in single file, Mother first, followed by Father, Tom, and Sam. Tom is sullen, and mostly stares at the floor. Sam, although not sullen, seems distracted and not quite there. The substance abuse therapist wonders if Sam is the "lost child" in this family. Mother enters purposefully, almost marching, and proceeds to the most distant chair, followed by her husband, to whom she says, "I want the kids to sit next to me; you sit at the end." Tom raises his eyes from the floor and looks at her hatefully but sits next to her. Sammy and Father make up the rear, taking the remaining seats just as they were told to do. Mom is the one who contacted the therapist, telling of Tom's return to drugs, and of her anger and despair and her fear (possibly her wish) that Daddy will "beat the shit out of him." Although her focus was on Tom during the phone contact, she expressed the wish that the whole family be present at the first session. The systemic therapist wondered, Is she an intuitive systems theorist or does she just want to set the stage and direct the play? The substance abuse therapist thinks, Perhaps both; from her entrance, it appears that she runs the show, but appearances aren't always reality and this may not be the case. All the therapists have the same information derived from Mother's call, and have observed the same behavior.

THE SESSION

MOTHER (pointing at Father): He was circumcised at age 26 for me. (Laughs) But that's not why we're here. I've been in love with Rob from the beginning, but I wouldn't have married him unless he had a *bris*. We did, and we've had a great time ever since. I'm in electronic parts and I make a helluva lot of money. I barely got out of high school, and I never expected to make so much money, but I turned out to be one helluva sales woman. Rob's in the best construction union in the city, and he makes out like a bandit. Sam is a doll. He gets great grades, he's going to be Bar Mitzvah, and things are great—except for that fucking kid. Two months out of New Start and he's back at it. ("Fucking kid" seems discordant, and is said without visible anger in the same animated, pressured voice she's been using all along.)

FATHER (angrily): I'm going to break his fucking neck if he doesn't stop. (His biceps harden as he says this, and he looks like he's about to get up and do it.)

MOTHER: We're not putting up with this shit anymore.

TOM (mutters): Fuck you! (Father starts to go for him, thinks better of it, and sits back down.)

COMMUNICATIONS THERAPIST (more to Mother, but to the entire family): You don't communicate directly. Tom's right here, but you talk about him instead of to him.

FATHER: Talking to him is like talking to the wall. What he needs is the strap, and he's not too big for it either.

COMMUNICATIONS THERAPIST: You're still talking about him, not to him.

FATHER: If I talk to him, he's not going to like what I say. I want that fucking kid to go to college. I didn't go, and he's going to go even if I have to kill him.

STRUCTURALIST: Mr. Baker, I want you to sit next to your wife. Tom and Sam, you sit down at this end.

STRATEGIST: I won't tolerate threats in the session. I want you to speak emotionally but civilly to one another. No threats.

SAM (giggles).

MOTHER (starts giggling too; to Sam): Come sit next to me.

STRUCTURALIST: No, I want you to sit next to your husband.

SYSTEMIC INTERGENERATIONALIST: Let's back off and find out a little more about your family. (To the parents): I'd like to know more about your families of origin. I'd like all of you to help me draw a "genogram"—a picture of the relationships in your family.

STRUCTURALIST (to Mother): What did you do with the tip?

SAM (still giggling): The rabbi gets the salary; the *Mohel* (ritual circumciser) gets the tip. (Mom puts her arm around Sam and seems to be flirting with him.)

OBJECT RELATIONS THERAPIST (to Father): How does it feel to have your wife tell us that you were circumcised for her?

TOM (trembling with fear but defiant): Daddy's a monk because Mom made him cut off a piece of his dick. (He runs out of the room.)

FATHER (Looking at Tom): He's a real asshole. (Shouts). Tom, come back in here! (Tom peeks in, realizes his father isn't really mad at him, and goes back to his place.)

MOTHER (to Tom): You should only be as much of a man as your father.

FATHER (beams).

BEHAVIORIST (unconsciously moves his hand to his crotch).

DYNAMIC THERAPIST (thinks to himself): *Mom reminds me of Judy, the lady I treated last year who couldn't understand why giving an enema to her 16-year-old son wasn't a good idea. This Mom's another phallic mother. If Tom relates to her as a phallic mother, that puts him way back developmentally—definitely preoedipal. So all the apparently oedipal stuff going on in this session isn't really oedipal. My association to the enema-giving mother makes me wonder if this isn't an anal family characterized by "messy" acting out. They need to "get their shit together." Is all their anger anal sadism and anal explosiveness? Should I say that and speak directly to their unconscious? That would also be tracking—using metaphors this family can understand.* (Speaking): You're here to get your shit together, but you can't seem to do it even here.

MOTHER (starts to cry): We can't get our shit together. This just goes on and on—counselors, getting thrown out of school, talking to him, beating him, the TC. Now he's smoking again. I can't stand it. I can't stand it. He's got everything. I was poor. My father was a shoemaker. Rob had it real rough. He ran in gangs, drank like a fish, went to reform school. I loved him from the first time I saw him, but I wouldn't go to bed with him unless he married me. Rob's a man, not like my father—or that damned kid. My father's a wimp. Never made much of a living and was pussy-whipped all his life. My kids love him, but they've known Grandma wears the pants almost since they were born. (To therapist): Yeah, that's the way we talk. We let it all hang out in *my* family. (All of the therapists wonder— is Rob pussy-whipped too, in spite of his supermasculinity and Mom's denial?)

STRUCTURALIST (mentally notes): *"My" rather than "our" family.*

MOTHER: My ignorant parents said they would sit *shivah* (observe the mourning period) if I married Rob. He was 25, tough as nails, and was he handsome! My mother said the tattoos made her sick. I love them. Anyway, Rob converted and we got married, and now my folks love him. Tom has had it good from the beginning. Everyone adored him. My parents really changed after he was born and accepted Rob. Rob stopped drinking— once in a while, he has a beer, but he doesn't even like that anymore.

TOM (mumbling): Yeah, Dad doesn't drink, so how can he understand why I smoke? Some macho! The only reason he doesn't drink is because my mom doesn't let him. (Starts to say, "He is a pussy," but looks at his dad and gets scared, so pussy doesn't quite sound.)

MOTHER: Then Rob got in the construction union. His family never did shit for him. His dad was a drunk; it killed him—shot his liver, and his mom's a doormat. She's got rosary beads up her ass. Always praying; never did a thing for the kids. Rob's lucky he's in the union; never graduated high school. He's done real good. Nobody works as hard as my Rob. The rest of his family is a total loss. All of his brothers drink and fight and are just horrible. We stay away from them. I'm really proud of Rob.

INTERGENERATIONAL, OBJECT RELATIONAL, STRATEGIC, AND STRUCTURAL THERAPISTS ALL THINK: *She regards him as a child—her child. What does that say to the kids? Can they be kids too? She presents Father on one hand as both castrated and pussy-whipped like her father, and on the other hand, as a 'real' man. The boys must have a very split image of Father and major difficulties in male identification. There is also an historical split between Dad, the delinquent drunk, and Dad, the heroic success overcoming his background to become the hardworking provider. Sam, the good boy,*

identifies with the hardworking father; Tom, the bad boy, with the
delinquent father.

MOTHER: Once the kids were in school, I got a job in the office of a defense industry plant. After a few years, they realized I had the gift of gab (all of the therapists think, *Yep, to the point where no one can get in a word edgewise*), and gave me a crack at sales. Boy, am I good at it! A woman too—the only one. So now we have plenty of money, a lovely home, two dogs and a cat—they always had all the toys in the world and a great life. Sam appreciates it—I don't know what went wrong with Tom. He was a good kid. When he wasn't, Rob would take the strap to his bare backside and he would straighten out quick. My dad used a razor strap on my brothers when my mother told him to. I think that's good for boys. But now when they get into it, Rob punches him in the head sometimes—and I hate that. Someone's going to get hurt, and that's one reason I called you. You tell Rob to keep his hands to himself.

Anyway, Tom's always had it real good. My mother still spoils him rotten. All we ever asked of him was a little respect and good grades. Sam's an honor student.

FATHER (with near rage and in a loud voice): And Tom flunks damn near everything. You'd think he was a real dumb kid but he ain't—just a fuckoff.

TOM (muttering, still looking at the floor): You can't even read.

FATHER: Like hell I can't.

MOTHER: Well, not too good, dear.

FATHER (blushes).

MOTHER: The only thing we want from our kids is that they go to college. We never had a chance to go, and that's really important to us. They can study anything they want, do whatever they want, as long as they graduate. That's not much to ask. (Cries.)

SAM (giggles): Zero point zero averages don't graduate.

MOTHER: The trouble started around 8th grade. Tom never did too good in school, but he got through; then all of a sudden, he started cutting classes and Rob spanked him good and hard, but that didn't work, and his grades went to F's. Then he found the grass.

FATHER: It was his scumbag friends.

MOTHER: Rob's right—his friends get worse every year. Nobody but the scumbags want anything to do with him. Anyway, we tried counseling; he was in a special class—what do you call it, the resource room?—I was always in school. Rob wouldn't go after a while. We yelled, we hit, we begged, we bribed, we told him we'd do anything for him if he just stopped getting stoned. Nothing helped. The school sucks, too. They kept putting him into the next highest grade, even though he hadn't learned anything. Then he was even more lost. You don't know how many times I've said, "Tom, please tell me what's really bothering you," and all he says is, "Leave me alone." And I just wanted to slap him. Sometimes I did, other times I cried. Finally the guidance counselor said he should go to New Life. That was last year, after he got caught shoplifting. He fought us like hell, but Rob said it was the cops or the TC. So he went. It was like a miracle. When we got to visit him, or went to their family days, he was a different kid. There was one family session when he and Rob were crying and hugged each other, and told each other how much they loved each other, and then cried some more. Tom even told us that he knew how much he hurt us and felt really rotten about it.

TOM: I must have been out of my mind.

MOTHER (ignores him): It was wonderful. No chip on his shoulder, no sullen, miserable attitude. He went through their whole program—18 months to reentry. Now he's home and back in school, and the same rotten kid.

FATHER: And his scumbag friends are back.

MOTHER: We knew he was smoking before we found it. It's his attitude. As soon as he smokes.

FATHER (interrupting): He starts acting like an asshole. We even let him bring his girl to his room, and he fucks his brains out. What other parents would let him do that?

STRUCTURALIST, INTERGENERATIONALIST, OBJECT RELATIONS THEORIST, AND ADDICTION THERAPIST ALL WONDER: *What kind of mixed message is being given here? It is also interesting to hear that Tom*

has a girl. All the therapists want to hear more about her. Is Tommy more together than we think?
MOTHER: You have to help us. I'm going to pull my hair out of my head.
EXPERIENTIALIST: You have the resources to help yourselves.
MOTHER: No, we don't. That's why we're here. What should we do?

Clearly the Bakers present us with a complex problem, or should I say problems? On the surface, there is only one problem—drug use by the identified patient. However, from both an intrapsychic psychodynamic and an interpersonal systemic viewpoint, a great deal more is going on and needs to be addressed. How can we understand the material presented by the Bakers? How would therapists from the various schools understand it? What would they do with it?

On one level, the system is unbalanced—skewed—by a domineering, perhaps castrating mother, and it is not unreasonable to think that her interaction with the family and their reaction to it may be a big piece of the action. Is Tom's drug use a maladaptive way of coping with Mother, of avoiding her, of ducking an adolescent second oedipal struggle, of rebelling, of expressing rage at her? As a communications therapist points out, the family members all too often talk about rather than to each other. Therapists of whatever school can't miss the lack of generational boundaries in this family. The parents' sex life is all over the room with Dad being simultaneously presented as a pussy-whipped castrata and as a hypermasculine stud. In either case, he seems to be defined by Mother. What sort of anxiety does this blatant and exhibitionistic sexuality stir up in the boys? To grow to manhood must simultaneously mean that one will be castrated and one can't possibly compete with a father with whom Mother is "madly in love" (or is she?), and who is not so implicitly presented as a great lover. Rather remain a helpless child, albeit a counterdependent, pseudoautonomous one by staying stoned, than be either castrated or inadequate.

The lack of, or at least seriously blurred, generational boundaries are in need of repair. Perhaps the reason this family is "stuck," unable to move to the next stage of its life cycle, is that the very absence of boundaries makes progression much too dangerous. Does the family need Tom to stay stoned so they can stay stuck? What about Dad's rage and his physicality with his children? After all, one of Mother's reasons for making the appointment is her fear that, "Dad will beat the shit out of him." What is Father so angry about? The wife's demeaning him (although she doesn't see it that way and maybe he doesn't either)? Her apparent dominance? His failure to be able to control his son? His envy of his son's "freedom" to act out after his renunciation of such freedom for family responsibility? Or is this historical anger? We know that his childhood was painful and deprived. What is his anger a defense against? Pain? Hurt? What sort of pain or hurt? Ancient wounds? Something about his marriage? The implicit rejection of his love in his son's disobedience? His renunciation of his youthful wildness? Pain experienced in the reformatory? I vote for all of the above, first and perhaps most significantly that his son apparently isn't going to vicariously fulfill his wish for literacy, for education, for entry into a middle class profession as opposed to a successful blue collar career. How much is his anger a defense against his feelings of shame, a shame accentuated by the contrast with his more educated or at least literate wife over his own deficiencies? Does he need to undermine his son in some surely unconscious way to prevent that son from surpassing him? Indeed one wonders at how good an approximation Father is to the role of Freud's (1913b) primal father with his rage and violence. On the other hand, much of that rage is culturally syntonic, and for the most part, meets the approval of his wife.

Let's look at Father from Tom's side. Father was a drunk. Being a pothead is thus both an identification ("I get high like Dad did"), and a disidentification ("Dad never used grass"). He can be Father and feel close to him in what is perhaps the only way he can feel that closeness and simultaneously feel safely removed from him. My "hunch" (and I tend to trust my hunches, although I know they may be completely off base) is that one of the most powerful factors keeping Tom stoned is his most likely semiconscious, but perhaps completely unconscious, belief that he, like Father, can safely live a drug-dominated, acting-out adolescence and easily and painlessly emerge from it in his early 20s. That may be a dubious proposition, at best; we frequently see a generational cycle in which the children, usually of "functional" alcoholic fathers, go rapidly downhill as either their drug use or drinking progresses to dysfunction. Rob and Tom don't quite fit this pattern, but they are perhaps close to it. Rob was a tough, heavy-drinking kid, "who made it on his own," both as a street child and later on, as worker, husband, and father. Rob always functioned in his world, whatever that happened to be. Tom fails in his world. Father stopped drinking easily, but there is no certainty that Tom will stop smoking as easily, and the damage that he is inflicting on himself is cumulative. The further down he goes in his addictive fall, the harder it will be to come back. It is also clear that whatever the problems in their marriage, Harriet has had a stabilizing influence on Rob, providing him with something of the family support he apparently lacked as a child. In Kohut's (1971, 1977a) terms, she has served a selfobject function in his life, particularly in late adolescence and early adulthood, crucial times in an addictive career—nodal points in which an adolescent externalizing acting-out lifestyle either becomes the prelude to a full-blown addiction or is reined in and becomes a developmental episode in the life rather than the first stage of a progression toward death. There is no guarantee that Tom will turn the corner as Rob did, and I planned to tell him that at some point.

A related aspect of Tom's magic thinking that he doesn't need to get clean yet, which is perhaps a denial of the fact that he can't get clean ("I can stop whenever I want, but I don't want to just yet") emerged in a later session. I also wondered if Tom believes that he doesn't have to get clean and graduate from high school because Daddy can always get him into the union where he can "make out like a bandit." Subsequent sessions proved this to be the case, although Tom's belief was not fully a conscious one, or at least one that he could not articulate. Closeness to Father, if not complete identification with him (cf. Freud's [1917] comment on regression and object relations, "An object relation regresses to an identification") gave these quasi-conscious fantasies additional saliency and power. This too I planned to interpret, although the timing of that interpretation was open.

What about Sam, the "good boy"? I worried most about him. Given the amount of attention Tom gets from this family, it will be remarkable if Sam is not tempted to go in the same direction. "Good boy" is, to say the least, not the easiest of roles. He did indeed seem "lost" in the session, ignored by both Mother and Father and seemingly having no alliance with Tom. His occasional use of humor would be consistent with his being in the "mascot" role. For all this seeming isolation, one wonders about the sexualized teasing by Mother. What's that like for a pubescent boy? Again, the boundary problem in this family. Minuchin would almost surely address some of his first interventions to Sam. What is Sam's role in the family's dynamics? Is he ever allowed to be "bad"? Does he occupy all the good space, leaving no "good" space for Tom? Does the family put Tom in a kind of "double bind" overtly enjoining him to be good while covertly telling him that his role is to be the bad boy? Perhaps Dad needs him to enact the self that he has relinquished. On the other hand, this is a session that has been convened to deal with Tom's drug addiction and perhaps Sam's neglect by the family is atypical and his silence is atypical. We can't be sure. This needs exploration, but it is very odd that Mother doesn't, for all practical purposes, mention him in her long monologues.

What are the internal mechanisms and forces in this family? What is keeping them stuck? Mother tells us that in practical ways they are far from stuck, being ambitious, upwardly mobile people. Has there been a failure of selfobject relating here, leaving Tom to form his selfobject relations with marijuana and "scumbags"? In the Scharffs' (1991) terms, there has been a failure of the contextual mutual transferences; the holding in this family is not strong enough to contain the centrifugal forces in this family. This seems to be so. Yet this may not be the case. Both Mother and Father deny it, however defensively; they passionately believe that they are loving, supportive parents. So this could be, in Steinglass's (1987) terms, a family with addiction rather than an addicted family. We don't know enough yet to be sure.

Then there is the intergenerational. Is Tom the least differentiated of the family members, or paradoxically, is it Sam, the good boy? Have Mom and Dad projected their undifferentiation from their respective families onto Tom? They don't come across as undifferentiated, so I don't think so, yet it is possible. The parents are people who struggled mightily to emerge from the pathology of their families of origin, and they have in some ways admirably succeeded, yet they may be unconsciously re-creating some of the undifferentiation in their own families. I wonder if some of Dad's rage at Tom is transferential as he sees his alcoholic father being re-created in his drug-addicted son. Is this interpretable to this unsophisticated, unpsychologically minded man? How can I track? Say this in a way that he can hear it, and how relevant is it anyway, given the strong here-and-now determinants of his rage? Who knows, but it's worth a try. This family is too angry and needs help chilling out. I also thought of Guntrip's (1968) "Hate is love made angry" in thinking of Father's rage at son. There is the hurt underlying the rage.

There is yet another aspect of the intergenerational drama. There is a significant amount of apparently exclusively male alcoholism in Father's family, and it sounds a helluva lot like Cloninger's (1983) male-limited alcoholism, which has a heavy genetic loading. Although the heritability of other chemical addiction is inferential, one wonders how much genetic loading predisposes Tom to addiction. Clearly he does not "smoke well." He is not a kid partying; he is an addict. How large a role does constitutional predisposition play in his addiction? Has he (and the family) been educated about his biological vulnerability in his previous therapy or at his TC? We don't know enough about this family, and regardless of school (experientialists and possibly behaviorists excepted), the therapist either needs to take a careful multigenerational history or to construct a genogram.

What are the existential issues here? What does Tom's addiction help him and his family avoid—separation, tension in the marriage, aging, the decline of the maternal grandparents who have become parents to both Harriet and Rob? Suspicion that their material success isn't enough and something—something in the realm of meaning or values—is missing? We don't know, and that is something we need to be on the lookout for. Struggling to care for a sick (i.e., addicted) kid gives meaning and purpose to one's life. Would Tom's cure leave this family at sea and directionless?

What about the object relations side of things? Tom is both an exciting and a rejecting object for each of the others. Mom is an exciting object, enticing and dangerous. Rob primarily plays the antilibidinal rejecting object, and Sam's role in object relations terms is less clear. Seen in this way, it becomes strikingly clear that there is no ideal object, and not a strong enough central ego anywhere to give this family the cohesion it needs to help Tom recover and to itself move on. That is why the family holding, selfobject function, contextual transference fails. It is an interlocking system of exciting and rejecting objects. I am speaking here of the family members as external objects for each other; they are of course also internal objects insofar as they are activating internal object relations, which are then projected onto them. The therapist is going to have to figure out (if he or she is working at all dynamically) what each is projecting on the others. What exciting and what rejecting objects are being projected on Mother by Father and Tom, by bad boy onto good boy and Mother and Father, by Father onto Mother and onto his sons? Who are the original objects and what are the splits in their respective selves? In short, what is the internal drama being played out in the external actions of this family?

Perhaps even more importantly, can the therapist provide the holding, build a strong enough contextual or selfobject transference to anchor this family and enable their growth? What can the therapist do to facilitate this, if anything? We know that Tom did well in the TC, which, if it was a good one, provided a powerful holding environment. This suggests that on the more behavioral level, Tom needs structure. One also wonders how much the TC functioned as a holding environment for the entire family. Mother talks of emotionally open family sessions there. This augurs well; if they could do it there, perhaps they can do it here.

Finally, what basic assumptions are being played out in this family? On the conscious level, this session is a task group working to help Tom get clean; at an unconscious level, there is a dependence of all on all and all on the whole, mostly unacknowledged or denied; fight and flight are all over the place; pairing is there, overtly between Mother and Father, Sam and Mother, and perhaps Tom and Mother or Tom and Father; and fusion/fission and defenses against them are readily apparent. All families work on both task and basic assumptions levels, but in this family, the basic assumptions group overwhelms the task group. This is a useful way of organizing the complex material of this session and of thinking of ways of working with it.

Similarly, Melanie Klein's developmental scheme throws light on this family's functioning. Rarely do they work from the depressive position of tolerance for ambivalence, mourning and reparation for damage done; they readily regress to the paranoid-schizoid position, perhaps also to the autistic-contiguous position. Of course, all of human action is a complex dialectical interplay of the various Kleinian positions; however, in healthy maturity, the depressive position predominates. That is not the case with the Bakers. This means that the therapist must be alert to the projections and projective identifications rampant in the family's interactions. They may or may not be interpretable, but awareness of them strengthens the therapist as understanding reduces the disabling consequences of countertransference. Now let us go back to the session and look at how the various schools might work with this family.

STRATEGIC/COMMUNICATION

The strategic therapist would immediately search for strategies for engaging and changing this family. The strategist would be concerned with taking control of the therapeutic situation. Antecedent to strategy is the question of strategy for what, so the first task of the strategist is to figure out what problems this family has, and what sort of dysfunction. This is not a why inquiry but a what inquiry. What are the dysfunctional behaviors? In common with the other schools and lay opinion, Mother's dominance is seen to effectively blunt communication in the Baker family. So the first strategy will focus on containing Mother and correlatively bringing out the other family members. The second problem is the behavior of the identified patient. Whatever function his addiction serves for the other family members, Tom's drug use is unquestionably problematic. It requires immediate attention and a strategy must be devised for dealing with it. Antecedent, though not entirely distinct from containing Mother and sobering Tom, is the strategic therapist's taking control.

Let us look at the control issue from the point of view of a strategist. First, it is assumed that each and every member of the family is vying for control within the family and without it—here in relationship with the therapist. This is an a priori assumption, since the struggle for power in every human relationship is axiomatic for this school. This is an important point. The therapist's knowledge of the ongoing, here-and-now struggle for power is not empirical; it is something "known," even before the family has been met. This a priori knowledge does not tell the therapist how the power struggle will manifest itself, merely that it will be inexorably present. Like any theory, Haley's (1990) tells the therapist what to look for. It was once empirical, too. That is, Haley presumably arrived at his belief in the universality of the drive for power and dominance from experience (rather than from personal hang-ups or bias), and made an inductive leap from that experience to a "rule" or a scientific generalization or principle or law, here the law of the centrality of power in human relations. The generalization now directs our attention to a new particular—the family relations of the family at hand, in this case the Bakers. But Haley's generalization more than directs our attention to the particular manifestations in the case we are treating. This is so because the generalization does more than state that power aspects of relations are universal; it states that they are the center and core of every human relationship. That they are the most salient thing happening. Further, there is a treatment corollary of this generalization. Haley's technique is directly derived from his theory. The implication of power for therapeutic technique is that the first task of the therapist is to gain control of the session and of the treatment. Concretely this means activity and directiveness on the part of the therapist.

Before saying how this might play out in an actual session, it will be useful to look at the Baker family through the prism of power-dominance-control, remembering that passivity can be extremely controlling and inactivity highly active. As the existential philosopher Martin Heidegger (1927) said in another context, "*Das Nicht nichts,*" "the nothing nothings." Let us look at how the Bakers dominate and nothing.

Mother's control is perhaps not only the easiest to see, but the easiest to deal with. She is up front, the "boss," making the appointment, presenting the problem, literally putting the family members in their place. An analytic or intergenerational therapist might wonder where she is coming from. Are her attempts to control an effort to reverse a position of powerlessness in her family of origin? Is she compensating for low self-esteem? Is she merely filling a void? The strategist is uninterested in all this. It is irrelevant. What counts is coming up with a strategy to defeat Mom at arm wrestling. Dad's style is physical intimidation. However much Mom appears to be boss, Dad may very well have the final say: "One reason I called is I was afraid that Dad would beat the shit out of Tom."

Haley doesn't much talk about it, but the strategist must be something of an analyst, at least in the sense of analyzing the real power relations in the family. Be this as it may, Dad has his own strategies for dominance and control, and the therapist must settle his hash also. One wonders if Haley would duke it out with him. Tom is perhaps the most interesting power broker. As the "perp," as they say in police circles, that is, the identified patient, Tom is at the center of things. That in itself gives him enormous power. In a very real sense, he, not Mother, controls the Baker family. This "secondary gain," to borrow a concept from another, the analytic, tradition, may very well be powerfully maintaining Tom's addiction. Getting the family's focus off of Tom may be curative, although he presumably would fight such a loss of control by escalating his acting out. Humans don't relinquish power easily or gladly.

Here is one place where interpretation so foreign to the strategic school makes sense, even from the strategic perspective. The family needs to be told that the tail is wagging the dog, and Tom needs to know that he is getting off on the attention his drug use brings him. In strategic therapy we don't ask why, only what and how. Yet we cannot help but wonder why Tom meets his power needs in this way. Are Mother and Father simply too powerful in their respective styles for him to have a modicum of power in any other way?

Or has he so undermined his opportunities for alternate satisfactions of his power needs that the interpersonal pull of his addiction is all that he has left?

Although the strategist isn't interested in, but does not deny, the reality of underlying process, Tom, in common with all addicts, knows and feels that he is out of control and powerless to control his addiction, making the "control" he exercises over his family and the feelings of empowerment he derives from it a stringent psychic necessity for him. The strategist may overtly ignore all of this, but whatever may be the case as far as Tom's conscious, semiconscious, and unconscious motivations are concerned, the strategist will rightly move in in some way on Tom's being the tail that wags the dog. Of course, Tom's drug use itself gives him the illusion of power and control. Again in common with all addicts, his chemical courage and his reactive grandiosity are camouflage for underlying feelings of worthlessness and powerlessness. This gives drugs an extraordinarily powerful degree of power over him.

In their 1972 book, *The Drinking Man,* David McClelland and colleagues convincingly argue that men drink in order to feel (more) powerful. Their argument has strong empirical support from its analysis of folk tales of preliterate cultures where they found a significant correlation between cultures with a strong conflict between obedience and autonomy (which presumably left the obedient men feeling powerless, since to be autonomous, that is, powerful, brought them into intolerable conflict with authority) and drunkenness, a state in which they felt powerful. The stories these cultures told were about what McClelland and colleagues called "egoistic" power, that is, self assertion, rather than "altruistic" power where the power is in the service of social goals. Drunkenness was depicted in their folk tales as a state in which men were powerful.

Interestingly, Child and colleagues (1965), studying the same cultures, found that societies that frustrated and/or punished the meeting of "male" dependency needs had the highest rates of drunkenness. One way to feel powerful is to "participate" in the power of others or of one's collective, so this study too supports McClelland and colleagues' assertion that "men drink to feel powerful."

206 ❖ COUPLE AND FAMILY THERAPY OF ADDICTION

Tom, of course, also fits the dependency conflict rubric, simultaneously asserting his "independence" and being totally dependent on family and on drugs. McClelland and colleagues present more direct evidence that men drink to feel egotistically powerful in a series of responses to Thematic Apperception Test (TAT) cards. In the TAT, subjects are shown situations that, unlike the Rorschach, are essentially realistic (the original set of cards had the look of old movie posters), and are instructed to tell what happened before the scene depicted, what is happening now, and what will happen. McClelland and colleagues conducted "cocktail parties" in which the subjects, Harvard graduate students, were told that they could drink all they wanted if they would tell some stories in "payment." The heavy drinkers told stories of egotistic power, and the more they drank, the more monothematic their stories became. Pot isn't booze, but it is not far-fetched to extrapolate from McClelland and colleagues' findings and to postulate that "men smoke pot in order to feel powerful."

Twelve-Step makes the issue of power central to its ideology. The first of the twelve steps of spiritual (emotional) growth states, "We admitted we were *powerless* over alcohol—that our lives had become unmanageable" (Alcoholics Anonymous World Services 1953, p. 5). Of course, this admission of powerlessness has a paradoxical Zen-like twist to it: the act of admitting powerlessness empowers. Twelve-Step further teaches reliance on a *Higher Power*, which, theological implications apart, is a didactic or cognitive intervention intended to enjoin (or teach) a healthy form of dependency. Bill Wilson is the AA cofounder and author of *Twelve-Steps and Twelve Traditions* (Alcoholics Anonymous World Services, 1953), known as the "12 and 12," a guide to and interpretation of the twelve steps, which Wilson modified from a similar set of steps expounded by the Oxford Movement. This was a sort of upper-class revival movement originating at Oxford University that Wilson joined when he first became sober, but found wanting insofar as it preached and talked down to alcoholics rather than sharing with them. He made sharing the central tenet of AA ("AA is a fellowship of men and women who *share* their experience, strength and hope with each other" says the AA preamble which is read at every meeting), and used the example of our dependence on electrical power as an example of healthy dependence.

Thus there is a reciprocal relationship between admitting dependency needs and relinquishing grandiose illusions of power. Instead of claiming power for self, the recovering twelve–step person "hits bottom," throws in the towel, admits powerlessness, and then meets his or her power needs relationally, in relationship with the group, with the program, with the sponsor, and for some with the Higher Power. This "epistemological shift," to use Bateson's categorization of it (see Chapter 1) can be conceptualized as a shift from a mirror to an idealizing transference. Interestingly, twelve–step literature mostly ignores the mirror and idealizing transference to the substance of abuse, although there are references in the twelve–step literature to "alcohol being the alcoholic's Higher Power," and to alcohol as the controller, with that control being the reality behind the alcoholic's insistence that he or she can control the controller.

Returning to the Bakers, it is clear that none of them has admitted powerlessness, whether that powerlessness be Tom's vis-à-vis pot or his parents' vis-à-vis Tom. A twelve–step approach would push for open recognition of what is clearly the case—Tom can't control his pot smoking and Mom and Dad can't control another human being, here their addicted son.

So the vicissitudes of power as central, salient, and determinative of behavior and dynamics of self and system, of addict and family, is not exclusively the insight of the strategist; in their respective ways, the social-psychological researcher McClelland, the alcoholic Wilson's self-help movement, and the Kohutian analyst subscribe to the same belief. The difference is not so much in the analysis of dynamics, as in what they do with that analysis. The strategist's form of "ego deflation" is direct, confrontational, and self-consciously aiming for control. The strategic school having grown out of the communication school of family therapy (recall that Haley was part of Bateson's team) strategists still pay extremely careful attention to communication and its disturbances. They make extensive use of paradoxical interventions, including therapeutic double binds. How would that work in our first session with the Bakers?

In common with therapists of all schools, our strategist would start by listening and trying to figure out what's going on. One thing that's going on is that the family talks "about" and "not to."

STRATEGIST: Nobody in this family talks to anyone else. You talk about each other, but not to each other.

MOTHER: Talking to him is useless.

STRATEGIST: I want you to pretend that he doesn't exist. (This is a paradoxical intervention.)

TOM: She never listens to me.

FATHER: Why should she? Your brain has turned to shit and you don't make sense. (Note that they are now talking to each other, and that the therapist has taken control of the session.)

What about a double bind? Are the Bakers telling Tom that if he continues to smoke, he is hateful and bad, yet telling him that if he quits, the family will suffer in some catastrophic way? There is certainly a subtext here, and some family needs are being met by Tom's continuing use—Mother's for power, Father's to stay angry and perhaps vicariously act out, Sam's to continue as good boy and favorite, and perhaps some avoidance of latent conflict say between the parents as well, yet this family sincerely wants Tom to stop and this is not a classic double bind situation. The Bakers' communications aren't that disturbed. So the therapist in this case isn't going to go after the double bind. What he will do is to formulate a plan, a strategy, to effectuate change and to take control by using directives, perhaps paradoxical directions.

STRATEGIST: I want you all to totally control Tom. Tell him how to run his life down to the last detail. Tell him when he's going to shit, when to get up, when to and what to eat, what programs to watch, what music to play.

This is a form of prescribing the symptom. The hoped for result is for the family to realize that they can't control Tom. As they let go, he will cease to have a reason to rebel and insofar as his addiction is driven by rebellion, will smoke less or not at all.

STRATEGIST (to Sam): I want you to do everything you're told, to clean the house, to help Tom in any way you can, to help Dad and Mom. I want you to be so good that your brother will learn how he should act. I want you to study more and work harder at your Bar Mitzvah lessons. You shouldn't go out with your friends so you will have more time to be at home to help your parents.

Presumably, our good boy Sam will be unable to stand such an overdose of goodness and will rebel. In his rebellion, he will gain some freedom for himself, shake up the family system, relinquish his form of control—good boys are rewarded and loved and parents jump through hoops for them—and occupy some of the bad boy space now exclusively occupied by Tom, perhaps driving him out of it.

STRATEGIST (to Tom): I want you to smoke as much pot as you can. Light up a joint when you get out of bed. Have one with breakfast. Stay stoned all day and all night and make sure you have a joint before you go to bed.

Presumably having permission to get high will take some of the kick out of it for Tom. No more rebellion. If he follows the instruction, he will be too stoned to get any pleasure out of it, and may voluntarily give it up—or he may rebel and be oppositional by not smoking—so if he follows the instruction he may get clean, and if he doesn't, he may get clean.

The strategist has now taken control. He is enacting his power in his paradoxical directives. He has a strategy. He may have laid the groundwork for his interventions by asking the family what they were prepared to do to solve the problem. If they say they will do anything, he has set them up and the Bakers are desperate enough to probably agree that they will do anything to get Tom clean. If the strategy works, things are certainly going to escalate in the Baker family. Things may become hellish, but the status quo—the homeostasis, which is also hellish—will be disturbed. All in all, it is not a bad strategy, but what about prescribing around-the-clock pot smoking for Tom? This has some support in the AA statement that, "John Barleycorn is the best convincer," and the not infrequent injunction to resistant members to "go out and tie one on." Nevertheless, I have my doubts. Tom's level of psychopathology is an unknown. He may be a borderline kid who could be driven across the border into a psychotic break by saturation cannabis intake. It is risky. But, Tom has had a lot of treatment and nothing has worked. He is already in danger. Desperate situations sometimes call for desperate measures, and a case can be made for the strategist's paradoxical directives to the Bakers, including the one to Tom to smoke pot around the clock. Note that the strategist takes power, he does not discuss it or interpret it. The power relations in the family are disturbed by the paradoxical directives, but there is no attempt to increase insight. It is not my way of working, but I have seen therapists work with families with chronic teenage drug users in exactly the way our strategist did with success.

STRUCTURALIST

The structuralist is also interested in power and control, both between therapist and family and within the family. Generally speaking, the structuralist will work to strengthen the parental dyad. (I tremble for my soul when I use phrases like "parental dyad," but such is the state of the art.)

> STRUCTURALIST (Early on, when Mom has described Dad's circumcision; mostly to Mom but directed at all): What happened to the tip? Do you still have it?

This intervention does several things. As we saw earlier, when all the therapists were speaking together, it elicited some rebellion and humor on the part of Sam. More importantly, it takes power away from Mother, essentially neutralizing her. Although not altogether apparent in the segment of the session we have, openness about sex verging on crudeness, bantering, humor, and informality are part of this family's style as is a certain degree of exhibitionism, and the structuralist here is "tracking," speaking in the family's style. The therapist takes control and at the same time "joins" the family, making a remark a family member might have made. This particular comment is closest to Sam's occasional near wisecracks. The castrating mother and presumably castrated father are recast as benign and intact, respectively—sort of.

From the structuralist's viewpoint, this is an enmeshed family. Differentiation is difficult, and one reason Tom may hold onto his addiction is to differentiate himself from the enmeshment and this may be true in spite of the strong element of identification with Father in Tom's usage. One way to demonstrate the enmeshment is to construct a structural map.

This family could be mapped in several ways using Minuchin's system of dashes for clear boundaries, dots for diffuse boundaries, one line for rigid boundary, two lines for affiliation, and three lines for overinvolvement. There are also symbols for conflict, coalition, and detouring. (See Figure 4–1.)

I have constructed the map (Figure 4–2) to demonstrate Sam's rigid boundary (apparent distance) from Tom and Father and his affiliation with Mother. One suspects that Sam is overinvolved with Mother and two parallel lines connecting Sam and Mom may change to three parallel lines in the structural map as we get more data. Mother is overinvolved with Tom, although also in conflict with him, but I choose to highlight the overinvolvement in my structural map. Mother has an apparently diffuse boundary with Father in which she defines him and in some ways assimilates him. His fury directed at Tom may be partly coming from his struggle to differentiate from his wife. Her "castrating" stance toward her husband can also be seen as a kind of engulfment, manifested in such behavior as speaking for him. Father seems to have a rigid boundary with his younger son and little relationship with him, but this may be an artifact of Tom's being the center of the present crisis, so this mapping too may have to be revised as more data become available. Father has a diffuse boundary

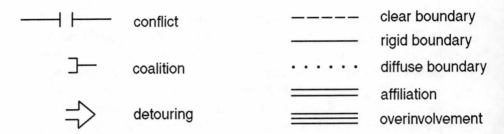

—⊣ ⊢— conflict	----- clear boundary
	——— rigid boundary
⊐— coalition	• • • • • • diffuse boundary
	═══ affiliation
⟹ detouring	≣ overinvolvement

FIGURE 4-1. Minuchin's Symbol System.

with his wife and is in intense conflict with his oldest son, with whom he is also overinvolved. In the map, I highlight the conflict. Tom, the identified patient (IP), is cut off from his brother, overinvolved with his mother, and in conflict with his father. Note the lack of clear hierarchy in the Baker family as here mapped. Contrast it with the Jones family (Figure 4–3), where Mother and Father have an alliance and each relates to, but has clear boundaries from each of their children, C_1 and C_2.

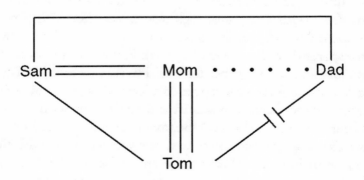

FIGURE 4-2. Structural map of the Baker family.

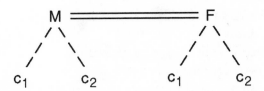

FIGURE 4–3. Structural map of the Jones family.

For didactic purposes, we have mapped the Bakers too early and are going to have to rework our map. Nevertheless, the usefulness of Minuchin's structural map is clear. The aloofness of Sam, the lack of hierarchy, and the weakness and confusion of the parental alliance are very clear in the map. The device is limited insofar as it is difficult to depict complexity in relationships, but this is also advantageous in that it forces the therapist to choose the most salient relational characteristic of the various subsets of the family (a subset can be an individual). How would you map the Bakers?

The structuralist would move to strengthen the parents in their alliance and to help them "control" the "bad boy." Here we see an exactly opposite approach to that of the strategist.

STRUCTURALIST (to parents): You have to stop Tom's drug use immediately.

MOM AND DAD: We'd love to but we can't.

STRUCTURALIST: You support him, don't you?

MOM: Of course.

STRUCTURALIST: You'll support him into the grave. Tell him he can't live in *your* home if he smokes and that you won't give him a cent until he stops except for treatment.

Here the structuralist is teaching "tough love." Note "*your* home," which simultaneously points to a source of parental power and speaks to parental alliance; they own their home together and have the power to decide who will live in it.

214 ❖ COUPLE AND FAMILY THERAPY OF ADDICTION

MOTHER: We can't just throw him out.

FATHER: Why not?

MOTHER: People will say we're monsters.

STRUCTURALIST: That's a cop-out.

TOM: You can shove your house up your ass.

STRUCTURALIST: If they do, you surely won't be able to live in it.

TOM (to structuralist): Fuck you.

STRUCTURALIST (to parents): Are you serious about wanting Tom to get clean? If you are, you have to be tough. Tell him he's out, and you won't do a thing for him if he uses.

MOTHER: Right now?

STRUCTURALIST: You bet.

FATHER (to Mother): Harriet, let's do it.

MOTHER (looking shaken): Okay.

STRUCTURALIST: Tell him.

FATHER: You're out of here if you use any more of that shit.

STRUCTURALIST: Mother?

MOTHER: I agree.

STRUCTURALIST (to Mother): Tell Tom, "Dad and I have decided no drugs in our house. And no users either."

MOTHER (weeping): Tom, the therapist is right. We'll worry about you, but Dad and I won't let you live with us if you keep smoking.

STRUCTURALIST (raising the ante): And you have to arrange urine monitoring. I'll tell you how.

TOM: A piss test too?

STRUCTURALIST: If you're taking piss tests, you can't get pissed.

TOM (to structuralist): Asshole. (But his bravado is crumbling. He is clearly upset.)

STRUCTURALIST (to Sam): Tell Tom you won't have anything to do with him if he uses.

SAM (gloating and joyful): I won't give you shit if you get stoned.

STRUCTURALIST (to Sam): You're really getting off on this, but that's not important now. The important thing is to get Tom clean. (To Tom): You have no place to go, kid.

TOM (cries).

Our structuralist is every bit as directive as the strategist, but his direction takes a different tack. For the structuralist, some of the strategist's paradoxical directives were just too dangerous, although structuralists typically are willing to take risks to move families off of ground zero. Our strategist assumes some degree of health in the parents' relationship and works to strengthen it and to establish or reestablish a hierarchical relationship between parents and children. Everything he does aims at establishing clear, but not overly rigid, boundaries and to disenmesh the family. Here the disenmeshment is unusually directive: sever your ties with the drug user if he won't stop. The Bakers didn't come to the session to conduct an "intervention," yet the structuralist has maneuvered them into (in effect) doing one. This structuralist approach would not have worked with a "sicker," that is, more enmeshed, family where the unconscious needs to keep Tom using were more powerful. It also assumes a certain degree of health in the parental relationship. Typically, the work a structuralist does needs some preliminaries, some loosening of Tom's symbiosis with Mother (however defended against) and some loosening of Father's projective identification with Tom. These are analytic terms, but they are perfectly applicable to the structuralist's analysis of enmeshment.

> STRUCTURALIST (to Tom): We will do anything to help you stop. Perhaps you can't stop—if you need detoxification you can have it; if you need medication, that can be arranged; if you need to go back into the TC or to a rehab, that's okay too; or you can keep coming here.

Here the structuralist is using a little paradox—"Perhaps you can't stop"—although that may be true, and he is being supportive. Structuralists often support or ally with the identified patient to "unbalance" the system. Another structuralist approach would do that.

> STRUCTURALIST 2: Being high must be great. What's it like?
> OR STRUCTURALIST 2 (to Tom): Your parents are really up your ass.

In both these interventions, the structuralist is tracking, joining the family, unbalancing, and forming an alliance with Tom all at once. Our first structuralist indirectly joined with Father in his question about the foreskin. A more direct approach would have been:

STRUCTURALIST (to Father, interrupting Mother): You don't get to say much, do you?

Or the first structural intervention could have been addressed to the "lost child" good boy:

STRUCTURALIST (to Sam): Do your parents ever pay any attention to you?

This also unbalances the family, disrupts their obsession with Tom, and shakes the homeostasis, making change at least possible. It may also serve to help the family member in the most long-term danger. Reframing is another typically structural intervention. If it were the case, the structuralist might say, "Tom stays stoned to keep the family together. If he gets clean, you two (indicating the parents) are going to have to talk to each other and deal with your problems. Tom is afraid you won't be able to do that and will divorce." There may indeed be some degree of this dynamic in the Baker family, but if present we do not have the evidence for it, and our structuralist wonders about this possibility, but goes to helping the parents put the screws on Tom. A more on-target reframing would be, "Tom uses because he thinks that's what everyone expects him to do, not only in the family, either, and he doesn't know how to fill any other role." This makes Tom less the "bad child," cuts down on the recrimination, and makes Tom's use a system problem, at least in part, which indeed it has to be, at least in part. It isn't used here because the structuralist chooses to address the "crisis," but that doesn't preclude its later use.

Our structuralist has done a good job. He has played to the strengths of the family, successfully joined them, made good use of tracking, clarified and strengthened boundaries, and given the family a means of dealing with their crisis. Tom is probably going to get clean. Would it be so easy! Usually it is not, but sometimes it is, and this sort of highly directive structural approach should be in the repertoire of the addiction family therapist.

INTERGENERATIONAL SYSTEMIC

The *genogram* is integral to the intergenerational approach, and the systemic therapist would make construction of the genogram one of his or her first therapeutic tasks. The Bakers spontaneously gave us a good deal of information about the family's antecedents and our systemic therapist would build on that information by asking questions to flesh out the genealogies. Bowen has a set of genogram symbols (Figure 4–4).

The genogram can be elaborated by indicating spouses of fathers and mothers, siblings and their children, and the IP's cousins as has been done in Figure 4–5. This was relevant in the Baker case, since two of Tom's cousins are drug-involved and he has a relationship with them. A systemic therapist will elicit as much information as possible to help in constructing the genogram.

> INTERGENERATIONALIST (successively to Dad and then to Mother, ignoring the children): Did anyone in your family of origin drink heavily? Who? Have there been any deaths associated with drinking or drugging? Divorces? (And so forth, going back at least to the parents' parents, and better, to the parents' grandparents.)
> DAD: My Dad's liver went and it killed him. My brothers are heading in the same direction.

The genogram vividly depicts the multigenerational problem drinking in Father's family and the equally salient fact that Father is the only family member who has recovered (or at least stopped drinking, Twelve–Step making a distinction between being "dry" [merely abstaining] and being "sober" ["working the program" to enable growth]). Whether the transmission be genetic, cultural, learned, psychodynamic, or the result of Bowenian intergenerational undifferentiation, the males in the Baker family are at high risk for addiction.

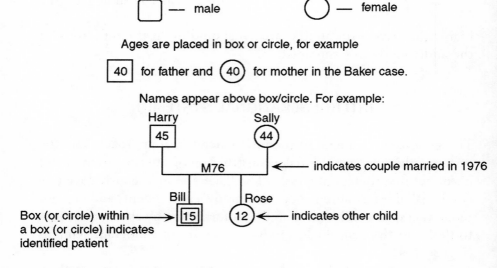

□ — male   ○ — female

Ages are placed in box or circle, for example

40 for father and (40) for mother in the Baker case.

Names appear above box/circle. For example:

Harry   Sally
45   (44)

M76 ←—— indicates couple married in 1976

Bill   Rose

Box (or circle) within ——→ |15| (12) ←—— indicates other child
a box (or circle) indicates
identified patient

Other conventional symbols:

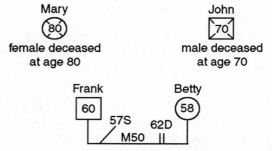

Mary   John
(80)   70
female deceased   male deceased
at age 80   at age 70

Frank   Betty
60   (58)
     57S   62D
      M50   ‖

Slant line with date followed by S indicates date of separation. Parallel lines
perpendicular to marriage line with date followed by D indicates date of divorce.

We will add symbols for substance abuse and religion.

(A) — alcoholic   (C) — Catholic

(D) — drug addicted   (J) — Jewish

(R) — recovering from   (C/J) — Catholic converted
      alcohol or   to Judaism
      drug addiction

FIGURE 4–4. Genogram symbols.

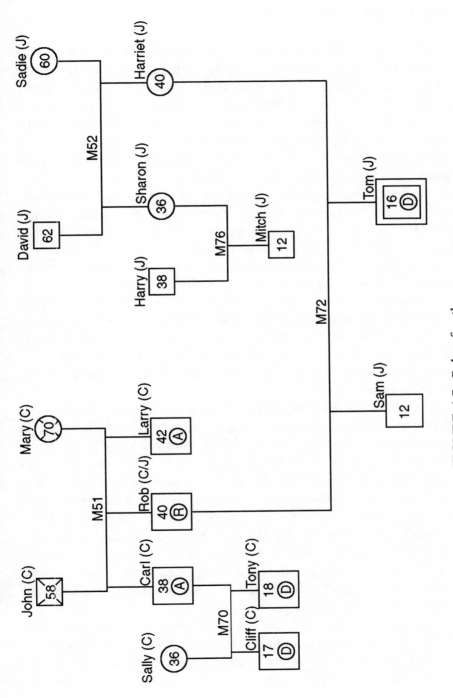

FIGURE 4-5. Baker family genogram.

The intergenerational therapist is definitely not a joiner, at least as incarnated by Bowen, yet like every other therapist, he needs to forge a therapeutic alliance. The construction of a genogram with the family enables this alliance. The therapist is definitely the expert here, yet is engaged in a cooperative venture with the family. Further, the construction of the genogram is not merely meaningful process, as important as that may be, to be left as therapy progresses. On the contrary, it is a tool that is repeatedly utilized. This is particularly so in substance abuse cases like the Bakers.' It can be used didactically to demonstrate the dim odds of Tom becoming an occasional pot smoker. Further, it is an objectification, an artifact that is hard to dispute and serves as a form of dispassionate evidence. In a family as volatile and as upset as the Bakers, this pacification function of the genogram may be important and powerful.

Since Rob's conversion is central to the Bakers' family dynamics, religion can be added to the genogram. The solidness of the Catholicism in the Baker family makes Father's conversion stand out. It clearly took courage—love, perhaps—for him to break with his family in this regard. Again, the genogram clarifies and vivifies the context of individual actions.

In the case of the Bakers, the information necessary for the construction of the genogram was easily elicited. The family's style of openness almost to the point of exhibitionism made the systematist's task easy. This is by no means always the case. Family secrets are not easily divulged, even within the family, let alone to strangers. This is particularly true of substance abusing families and, to a lesser extent, of families with a substance abuser, to again use Steinglass's differential. There is a twelve–step slogan, "You are as sick as your secrets," with which I agree. It isn't so much the content as the secretiveness itself that sometimes literally, and always figuratively, drives people crazy. Families that lie, distort, deceive, and withhold often make the construction of a meaningful genogram difficult, if not impossible. Substance abuse in significant others or even remote others and its frequent concomitants—spousal abuse, child abuse (physical and sexual), and suicide—are not readily shared. Additionally, secrecy within the family, particularly in earlier generations, may make the necessary information unavailable to the family in treatment. So ignorance, unconscious repressive processes, and conscious deception and denial all contribute to the genogrammer's woes.

The prevalence of conscious deception in substance abusing families in treatment brings to mind Freud's (1905) story of the Jewish man in Eastern Europe deeply into *yiches* (social status) who goes to the *shadchen* (marriage broker) to arrange a marriage with a woman of good pedigree. The marriage broker assures the prospective groom that all the candidate's relatives were upstanding and outstanding people, including the prospective bride's dead father. The deal is made and the wedding takes place. Several months later, the groom infuriatingly accosts the marriage broker, "You're a liar and a thief. You told me that my father-in-law was dead and I just found out he's alive and in jail." Nonplussed, the marriage broker replies, "You call that living?" Many families are just as honest as the marriage broker.

You don't have to be an intergenerationalist to love genograms. Therapists in many schools find them useful and incorporate their use into their technique. This is particularly true for substance abuse therapists who are rightfully interested in addiction in the family. A word of caution here. Overzealous addiction counselors press extraordinarily hard to unearth the family antecedents of addiction, searching out the alcoholic in grandparents or great-grandparents with the passion of a McCarthyite seeking out Communists in a government agency. Usually such counselors are committed to the heritability wing of the disease model contingent of counselors. If you look hard enough, you will find addiction or compulsion in any family, and the result is trivial. Not only is it trivial, but it blurs the differential, obscuring the saliency of familial, intergenerational addiction in the treatment of the family at hand. In the Bakers' case, that history is indeed salient.

Our systemic intergenerationalist would work in a dispassionate, researcherly manner in eliciting the information needed to construct the genogram. Further, he or she would work individually, that is, question each family member individually rather than solicit a familial response. The intention here is to encourage individuation or, to use Bowen's word, *differentiation*, to sculpt individuals out of the family mass. (I always misread "family mass" as "family mess" and envision the differentiated ones as fecal dolls, but no doubt that's my problem.) From the systemic point of view, the therapist's stance and style is more important than the content of his/her interventions. Nothing is more relevant to the proper therapeutic stance than the therapist's own differentiation. In common with most other therapists, but more so, the intergenerationalist's goal in this first session is *evaluation*. Construction of the genogram is an essential part of this evaluation.

INTERGENERATIONALIST: Mr. Baker, can we analyze the drinking in your family? If we do, we can clearly see that all of the men have trouble with alcohol. Your son's drugging is entirely consistent with your family history.

MOTHER (humorously, to husband): I knew the problem was on your side. (To therapist): Okay, it runs on Dad's side. How does that help us?

INTERGENERATIONALIST (refusing to be "triangulated"): Mrs. Baker, I'm talking to Mr. Baker about his family.

MOTHER (to Tom): You see, you just can't get high; you have the addiction gene from Dad.

INTERGENERATIONALIST: Mrs. Baker, you're bringing Tom into it because you don't want to deal with my saying to you that I was talking to your husband. First you broke up my dialogue with your husband, and now you're bringing in your son. It's hard for you to stay with or tolerate two-person relationships. You either become or bring in a third person.

Here the intergenerationalist interrupts the elucidation and elaboration of the intergenerational analysis to comment on and indeed arrest attempts at triangulation in the here and now of the family session. In his analysis, he sees triangulation rather than castration by Mrs. Baker. In her own undifferentiation, she has trouble allowing the differentiation of others. From this point of view, although her aggression appears to be in the service of separation, it is actually driven by the need for fusion, which is seen as central to the family dynamic. Tom is a clear case of "emotional cutoff," resulting in a false self or a pseudo–self-sufficiency. He is neither fused nor differentiated, and uses drugs to do both. He fuses with the drug and simultaneously isolates himself from his family. I would comment on this early in treatment, perhaps in this first session. I assume an intergenerationalist might say something like this:

INTERGENERATIONALIST (to Tom): When you get high, you feel independent. You are able to get some distance from your family. But then, just as you're feeling like yourself, you lose yourself in the fog of your high.

But then again, he might not. More typical of the Bowenian approach would be to see Tom's drug problem as a correlative of his parents' relative undifferentiation and projection of undifferentiation onto him, this being so in spite of the relatively high degree of differentiation in the Baker family when compared to, let us say, a schizophrenic family. So the Bowenian therapist is much more likely to say:

INTERGENERATIONALIST: In our session today, I have been able to see some patterns both in your immediate family and in your extended family. I would like to coach you in ways to change some of those patterns, the ones that are making it difficult for Tom to grow up. The best way I can do that is by meeting with Tom's parents. Mr. and Mrs. Baker, would you be willing to meet with me without the children?

MR. BAKER: If you're trying to put it on us, you're crazy, doc.

INTERGENERATIONALIST: Not at all. I always suggest meetings with the parents to help them help their children become independent.

TOM: If you want to cook up some scheme for my folks to run my life, go ahead. It ain't going to work.

INTERGENERATIONALIST: My meeting with your parents scares you, so you butt in.

TOM: Fuck you.

MR. BAKER: Let's do it.

MRS. BAKER: What the hell, okay.

224 ❖ COUPLE AND FAMILY THERAPY OF ADDICTION

And the arrangement is made. Presumably the intergenerationalist will coach the parents in differentiating themselves from their families of origin, thereby reducing or eliminating their need to triangulate Tom and to project undifferentiation onto him. Sam, who may actually be the less differentiated child, although not caught up in emotional cutoff, would also benefit from this strategy.

An alternative intergenerational strategy would be to "coach" Tom individually, focusing not on his drug use but on his lack of differentiation. This has merit, but I have my doubts how well it would work without Tom's abstinence.

Yet another intergenerational strategy would be to continue to work with the genogram to increase the Bakers' awareness of, not the neurochemical genetic, but the intergenerational transmission patterns culminating with Tom's addiction.

EXPERIENTIAL

Unlike the Bowenian intergenerationalist with his coolness and analytic detachment, an experientialist would wade right in, joining and engaging in the "political battle."

EXPERIENTIALIST: Shit, I can't even control my own kids, how the hell do you think I'm going to control yours? Half the time, I can't even control myself.

FATHER: I can kick his ass the fuck out of the house.

EXPERIENTIALIST (Thinks, *I won that political battle. Dad's taking responsibility*; to Dad): That's not a bad idea.

MOM: We can't do that.

EXPERIENTIALIST (Thinks, *I should have known that was too easy*; to Mom): Well, if you don't want to exile the kid to Siberia, you could try to make things more peaceful at home.

MOM: How?

EXPERIENTIALIST: You could build him a greenhouse to grow pot in.

FATHER: You're nuts.

EXPERIENTIALIST: Dad, you could design it, and all of you could build it. It would bring the family together. You could all work on it. Mom could order the best seeds, Tijuana Gold. And Sam, you could water them every day. Dad, you could run in the electric power and pipe, and Tom, you could hoe. And it should have air conditioning and a state of the art stereo system.

MOTHER: We couldn't do that; we'd go to jail.

EXPERIENTIALIST: That's good. Tom's heading for jail, so that would help you understand him.

TOM: Assholes. He thinks you're helping me use by letting me live in the house, so he's making fun of you.

EXPERIENTIALIST (to Tom): Who, me?

SAM: I think we should build a tower on the greenhouse for Tom to hang himself from.

EXPERIENTIALIST: Maybe your parents could hang themselves too.

MOTHER (starts crying): I really do wish I was dead. I am so ashamed. I am so scared. I know Tom's going to die if he keeps this up and I can't live through that.

EXPERIENTIALIST (to Tom): What kind of funeral do you want? Shall we throw grass seeds on the grave?

TOM: Let me out of here. He is nuts.

EXPERIENTIALIST: Or maybe you'd like to go to Mom's funeral if they let you out of jail to attend.

TOM: Oh fuck.

FATHER (to therapist): He ain't no tough guy. I've been on the street and in the can. I know what it's like. It sucks, it really sucks.

MOTHER: Stop! I don't want to hear about it. Oh. Oh. Tom, you can't live in our house if you get high. You're out.

EXPERIENTIALIST: What would become of the greenhouse?

TOM: I can't stop. I feel like shit when I don't smoke. (Pauses). Just don't make me go back to that school and I'll try.

FATHER: Trying is bullshit. You can stop.

MOM (sobbing): Tom, just stay clean and I won't ask anything else.

TOM: Yeah, okay.

MOTHER (embraces Tom. He pulls away, then returns the embrace.)

SAM: Oh, shit.

MOTHER (pulls Sam into the embrace).

FATHER: Maybe it'll work this time.

EXPERIENTIALIST (to Dad, wiping away a tear): Maybe. (Looking at Mother and the boys.) I feel left out. How 'bout you and I hugging? (They do.)

Here our experiential therapist tries some theater of the absurd. Sensing that the family is enabling Tom in one way or another, he makes that enabling transparently clear, and that clarity shakes the family, moving them to remove their destructive support. The experientialist also intuits some of the subterranean themes in the Baker family: their fears (and perhaps wishes) that Tom would die, Dad's acquaintance with the night, Sam's hostility to Tom, and the desperate need of all four for love. A great deal of this surfaces in response to the experientialist's absurdity. This openness could be therapeutically exploited and expanded in a variety of ways, perhaps by probing for the parents' fears of death, which may be motivating their ambivalent enabling; for Tom to move toward adulthood underscores their own passage through time and the life cycle. There is some mourning work to be done before they can let Tom go.

Sam's comment brought to mind a particularly acrimonious divorce hearing in which I was an expert witness. Jane claimed Ken had put a quarter of a million dollars "up his nose" during his cocaine addiction. Ken was claiming disability and asking for support payments. Jane bitterly told the court that their assets were gone except for their condo, but that even that was virtually worthless because Ken had trashed it during one of his cocaine sprees. In the most innocent of little boy voices, Ken interrupted her to say, "The only damage I ever did to the apartment was to leave a hole in the ceiling when the hook pulled out when I tried to hang myself." The judge barely managed to restrain her laughter.

BEHAVIORAL

In contrast with the communication/strategic, structuralist, intergenerational, and experiential approaches, the behaviorist would focus on Tom's problem behavior. The IP is indeed the IP, although the family may be unwittingly reinforcing the objectionable behavior. So our behaviorist's work will be with the whole family and yet will focus on Tom. He will attempt to elicit drug signals, teach coping skills, and suggest ways the family can help Tom achieve abstinence. Constructing contingency schedules and the like are the essence of his approach. His role is teacherly.

BEHAVIORIST: There is an awful lot of anger directed at Tom. It's hard to stay clean when everyone is putting you down. I wonder if you would agree to say something positive to Tom three times each day until our next session.

DAD: I've heard that positive reinforcement shit before. He never does anything right, so what could we reinforce?

MOM: He's not that bad.

SAM (giggles).

BEHAVIORIST: Mr. Baker, I'm not asking you to reinforce behavior, just to say something positive. For example, "Thank you Tom for coming to therapy tonight." Or, "You look spiffy today."

SAM: Spiffy?

MOM (to Dad): You're too quick to hit. Why not try this? Do it for me.

DAD: Well, he's handsome when he doesn't look strung out. That's not surprising since he looks like me. I'll tell him that.

BEHAVIORIST: Sam, what about you?

SAM: Yeah?

BEHAVIORIST (Hands out forms): There are three blank spaces in each of the two columns on these forms. I want you to write down your positive comments to Tom in the first column and we'll discuss them next week. (To Tom): Tom, I need you to do something, too. I want you to tell your parents and your brother that you appreciate their saying positive things. Just check it off each time you do that on this form. (Hands form to him.)

TOM: What if I don't feel it?

BEHAVIORIST: Say it anyway.

TOM: That's like the NA (Narcotics Anonymous) slogan, "Bring the body and the mind will follow."

BEHAVIORIST: Exactly. Will you do it?

TOM: Okay.

Our behaviorist approach and the NA slogan are interesting. If you want to get fancy, the social scientist Darryl Bem (1967) reports having empirical evidence that we determine our attitudes from our behavior in exactly the same way that we determine other people's attitudes from their behavior. I believe that similar work was cited in the Supreme Court desegregation decision or in the brief supporting it, the idea being that if you change the behavior—go to school with blacks—your attitude will be changed, too. This is classically behavioral stuff.

Notice how the behaviorist, somewhat like the intergenerationalist, cools the situation by being rational, calm, and reasonable, and ignores a lot of the emotion coming from the Bakers. He elicits cooperation by asking little, and his minimalist approach may open a door allowing broader change. He goes on to deal with drug signals.

BEHAVIORIST (to Tom): You don't want to get high all the time, do you?

SAM: Yes, he does.

TOM: Shut up, creep. No, not all the time.

BEHAVIORIST: So something must happen to make you want to smoke. We call that something a "trigger"; NA speaks of "places, people, and things" that make people want to use drugs. I would add "feelings" to that list. I want you to notice when you want to get high and write it down on this chart. (It may take a whole forest to provide the paper the behaviorist needs for his schedules, contingency charts, self-observational charts, and so forth.) As you can see, there's a place to write down the people, places, feelings, or things that proceed or accompany your urge. For now, I am not asking you to stop getting high, only to record each urge, each usage, and what set you off. It's kind of like a scientific experiment. Are you game?

TOM: I don't have to stop using?

BEHAVIORIST: Not this week.

DAD (to therapist): Are you sure you know what you're doing?

BEHAVIORIST (to Dad): I'm sure.

SAM: Why don't you give me some pot and those forms, and I'll do the experiment too.

BEHAVIORIST: Now Tom, I have one more chart for you. This one is to record how you feel after you use, if you do.

MOM: He'll be so busy writing it all down, he won't even get a chance to light it.

BEHAVIORIST: Now Mr. and Mrs. Baker, you have to agree to let this run—not to yell at Tom if he smokes this week.

MOM AND DAD: Okay.

BEHAVIORIST: Now Sam, I have a chart for you, too. I want you to record Tom's behavior and moods before and after he smokes as you see them, if he does smoke grass. All you have to do is put a check mark next to the word that describes them best. See, column one, date and time, column two, before, column three, after.

SAM: Most of the time he gets high out of the house.

BEHAVIORIST: But I'll bet you know when he does.

SAM: Yes.

BEHAVIORIST: Then record as much as you see.

SAM: I love this.

BEHAVIORIST: I think we have a deal. I call it a contract, and I want everyone to sign it. Mr. Baker, you agree to say three positive things to Tom each day, record them, and not interfere with Tom's use or nonuse this week. Sign here. Mrs. Baker, the same for you. (They sign.) And Sam, you're going to try and say one positive thing to Tom each day, record it, and if you see him high, check what you see. Okay? (Sam signs.) And Tom, your contract stipulates that you thank Sam and your parents for the positive things they say to you, and that you record your urges and usage just as I explained.

TOM: I'll sign.

BEHAVIORIST: Great. I think we're on the right track. I'll see you all the same time next week.

Well, our behaviorist has laid it all out. Next week he can go on to contingency contracting—rewards for abstinence and sanctions for use—and start to teach coping behaviors, self-efficacy skills, and alternate (to drug use) behavior to Tom, and teach the family ways of helping Tom cope as well as going over their homework, both for its intrinsic value and as a way of building a we-ness in solving Tom's problem without undermining Tom's responsibility for his own behavior. Our behaviorist will also use Tom's self-observations and Sam's observations as feedback loops to make triggers that are presently automatic and out of awareness, self-conscious and in awareness. The next step is to work on alternate responses to those triggers. Notice that the family "craziness" is ignored, and the behaviorist focuses almost entirely on the IP's problem and the family's response to it. This elicits cooperation and lowers resistance by turning the whole thing into a kind of game. It is also "shaping," approximating the desired behavior—abstinence—rather than expecting it prematurely. In reality, things would rarely go so smoothly, yet our behaviorist's approach sometimes succeeds and is worth trying. At some point, there might be a contract in which Tom's attendance at NA's young people's meetings would be rewarded, say with a trip to a professional hockey or basketball game with Dad or with the whole family.

Twenty years ago, I attended a program called Smoke Enders. I was a three-pack-a-day Marlboro man when I entered the program, which consisted of eight sessions culminating in the dreaded "cutoff" (abstinence day) followed by five more reinforcement sessions. I was angry as hell because I knew that I would leave smokeless. Something was being taken away, albeit by me, and I didn't like it. Be that as it may, Smoke Enders worked for me, and with the exception of one cigarette the day after cutoff, I haven't smoked since. Smoke Enders was a kind of amalgamation of behavior therapy and borrowings from AA such as "sharing," "telephone therapy" with peers, and group support. One of the more behavioral techniques was a rather simple one of having people wrap a paper marker around their packs of cigarettes and having them record each cigarette smoked and whether or not smoking that cigarette was pleasurable. In common with my fellow Smoke Enders, I was amazed to discover how very few cigarettes I actually enjoyed. This simple self-observation device constituted an extremely powerful feedback loop. Smoke Enders also used shaping— successive approximations to a nicotine-free state (there were no patches then) engendered through switching to low nicotine cigarettes, progressively restricting times smoking was permitted, forbidding carrying matches or a lighter, carrying your cigarettes in a different place, smoking with the other hand, and so on. Some of this was done to break habit patterns, and some of it to sever the connection between stimulus and response—between trigger and cigarette. The contract was an agreement to abide by the progressive restrictions imposed by the leader each week until cutoff. A reward system was built into the sharing and mutual reinforcement of the group meetings. It worked for a good number of people. Having beaten an addiction through participation in a behaviorally oriented therapy, I can hardly devalue the behavioral approach, however uncongenial I may find it.

DYNAMIC

The psychodynamic approach to the Bakers is here represented by an object relations therapist. It doesn't mean that our dynamic therapist will ignore drive, ego, and self understandings of the Bakers; on the contrary, he will integrate them into his object relations perspective. In general, dynamic therapists are not too active in an opening session, since interpretation requires knowledge of the family's dynamics and the acquisition of this knowledge is a time-bound process. Additionally, the creation of a holding environment and the unfolding of the transferences require time. Having said this, it is important to remember that the opposite of activity is not, in this case, passivity; rather, it is receptivity and therapeutically tactful interpretation. Typically, the dynamic family therapist provides drawing materials and if there are younger children, play materials. Our object relations therapist has done so, and Sam has been "doodling" during the session (Figure 4-6, parts I and II).

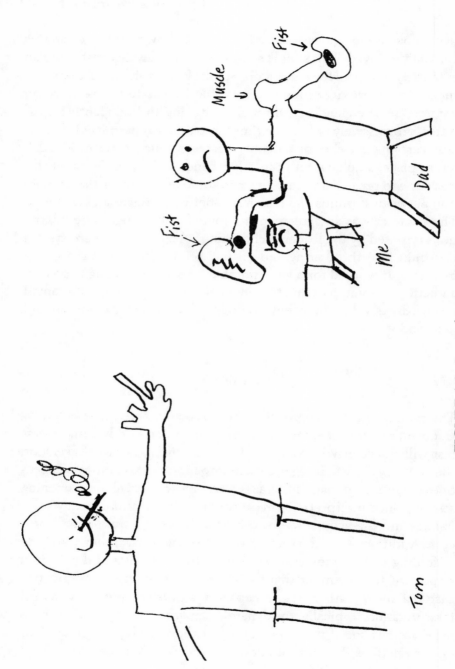

FIGURE 4-6. Sam's drawing, Part I

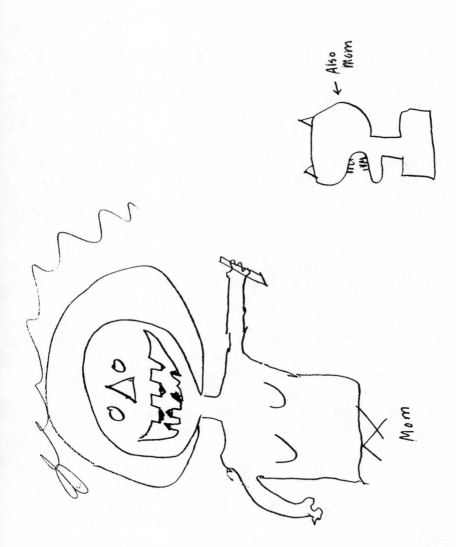

FIGURE 4-6. Sam's drawing, Part II

OBJECT RELATIONS THERAPIST: Would you share your drawing with us, Sam?

SAM (blushes but hands over the drawing. The therapist passes it around.)

OBJECT RELATIONS THERAPIST: Any thoughts about Sam's drawings?

MOM: I'm all teeth. Twice.

DAD (to Sam): You got Tom right with that smirk and that joint hanging out of his mouth.

TOM: You sure can't draw.

Fascinated by Sam's representation of his mother as a semihuman devouring beast, the object relations therapist's thoughts went to an early sexual encounter with an inexperienced partner who bit his penis as she attempted fellatio. He remembered his comment, "Teeth kitty" that later became a joke between them. Thinking along his counter-transferential associations, he realized that he was condensing Mother's castrating tendencies, "He was circumcised for me" with her cannibalistic tendencies as experienced by her younger son. Going with his own unconscious process, which had associated a moment of personal sexual anxiety with Sam's drawing, he went with his intuitions and played a hunch that Tom was so afraid of his castrating, devouring Mother that he needed to get high in order to have intercourse. Mother's well-fanged mouth was also her vagina dentata. Having made this connection by assessing his own experience and actually feeling anxiety when he looked at the drawing, he recovered, moving back into a stance of professional neutrality and objectivity. Now working from a central ego rather than an antilibidinal ego stance, drawing more on consciousness rather than from the unconscious process, he debated whether or not to make a "wild" (Freud 1910) interpretation. Knowing that creating a holding environment takes precedence and that interpretations require context, he at first decided to hold his insight, but reconsidered. Tom was so isolated both in the session and in the drawing that the object relationist decided that making contact with Tom was what most needed to be done, and that perhaps Sam's drawing and his own associations to it just might be the vehicle of such contact. He played his hunch.

OBJECT RELATIONIST: Sam's drawing makes me anxious, and my anxiety must be mild compared to yours. Your whole family lives in a condition of high anxiety. Tom, I don't quite know why, but when I realized how anxious everyone is, I thought, "Tom smokes to control his anxiety," and I wondered if you were so anxious that you had to get high to have sex. Have you ever had intercourse straight?

TOM (blushes beet red): No, I never got laid unless I was high. It makes it better. (Angrily.) You ought to try it, doc.

OBJECT RELATIONIST: That's kind of sad, Tom, that you can't even enjoy your own body without getting high. Really sad.

Our object relationist has scored a bull's eye. Pot not only allows Tom to be sexual; smoking it is a sexual act. Although smoking pot, as in the use of any inhalant, could be viewed as a form of respiratory eroticism, I have sometimes wondered if smokers—of crack, pot, tobacco—aren't unconsciously attempting to master the anxiety they felt when they first attempted to breathe on their own, surely a core component of the birth trauma, if there be one. In their anxious inhalation, they quell that anxiety through the physical act of inhaling and through the pharmacological effects of the inhalant. Smoking is also an oral act, both physically and symbolically, and it is interesting that Mother has something of the aspect of a smoking dragon in Sam's representation in which Tom also smokes. Is there some sort of identification here? Is Tom's smoking the turning of a passive experience into an active one, taking in the smoking dragon where she can be tamed and contained rather than being devoured by her? In all probability, some such dynamic is at work here. Of course, Sam's drawing is a representation of his internal object relations as well as his experience of the external objects constituting his family, and Tom in his usual closed, defensive manner has made a critical comment rather than associating to his brother's drawing. The avoidance is more salient than the hostility. Our object relationist is feeling guilty. This is really bad technique. Instead of providing a safe place for Tom, he has stirred up enormous anxiety. Yet he has made contact. Putting aside his self doubts, he continues.

OBJECT RELATIONS THERAPIST: Tom, you haven't told us your thoughts about the drawing.

MOTHER: The doctor is right. It really is sad that you can't get laid without getting high.

FATHER: He can't do anything without getting high.

OBJECT RELATIONS THERAPIST (again feeling guilty; to Father): Do you realize you are attacking Tom when he has made himself vulnerable? No wonder he closes down emotionally.

TOM: He's like that. That's why Sam drew him with his fist cocked.

OBJECT RELATIONS THERAPIST (thinks, *Mother's all sexual aggression; Dad, aggression aggression. If I were Tom, I'd be stoned all the time too.* Then catching himself, he thinks, *I'm overidentifying with Tom. Both of these parents are capable of loving concern and care of and for their children. That was amply demonstrated in the material emerging earlier in the session. My mother was sometimes seductive, and I wished my father was more aggressive. The Bakers really do make me anxious; too much id. Too little central ego. How can I use myself to understand and help, rather than act out? I think I do understand a piece of Tom anyway; if I don't lose my boundaries, I can exploit my identification with him therapeutically. Now I think I know what happens in this family that makes their holding not good enough. At their best, they can operate from the depressive position demonstrating Winnicott's capacity for concern, but when their anxiety gets too high or the rage too intense, they regress to the paranoid-schizoid position and attack and project their hostility and libido. Of course, we all do that and the dialectic between the depressive and paranoid-schizoid positions enriches our experience* [Gabbard 1996, Scharff 1992]. *But there is too much paranoid-schizoid functioning in the Baker family. At times they fragment and regress further to Ogden's* [1986] *autistic-contiguous position. The Bakers need help augmenting their capacity to function in the depressive position*; to Dad): Mr. Baker, any more thoughts about this drawing?

FATHER: I always said my wife had a big mouth. But it bothers me that Sam sees me as all fist. I got a heart too, you know. Hey, doc, what's the kid so anxious about? Like I told you, he's got it made except for the grass.

MOM: Sam, you drew yourself like a baby. You're kind of lost, too.

SAM: Who'd want to grow up in this family?

OBJECT RELATIONS THERAPIST: I don't understand that. Do you mean it feels better to be a baby?

SAM: Naw, I just meant I don't want to be like him (sticks his tongue out at Tom).

OBJECT RELATIONS THERAPIST: Tom, what's it like to have a dad with such big fists?

TOM: Scary, man, scary. He's violent.

FATHER: Don't scapegoat me, you asshole.

OBJECT RELATIONS THERAPIST: You need to be angry at each other.

MOM: Yeah, they're always fighting.

OBJECT RELATIONS THERAPIST (to Father): I think you see a part of yourself you don't like in Tom, and that infuriates you.

FATHER: Yeah, he's the asshole I used to be. I don't like to think about what a punk, total-loss kid I was.

TOM: Dad, I'm not you. I don't know how to be you. You make money. People respect you. You can go to a party and nurse a beer all night.

OBJECT RELATIONS THERAPIST (to Father): That punk kid's still a part of you. You must have had it pretty rough. Can you feel any compassion for him?

FATHER: No, he's just a loser.

OBJECT RELATIONS THERAPIST: Seeing him in Tom infuriates you.

FATHER: I get it. You want me to lay off him.

OBJECT RELATIONS THERAPIST: I wonder if you also see something of your drunken father in Tom and then you really hate him.

FATHER (looks shook, even shattered. His hands shake): Christ, you're right. I'm afraid of Tom when he's stoned out of his mind, and I ain't afraid of anything. I don't like admitting that.

OBJECT RELATIONS THERAPIST: So you're afraid of each other.

TOM: I'm not afraid. (Hesitates.) Shit, yes I am.

OBJECT RELATIONS THERAPIST (to Tom): I think you're sitting on so much rage you're afraid you're going to explode, so you tranquilize your rage with pot, run away from it, or put it on your dad. The way you do that is to provoke him until he is in a rage, which isn't too hard to do. And then your rage, which you can't handle, is in him and not you, and you can run away from it. You can't run away from the rage inside, but if you put it on him or in him, it's outside you and you can deal with it. Besides, having Dad foaming gives you a reason to get high and you want to do that for other reasons, including the fact that you're hooked. So each of you puts a part of yourself into the other because it's easier than having the rage inside for Tom and the hurt, confused, wild child within for Dad. Mr. Baker, in a funny way, except it isn't funny, you need Tom to stay a stoned, hurt, lost kid, although I know that another part of you really and sincerely wants him to get clean, to protect you from feeling the sorrow and pain inside you.

TOM: Dad, I need you. I know you love me, but I can't get close to you. You're too strong.

OBJECT RELATIONS THERAPIST: And frightening.

TOM (weeps).

MOTHER (rises to comfort him).

OBJECT RELATIONS THERAPIST (gently): No, Mother, this is man's stuff. Don't get between them. You're afraid to let your husband be emotional, to be a wimp like your father. You need him to be "strong," so you rush in, and Tom and Dad never make contact.

MOTHER (sits on her hands): You're right. That's why I love Rob, he's so masculine. I'm the boss, but that doesn't make him a wimp.

FATHER AND TOM (talk to each other intensely but not audibly).

FATHER (embraces Tom): So you have to stop. I don't want you to die like my Dad.

Once again, our object relations therapist interprets very early in treatment, which is somewhat atypical for this school. His long interpretation to Tom and Dad is an interpretation of mutual projective identification. It results in a strengthening of the contextual transference, since both Tom and his father feel understood without being judged in spite of the fact that the content of the interpretation is painful and anxiety provoking. Following the interpretation, Tom and Dad and later Mom move from a paranoid-schizoid stance to a depressive one. As the therapist "holds" the family, the family becomes better able to hold Tom. There is little focal transference as we would expect in this first session, but there may be intimations and precursors of it manifest in some of the comments family members make to the object relationist. Note the extensive use the object relations therapist makes of his countertransference. He also wonders if he was somehow represented in Sam's drawing or in the family's associations to it. Although nothing surfaced, he wondered if the doubled maternal figure, which at a manifest level served to make Mom a relatively benign mascot or pet, might also be a representation of him, reflecting both Sam's fear of him as a toothed beast and his mastery of that fear through the diminutive nature of the representation. All of this is too speculative to be of any use, yet at some level the therapist must be represented in the drawing.

Our object relations therapist is pulling for more central ego functioning so the family can get on with the task of helping Tom achieve sobriety rather than functioning predominantly on the "basic assumption" level (Bion 1961; cf. Chapter 1). But that doesn't mean that split-off internal objects and object relations are not constantly being enacted by the Bakers. Sam's drawing makes crystal clear Mother's ready availability for projection of both rejecting and exciting objects by all of the Bakers. Additionally, their antilibidinal egos suppress their libidinal egos' exciting objects. Another way of understanding this is to say that both boys repress their oedipal yearnings for Mother, and convert her into a witch-like rejecting object to avoid dealing with those yearnings. Given Father's rageful jealousy, which Mom continually provokes, the boys' avoidance/repression of oedipal yearnings is entirely rational. Her personality, style, and internal world make this easy. One wonders what Mother's early object relations were like and what sort of relationship she had with her infant sons.

Tom uses marijuana to augment the repression of his antilibidinal ego at the same time that it allows some expression of his libidinal wishes/fantasies/drives. Our object relations therapist has partially interpreted this to him. Pot is also an ideal exciting-rejecting object for him, ideal here used not in Fairbairn's sense but ironically. It tantalizes, excites, and then tranquilizes that excitement before it becomes too dangerous, giving marijuana a power and allure hard to find in this world. It has multiple hooks which fit all too well Tom's internal objects. Similarly, Tom's smoking pot expresses aggression and quells and quiets it at the same time. In the long run, and by now the long run is not very long for Tom, marijuana turns into the rejecting object, giving him a pseudo-opportunity to work through his relationship to his "bad" rejecting objects as his smoking punishes him in myriad ways, including the castration of not being able to function. Thus his marijuana smoking simultaneously permits some expression of forbidden libidinal and aggressive wishes, and punishes him for having those wishes. Such simultaneous gratification of id and superego, or in Fairbairn's terms of libidinal and antilibidinal aspects of ego, is hard to find in this world. It is all too good a deal. This makes it extraordinarily difficult for Tom to achieve abstinence.

Dynamic therapists of ego and self-psychological schools would understand Tom's relationship with pot as fusion with the symbiotic mother, and as a selfobject with which Tom has both mirror and idealizing transferences, and interpret it so. The rampant, multiple mirror transferences and the narcissistic rage consequent upon the failure to mirror adequately, so characteristic of this family, are also interpretable. Our object relations therapist, unless he is unusually doctrinaire, would have no difficulty with these alternate conceptualizations. Interpretation along ego and self-psychological lines might be quite useful, even mutative. Mutatis mutandis, Sam's drawing would be interpreted differently by these schools. The dragon, orally ingestive mother would be seen as a wish fantasy by an ego psychologist, and indeed the anger, the fighting, and Tom's substance abuse could all be accurately interpreted as a defense against active and passive oral incorporative wishes and perhaps more fundamentally, a defense against merger/symbiotic wishes, which are of course enacted even as they are defended against by Tom's pot smoking.

All of this will be fodder for the object relations therapist's interpretive mill in future sessions. He will also encourage participation in supportive and structuring therapeutic activities such as twelve–step meetings for both Tom and his family (Al-Anon for the parents, Al-Teen for Sam).

In this session, there was almost no interpretation or comment about the family's relationship to the therapist, although we have seen some of the therapist's thoughts about what might be going on in that area. We would anticipate such transference interpretation playing an increasing role as the object relations therapy proceeds.

The Bakers offered us no dreams. In dynamic family therapy, each of the family members associates to the dream and then associates to each of the others' associations. Generally speaking, dream interpretation is minimally useful in working with "actives," individually or in family sessions, however mutative it can be in working with the recovering. But there are exceptions.

Steve, a middle-aged safety engineer, came to therapy for depression. His presenting problem was writer's block. Since he was supposed to be writing safety reports for a nuclear facility, this was of some salience. Drinking was never mentioned. After several months, he reported the following dream.

"I was in my underpants. They were on backward and inside out. They had shit stains on them. I was afraid people would see me."

The patient, who had significant anal conflicts and who remembered excitingly showing his mother his feces appropriately evacuated into the potty and failing to elicit her interest, a traumatic disappointment, was certainly anally exhibitionistic. It was not without significance that he could not "produce" on the job. He associated desultorily and neither of us was able to "do" much with the dream. The session went elsewhere; then, just as we were about to "end," Steve suddenly snapped his fingers and said, "I know what that dream was about. I got shit-faced last night." In dreaming the dream and telling it, Steve "told" me about his alcoholism. More importantly, he told himself that he had a drinking problem.

Classical analysts spoke of regression to anality or orality as a defense against genital (oedipal) conflicts. We don't hear much about regression as a defense these days. Yet it is often a dynamic in addiction. Perhaps, Twelve–Step intuitively speaks to the addict's developmental level in its injunction to "become clean and dry." Steve's interesting oral-anal condensation in being "shit-faced" presaged our understanding of his drinking as, among other things, a defense against oedipal conflict after he achieved sobriety. Similarly, Tom's pot addiction served as a regressive defense against genital conflict.

SUBSTANCE ABUSE APPROACH

The substance abuse therapist would be likely to incorporate elements of all of the schools in his/her treatment, yet would keep the focus on the substance abuse in a way none of the schools does. He or she might also wonder about Tom's using some of the object relations therapist's interpretations as rationalizations for his continual use in somewhat the same way as the kids in "Dear Officer Krupke" in *West Side Story* rationalized their delinquencies, in Tom's case, "I'm so anxious I have to get high." I think in a real session, the object relations therapist would have done all he could to prevent that by saying, "Tom, I know you smoke to control your anxiety, but there are other ways to reduce anxiety and I can help you learn them." That moves him away from the neutrality of the object relations school into a more active, didactic stance.

Although most dynamic therapists would modify their technique in a didactic direction if they are working with a teenage addict, there is some conflict here which would not exist for a substance abuse therapist. Tom and his family have had a great deal of treatment, including Tom's extended stay in a therapeutic community, which doesn't give our substance abuse therapist his usual scope. Such typical interventions as exposition of the disease model of addiction, explanation of and referral to Twelve–Step program meetings, making the family aware of their enabling, and giving the family members an opportunity to express and work through their feelings of shame, rage, and guilt, enlisted by and directed toward the substance abuser, have been repeatedly made. That doesn't mean that all of that doesn't need to be done again. Given the power of resistance and denial and of the need for working through, reiteration is certainly in order, yet this family is not a "virgin" and none of this has worked before. Perhaps, the substance abuse therapist needs to do something different or at least something additional. As with all of our therapists, the substance abuse therapist listens very carefully, and he asks some characteristic questions.

SUBSTANCE ABUSE THERAPIST: I need to know a lot more about Tom's treatment and your treatment as a family as well. (The Bakers detail the therapists, the programs, the experiences they have had.)

SUBSTANCE ABUSE THERAPIST: Did anything help?

DAD: Only the TC, but it didn't last.

SUBSTANCE ABUSE THERAPIST: Tom?

TOM: I hated the TC. They shaved my head and made me wear stupid signs.

SUBSTANCE ABUSE THERAPIST: They used shame as a therapeutic tool.

TOM: Well, I didn't feel shame. I felt rage.

SUBSTANCE ABUSE THERAPIST: And you started smoking again to get back at them.

TOM: You're damn right.

SUBSTANCE ABUSE THERAPIST: That's pretty stupid, isn't it?

TOM: Yeah. I know that.

SUBSTANCE ABUSE THERAPIST: And to get back at your parents for putting you there.

TOM: Yeah.

SUBSTANCE ABUSE THERAPIST (to all): Do you know addiction is a disease?

BAKERS: Yeah.

SUBSTANCE ABUSE THERAPIST: Tell me what you know.

BAKERS (demonstrate a good collective and individual understanding of the disease concept of addiction).

SUBSTANCE ABUSE THERAPIST: Tom, if you really believe addiction is a disease, then you know that you have lost control, and if you continue to smoke, you're going to go down the tubes.

TOM: Yeah, I know.

SUBSTANCE ABUSE THERAPIST: Your smoking is like getting back at somebody by giving yourself cancer.

The substance abuse therapist is concentrating on the identified patient, yet he involves the family. They are seen as part of the solution, not part of the problem. For the moment, their pain and rage is ignored or acknowledged but not dealt with. In this style of family therapy, they will have ample opportunity to deal with their issues after Tom gets "clean"; right now, those issues are put aside. Of course, enlisting them as helpers raises their self-esteem and generally strengthens them.

The substance abuse therapist takes Tom through his experience in the TC in considerable detail and elicits the information that it was not altogether a negative experience for Tom. In particular, Tom pleasurably bonded with some of his fellow TC-ers. To say that he made friends is perhaps saying too much, but his ties however transitory were important to him. It also became clear that Tom found the rigid structure of the TC helpful, however much he hated the highly questionable therapeutic methods of that TC. This argues that firmness would be helpful for him.

SUBSTANCE ABUSE THERAPIST: I want to hear from all of you and from Tom himself just how he got into drugs and what his relationship to drugs has been over the years.

The taking of a painstakingly detailed drug history, bolstered by many questions from the substance abuse therapist, constitutes both a cooperative effort of the family and therapist and a vital source of information. It differs from the detailed history-taking of the genogram drawing intergenerationalist in that it concentrates on Tom's drug history. As Tom's drug history unfolded, it became clear that Tom was enacting a dismally familiar story. The marginal kid, always the outsider, academically pushed by his upwardly mobile parents, yet with scant academic skills and limited potential. (The therapist wondered about learning disability and/or attention deficit disorder, even possibly hyperactivity-attention deficit disorder, common comorbidities with substance abuse and the possibility of remediating/treating them.) This marginal kid finds pot, acceptance, even leadership, and an easy escape from self-esteem–deflating activities all at once at age 13. It was love at first sight. Within a year, Tom was trapped, incorrigibly identified with what he and his parents call the "scumbag crowd," hopelessly behind in school, and completely scorned by the college-bound crowd. There was no way back. The rest followed as the night the day, three years of progressive decline, rageful arguments at home, trouble in school, eventuating in around-the-clock pot smoking, Tom's collapse, and his entry into the TC.

For all his hatred of it, the TC had possibly saved Tom's life. Whatever its merits, discharge planning doesn't seem to have been one of the TC's strengths. Tom's reentry into school with which he could not cope socially or academically left him with no place to go except back to the scumbag crowd and he quickly relapsed. Angry at his parents for putting him into an impossible situation, furious at being pressured into the TC, retaliating against the TC, finding acceptance and self-esteem in smoking and dealing (a further step down the addictive staircase), Tom was in deep shit, caught up in the addictive cycle and going nowhere but down. The family's intervention in bringing Tom to the session may be literally lifesaving for him, and from this substance abuse point of view, the family's dynamics are irrelevant, at least for now. As a committed subscriber to the disease model, our substance abuse therapist sees no possibility of Tom becoming a "social smoker." He is an addict, and according to the disease model, his disease will progress, or should I say retrogress, and he has lost control in the sense that he cannot regulate his substance use. His only option is abstinence. The fact that his father can sip an occasional beer in spite of his youthful history of alcohol abuse is a pernicious model for Tom. He clearly cannot do what his father has been able to do. In the course of this history-taking, it also became clear that Father is functionally illiterate and deeply ashamed of it, in spite of his financial success as a skilled craftsman.

Equipped with this knowledge, this detailed history of Tom's drug use and treatment, and remembering Tom's pleading to leave school early in the session, the substance abuse therapist made a dramatic, early move, intervening in a directive way with the Bakers. Further, sensing Tom's unconscious or barely conscious belief that he, like his father, could recover, join the union, and live happily ever after whenever he wanted to, so he didn't need to stop smoking pot, the substance abuse therapist wove a firm repudiation of this belief into his interventions.

SUBSTANCE ABUSE THERAPIST: Tom, I'll make a deal with you. You want to drop out of school but you can't without your parents' permission. I'll help you get that permission.

MOTHER/FATHER: Over my dead body.

SUBSTANCE ABUSE THERAPIST: If you agree to get a job, to go to Twelve–Step meetings, and to stop smoking grass.

SAM: He's too dumb for school anyway. I get A's.

TOM (to Sam): Shut up.

SUBSTANCE ABUSE THERAPIST: Will you do it?

TOM (remains silent).

SUBSTANCE ABUSE THERAPIST: You think you can do anything you want, stay stoned right around the clock, then get clean when you're ready, and your old man will get you a job in the union, and you'll be just fine. I think your family believes that at some level, too, though they don't know it. It isn't true. The longer you smoke, the sicker you will get, and there may be no turning back. Or you'll have so much catch-up to do that you'll be overwhelmed and really screwed. Each day you smoke, you get sicker. How about a deal? I'll help you get your father's permission. We can work together in therapy and you'll be out of an impossible situation.

TOM (screams): Okay! Okay! Just get them to agree.

MOTHER/FATHER: No!

SUBSTANCE ABUSE THERAPIST (to parents): I know it breaks your heart to have Tom drop out of school, but you *have* to let him. He just *can't* do it. He's too far behind academically. The straight kids won't accept him and he has no place to go except back to the scumbags, and that means being stoned. I know how much you love Tom, and I know you'll do this for him. He can get a high school equivalency (G.E.D.) at night when he's in stable recovery. I'll get him into the G.E.D. program when he's ready.

MOTHER (cries).

FATHER: Okay, but he's got to get a job.

MOTHER: I can get him a job in the warehouse where I work.

TOM: I'll take it.

Notice how strongly our substance abuse therapist speaks. "You *have* to let him," and how much responsibility he takes for Tom's life. Many, perhaps most, therapists wouldn't be comfortable with this or see their role as being directive in this way. The therapist may be wrong, dropping out could be a disaster for Tom, but the substance abuse therapist senses that the present situation is hopeless, and there is nothing to lose by taking such a bold step. It is highly doubtful that Tom would be allowed to continue in school for very long in any case. Notice also how direct he is with Tom, and simultaneously how unashamedly manipulative he is in forging an alliance with Tom. He is similarly manipulative with the parents, appealing to both their love and their guilt. All he needs now is closure.

SUBSTANCE ABUSE THERAPIST: I'll see Tom individually for two weeks and then we will have another family session. Okay, Tom? (Tom nods.) And we will keep that format—two sessions with

Tom and then a family session. Tom has absolute confidentiality, unless his life is in danger, so he can be free to say anything here.

I find this format of several individual sessions alternating with a family session extremely useful in treating adolescent substance abusers.

SUBSTANCE ABUSE THERAPIST: I try to respect everyone else's confidentiality, but since we will be meeting as a family, it is less of an issue and Tom is the primary patient. I'll see you next week, Tom.

As therapy proceeds, the substance abuse therapist will engage the Bakers to give them an opportunity to express their feelings about Tom's addiction and to give them some support. The substance abuse therapist will probably be especially supportive of Sam, who, as a lost child, needs bringing out, but for now Tom is the primary patient and the family's role ancillary to his recovery.

Each of the therapeutic approaches—communications/strategic, structural, intergenerational-systemic, experiential, behavioral, object relations/dynamic and substance abuse—has its place in working with addicted families and families with addiction. If I were not so fond of felines, I might say, "There is more than one way to skin a cat." Instead I will say, "There are more ways than one to hang people."

Couples

C ouple therapy plays a large role in addiction treatment. The most common couple therapy scenario involves the "active"(ly using) partner being coerced into treatment by the sober partner. This is a tricky one. My experience is that in most cases, the user agrees to treatment to pacify or mollify the nonuser. Although many patients who enter treatment under a mandate of one sort or another—court referral after driving while intoxicated (DWI), or an employee assistance program (EAP) making treatment a condition of continued employment, or a spouse making treatment a condition of continuing the marriage—achieve stable sobriety, and research shows no difference in treatment outcome for voluntary and involuntary patients in a variety of programs, the resistance here is formidable.

Some addictions therapists maintain that every patient is "mandated," even if the mandate is not readily discernible to patient or therapist. Nevertheless, I have found that this paradigm rarely works. The sober partner usually gets to express a great deal of anger and outrage, which may (or may not) in itself be helpful, even if it changes nothing, while the user plays various games. A frequent outcome of this scenario is for the drinker/drugger to leave treatment after a few sessions and for the codependent to become a patient in individual therapy.

It is well to remember that marriage to an addict does not necessarily mean codependence. People get into and stay in such relationships for a wide variety of reasons, ranging from ignorance to economic necessity to unconscious reenactment. I would reserve *codependency* for the latter. I am reluctant to undertake couples treatment in which one partner continues to drink or drug if that use is seriously disabling. Unless the user makes a commitment to sobriety and has a realistic plan to achieve that goal, I would disengage, offering individual therapy and/or a referral. In cases where the alcohol/drug use is less disabling, I feel differently and will work with the couple for more extended periods, the goal being to make manifest the role the use plays in the relationship and the role the relationship plays in the use. In a surprisingly high number of cases, the "sober" partner turns out to have a substance abuse problem of his or her own.

Generally more fruitful is work in which one or both partners are in recovery. Given the extremely high rate of divorce in recovering couples, exploration of the nature of the bond and the role substance use plays in it is always in order. In cases in which one addicted partner gets sober while the other continues to use, divorce often makes perfect sense. In fact, remaining in such a relationship is far more pathological. So couples work involves every permutation of sobriety and use possible: active–sober, active–active, recovering–active, recovering–no substance use problem, and recovering–recovering. It is well to remember in working with recovering persons that they have been "reborn." They are substantially and truly different in sobriety, and this can be a highly dissonant experience for both the recovering person and the spouse.

The cases that follow as well as the cases in Chapter 6 are composites or otherwise altered so that although inspired by real people in treatment, they are not those real people. Rather, somewhat like characters in a novel, they are drawn from multiple sources, sometimes including aspects of myself. I hope that this does not lessen their verisimilitude or reduce their heuristic value.

MEGACREEP

"Casey, do you know what you are? You're a megacreep," said Amy. It was a label that stuck; forever after I thought of him as "mega-creepee," Amy's semihumorous diminutive which she invoked when she wasn't raging at him.

The case seemed to have no relation to substance abuse. They had been referred by Amy's analyst because of her near suicidal depression furthered by Casey's threat to leave her for another woman. He expressed a willingness to try to work things out, and she jumped at it. Stuck in a sort of developmental arrest, they were fortyish hippies perpetuating the 1960s in the 1980s. Drug use was so ego-syntonic that it never occurred to either that Casey's frequent (I came to suspect daily) cocaine sprees had anything to do with their problems. Nor did they consider their "recreational" pot smoking in any way problematic. It wasn't even denial in the usual sense. Rather it was that substance abuse was not a category extant in either of their cognitive maps. Both maintained that they were perfectly functional people, indeed vastly superior people who had some marital difficulties. They weren't defensively insistent upon it; it was simply their (conscious) experience of themselves.

Amy's pot smoking may indeed have been "recreational" and innocuous. I was never quite sure, but given her many borderline traits and probably borderline character structure, I had deep concerns that like so many borderlines, she would find the hazy soothingness of marijuana so seductive and so potent in quelling her ego-dystonic, intensely uncomfortable rage that she would become addicted to it. She had, however, been smoking for 25 years without clearly crossing the line into addiction. Perhaps, in *DSM-IV* terms, she was a substance abusing rather than a substance-dependent person. Having a history of psychiatric difficulties dating back to several hospitalizations in adolescence, she had "stabilized" after her marriage to Casey. A tempestuous idyll, the liaison had provided just the right mixture of stimulation and pacification without threatening too much intimacy.

Now Amy was the mother of pubescent and adolescent daughters, and her husband lauded her parenting, describing Amy as "a great mother." His standards of adequate parenting notwithstanding, this may have been true, or at least true when the children were younger and their demands less emotionally stressing. Amy was quiet when not raging and extremely attractive in a stylized way. She emanated sensuality and sexiness without ever being in poor taste, and one of her most painful injuries was Casey's now long-standing sexual rejection. She had verve and a sense of humor, evidenced in the comment that the surgery she faced for a reputedly benign brain tumor would mean, "operating on where I hang out." Not exactly a philosopher of the self, her intuitive neuro-hermeneutics were surprisingly on target. I thought her way of talking about her imminent surgery, which in the event turned out well, was courageous. She was also capable of totally irrational acting out, particularly when her rage took over. She seemed to thrive on the storminess of their relationship, which was already a long-established pattern when Casey insisted that they each sleep with other people the night before their marriage. He cheated on her during their honeymoon, but didn't try to inveigle her into "swinging," as he had in their prenuptial ritual. I felt some envy of their "freedom." What she couldn't stand was rejection and abandonment.

Control was of transcendent importance to both. They engaged in mutual control games and "controlled" their substance use. To the end of treatment, Amy and Casey both insisted that they had control of their marijuana and cocaine use. Of course, that's what they all say. I was probably gullible, which given my experience in such matters says something about their persuasiveness, especially Casey's, and my need to embrace their myth, a need the source of which I never identified in my sporadic efforts at self analysis during the course of their treatment. In any case, I almost bought that myth.

If Amy was a borderline charmer, Casey was a narcissistic, perhaps sociopathic, one. As grandiose as she was modest, he poured out a long litany of the famous people he had known, the trips (chemical and geographic) they had taken, the fantastic hotels they had stayed in. A rock music producer with a loft in Soho, he evidenced the taste of a millionaire, their post-hippie style notwithstanding, although it was far from clear that he had a pot to piss in. I figured out fairly early that whatever he said he was, he was a con man, but something about him made me want to be conned. In short, I was seduced by the "glamour" of his lifestyle and wanted the vicarious pleasure of participating in it. It turned out to be an expensive pleasure since he stiffed me. I was more angry at myself than at him.

It was difficult to keep Casey on track. What he wanted to do was to rave about his accomplishments, his voracious taste for art, his appeal to women. "I start my day with Bach, go on to the Stones, then Messiaen, then rap, then Sessions, then the Dead. I have to have music. I have a musical soul. I live for art." He was in fact physically unprepossessing. Overweight, pasty, uneven smile. Yet he, like his wife, had charm. According to Amy, he was impotent with her on the rare occasions he agreed to try. I wondered if he was impotent with all of them.

I thought that he had come to therapy to get Amy off his back. She lived in the country in an expensive home provided by her wealthy "witch mother," a description they agreed on although they had no trouble taking her money. Periodically, Amy would descend on his love nest with, literally, a hatchet to break down the door, and Casey would go down the fire escape in what seemed a pretty good imitation of a Marx Brothers movie. They both laughed when describing their escapades. Their sometimes near-violent interaction seemed to provide some relief from the underlying tension inside each. But that didn't last long and the cycle repeated. Once again I wondered why Casey was there. Partly to placate Amy, but I also came to believe that he had a remnant of real feeling for her and couldn't abandon her while she was facing possibly disabling or even fatal surgery. Such abandonment was also incongruent with his self-image and his "persona"—to rip off creditors and his mother-in-law was hip; to appear a coward by leaving his ill wife would hurt his public image and was incongruent with his self-image.

Casey, the son of a brutal father and a passive mother, came from bitter poverty. He had run away in his early teens, hitchhiked across the country and wound up a homosexual prostitute on the LA

"Strip." Eventually making the "creative scene," he had had some early successes in the rock music world including producing a successful play, but he had been down on his luck for a long time. He felt infinitely entitled by his deprivations, and compulsively reiterated how he cringed whenever anyone made an unexpected move in anticipation of his father's crushing blows. Blows there had been, and Casey's fears were real enough, yet he shamelessly used the cringing routine to justify whatever outrage he was into at the moment.

Casey discovered cocaine at a young age and it was love at first sight. Sensing the abyss beneath that he could return to any time, and seeing so many around him destroyed by drugs, he early hedged his use by snorting only, not getting high when he was working, and not dealing unless he was flat broke and without prospects. He had kept his control, and unlike so many of his friends, remained the "master" rather than the slave of cocaine. Or at least so he said.

There was another reason Casey had returned to Amy to work things out. He was having trouble with his current girlfriend.

CASEY (to Amy): I couldn't leave the kids. And I couldn't have them with me once she started dancing bottomless.

AMY: Bottomless? You knew she was a topless dancer.

CASEY: I didn't mind that, but then she got a job in a joint where she had to go bottomless and sit on men's laps.

AMY: She's a whore, megacreep, and you're a pimp. You were living off her.

CASEY: Fuck you. You know I'm promoting a new disk, a million dollar proposition. What a contract. Next week I fly to Hong Kong and then Paris to promote it. Why would I take Betty's money? I just don't like bottomless.

AMY: Oh, Casey. Only you would draw the line at bottomless. I love you, Megacreepee.

CASEY (laughs): Topless straight up; bottomless it's over. (They both giggle.)

AMY: So you're coming back.

CASEY: I didn't say that. Maybe after Hong Kong.

I thought, truly a marriage made in purgatory, or maybe a narcissist and a borderline could make each other happy.

The sessions went nowhere. There was screaming. There was raging. There was giggling. There was crying. I was surprised at how much Casey wept, but he was a slouch compared to Amy. If his emotion was shallow, I thought it real. Hers was truly deep, desperate yet histrionic. More and more I heard about getting high. Getting high was simply a part of their lives. They thought it was part of the solution; I increasingly thought it was part of the problem. I bided my time, making comments on their reenactments of their conflicts with their families of origin. My attempts at interpretation fell on deaf ears. They were totally ignored. My attempts at pacification were more successful, lowering the volume and reducing their anxiety and rage. Typically my comments took the form of commenting to the effect that each was furious (and/or deeply hurt) because the other said or did something that attacked the other's self-esteem. I commented on their respective vulnerabilities and took a self psychological approach, offering interpretations around threats of fragmentation and defenses against it. I repeatedly suggested that various of their behaviors, including their drug use, served to maintain cohesion and continuity, and pointed out how easily each could disorganize the other. This played better than my attempts at genetic and object relational interpretation.

They started treating each other less savagely. There was more giggling and occasional spontaneous expression of affection. Amy underwent her surgery and Casey was there for her. We resumed after her recovery, and things deteriorated. He was absent more on his world travels to promote the million dollar contract. He paid one of his daughter's prep school tuition with a bad check, which Amy's mother eventually covered after much humiliation for wife and daughter. He paid me with a check signed by "Bottomless." That put me in an untenable position. Clearly Casey was lying to Amy and I knew it. Should I spill the beans? Amy started paying me with her mother's checks. When later Casey was supposed to pay me with his own money, he disappeared. I asked Casey to see me privately and he did, maintaining that his ex-girlfriend was truly ex, but that she owed him money for cocaine and that was the money he had used to pay me. I didn't believe him, but decided to use the opportunity to focus on his cocaine use. I wondered if Casey's trips to "promote" his "disk" were in reality drug runs. I asked him. He laughed and said, "That's a good way to mold concrete—not for me. I'm too much of a coward." I, probably foolishly, believed him.

He moved back to his loft. Amy wept and pleaded in a couples session. He maintained that he needed privacy for "creative purposes." Shortly thereafter, Casey took his younger daughter to the loft. Whatever she reported to her mother resulted in Amy's visiting the loft. This time with an ax. She broke the door in; Casey broke an ankle jumping from the fire escape. Amy and Bottomless, who turned out to have the improbable name of Claire—Claires for me are prim and proper—assaulted each other verbally and physically, and after considerable slapping and hair pulling, began to commiserate with each other. They wept and embraced, had a drink together, and toasted "that bastard, Megacreep." In our next session, Amy hinted that there was something sexual between her and Claire. Casey looked sheepishly down at his cast, enjoying every moment of Amy's recitation of the "raid." I suggested that he got off on being a "bad boy."

In his individual sessions, I had insisted that Casey pay for his part of the therapy with his own money. He had agreed, but after a month, no money was forthcoming. I was more and more active in the individual sessions, focusing on Casey's cocaine use and how it kept him broke. When I made similar comments in the joint sessions, Amy showed not the slightest interest in my comments on the deleterious effects of cocaine on their relationship. They were sort of lovey-dovey after the raid, although Casey returned to the now empty loft.

I talked more and more about cocaine, and how it fed Casey's grandiosity. I also spoke once again of how it kept him broke. He spoke of how he lived for art. Amy had stopped clinging and begging for him to stay; he became increasingly depressed. I said I could not continue without payment. Amy offered to pay with her mother's check, which I (probably foolishly) refused. Casey failed several sessions. I told them we couldn't continue unless Casey attended Narcotics Anonymous (NA) or proposed another plan to deal with his habit.

They both thought that quaint, but I could see the fear behind Casey's flippancy. I never saw him again. Amy attended several more sessions, increasingly chipper.

Not long after termination, her analyst told me that she was going with an "East End redneck," as the sophisticated refer to the locals in the Hamptons, twenty years her junior. For the first time, I felt empathy for Megacreepee. My fantasy was that abandoned by both women, he would commit suicide. Aside from the sadistic pleasure inherent in my fantasy, it had all too much reality potential. The therapy had started with him riding high and her suicidal, unable to handle his abandonment; now he was, or so I thought, suicidal and she was riding high. Quite a seesaw. I was not sorry to be off the ride.

Later I wondered about my role in the whole crazy therapy. What was my countertransference? There was certainly voyeuristic pleasure; there was envy, there was contempt, there was judgment, there was sadism, there was masochistic submission and passivity on my part. How much was induced? How much was projective counter-identification? Casey and Amy were certainly exciting objects for me (they were also rejecting objects), activating my libidinal and anti-libidinal egos.

I wondered about the original external objects that had become my internal objects. My associations went to Asshole McGurk, actually Sonny McGurk, although everyone including my mother who almost never cursed called him Asshole. Asshole was the neighborhood delinquent, universally believed to be headed for the electric chair. A real bad actor. I was terrified of him, yet desperately yearned to participate in his escapades. I wanted to be a playmate of Asshole McGurk. He scorned me, and probably didn't know I was alive. In my relationship with Casey and Amy, I finally got to play with Asshole, and I thoroughly enjoyed it—among other feelings and reactions. I am sure that there are more primitive and salient exciting and rejecting objects in my past, but what I got in touch with was my relationship or desire for relationship with two wild Irishmen. Like Casey and Sonny, I wanted to be a bad boy and be admired for it.

258 ❖ COUPLE AND FAMILY THERAPY OF ADDICTION

Casey and Amy also took me back to my days in the East Village, replete with motorcycle and counterculture panache. Part of my antitherapeutic bond, my loss of objectivity, and my inability to set limits and maintain boundaries with Amy and Casey was driven by nostalgia. I wanted to be young again. I came to realize that I have all the stuff they have, albeit usually more under wraps, and that my ironic distance from them was a way of denying that. Could I have been more effective with them if I had been more aware of my countertransference and its enactment at the time? I don't know. There is only so much a therapist can do, and they were a tough nut indeed.

Working with deeply disturbed, acting out substance abusing couples is dangerous work. With the keenest self-awareness, it is all too easy to be caught up in the vortex and drowned in the maelstrom. At the end of my work with Casey and Amy, I had much more feeling for F. Scott Fitzgerald's Dick Diver, the psychiatrist driven mad by his patient in *Tender is the Night*. If you work with couples like Casey and Amy, and you will if you do much substance abuse work, be zealous for your own sanity, for it is truly in jeopardy.

Some months after our last session, I ran into Amy's analyst. She was ecstatic about my work with Amy and Casey. "You saved Amy's life. She would never have gotten through the separation without the couple sessions. How can I thank you? I was sure I was going to lose her." Go figure.

Casey's still flying around the world promoting God knows what. Some manic defenses, brief decompensations notwithstanding, go on forever.

The example of Casey and Amy was illustrative of some of the problems of working with couples in which both are actively using. Casey's cocaine use was highly contributive to their marital difficulties, while Amy's marijuana smoking, though certainly contributing, was not central to their difficulties. Our next couple, Tom and Sally, are illustrative of the vicissitudes of a marital relationship in sobriety.

THE PATHOLOGIZATION OF MALENESS

Sally, a compulsive workaholic alcoholism counselor, sent Tom, a blue-collar recovering alcoholic with seven years' sobriety, to therapy to be "fixed." He was alleged to be insensitive, inattentive, self-absorbed, indifferent to her feelings, and hostile. It quickly became clear that Tom didn't want to be fixed. Although he copped to having the traits Sally attributed to him (I thought insincerely), he said, "Things aren't nearly as bad as she says. I'm sorta like she says but I'm not all that bad . . . " He trailed off. Then no longer sounding like a small boy trying to talk his way out of being punished, he became assertive. "I really work the program. I do the steps, talk to my sponsor, go to a lot of meetings. What does she want? I don't need no counseling, and I don't want any, but I'll come to shut her up. I don't want no divorce."

I didn't know if it was true that he "didn't need no counseling," but by the end of the session, I was clear that working with him would be torture. I could try to mute his resentment by redefining myself as something other than a punitive father or schoolmaster, or I could interpret his transference, but my gut feeling was that it wasn't going to work. I empathized, indeed agreed, with his contention that it didn't make much sense to try to "fix" him if it was a relationship problem. I didn't want to struggle with his sullen, if understandable, resistance, somewhat masked by affability and an engaging smile. He struck me as a kind of concrete guy who wasn't going to respond to analytic interpretation, and he didn't really believe that there was any reason for his being there. Trying to convince him that I was an ally, not his enemy, might be possible, but I just wasn't into it. Instead I said, "Tom, this is a marital problem. It would make a lot more sense if Sally came too, and if we had couple sessions." He beamed. If I didn't feel up to dealing with his resistance, I should have quit while I was ahead. Sally made Tom look like a piece of cake.

It was with great reluctance that Sally agreed to participate in the couple sessions. Since she saw the problem as residing entirely in her husband, the only reason she could see for being there was to explain his deficiencies to me. She felt that she had already, so to speak, sent a note to the principal when she sent Tom to me; she could see little reason to come in person. But she was trapped by her own ideology. Being a counselor, and totally committed to openness, honesty, communication, free expression of feelings, the twelve steps, belief in a Higher Power, and onward and upward, she could hardly refuse. After a session or two, I wished she had. I'm just not a let-it-all-hang-out guy. Civility and tact are greatly underrated virtues these days, especially in relationships where it is alleged that complete openness is the only possible value. I, on the contrary, believe that there are things that are best not said. Such Sallyisms as, "Tom, you need to know what your impact on me is," and "I know you don't like to hear it, but I need to tell you—for both our sakes—that you are an insensitive" drove me up the wall. She talked "program" relentlessly when she wasn't therapizing. "Tom, if you worked your tenth step [the one about taking a daily moral inventory] harder, we wouldn't have these difficulties. You should do some anger work with Dr. Levin instead of taking it out on me." My repeated suggestion that she infantilized Tom and treated him like a patient fell on deaf ears. Tom alternated between variations on "Yes, dear," and anger. I couldn't see things going anywhere.

I was puzzled at Sally's huge professional success. She was an addictions counselor, without an advanced degree. She had a "cut-rate" business, working very long hours for low fees. I knew that she was esteemed, even loved by many, and I felt like an ingrate for disliking her since she referred paying patients "who could afford it" to me from time to time. She was a rabid Al-Anon member, and my association was to another recovering husband who referred to Al-Anon as "the church of the holy revenge."

Sally had many of the characteristics of the "true believer," a type that is anathema to me. I wondered if I shouldn't refer her since I genuinely disliked her. I have hated patients I worked with, but dislike has a different quality than hate. It is quieter but (for me) more enduring and less subject to revision. I wondered about my transference. My mother shared few of Sally's traits and none of her style; my wife is one of the least ideological of women, although strongly assertive of her and all women's rights. I couldn't quite figure out where I was coming from. My reaction couldn't be entirely objective. It did occur to me that I spent a great deal of my professional life listening to women complain about their husbands, and with the passing years I have become impatient with it, but that didn't quite account for my reaction.

After a dozen sessions, Sally discovered the "answer." "I've been discussing Tom with my friend, Muriel. She put me onto *Driven to Distraction*, a best-selling book on attention deficit disorder (ADD). Tom fits the rubric. He has every characteristic on the list. He is an adult ADD. He was a hyperactive kid who self-medicated with drugs. That fits too. Tom, you have to go on Ritalin." Tom replied, "I'm a program person. I don't want any drugs." That went back and forth for a while, including the few rounds of "If you love me, you'll do it for me" from her, and "Get off my back, you bitch!" from him. Ensuing sessions were less adversarial. ADD was like alcoholism in that a host of difficulties could be attributed to the DISEASE. Or as the Albert Ellis–inspired Rational Recovery (RR) movement would have it, the BEAST. This sort of attribution was ego-syntonic to both of them and took the focus off of personal fault. He weakened, and at least paid lip service to seeing a psychiatrist about Ritalin, although I took note that week after week the appointment wasn't made. They bonded, tensely and tentatively, around program talk, working the steps and the disease. I pointed out the resistance side of that (and was ignored), and found myself reflecting on the joys of cab driving and worm picking, relatively blissful previous occupations. I found that odd, since I believe that the disease model of addiction is highly heuristic and therapeutically powerful. Perhaps I was reacting to my exclusion.

Our peaceful interlude soon ended. Sally attacked Tom's resistance to actually doing anything about his alleged hyperactivity and attention deficit. I commented on their vicious cycle of Sally's attacks, his passive resistance, his growing anger, his deeply passive aggression culminating in an explosion followed by her threats of divorce. They acknowledged that I was right and that indeed this was their pattern, but showed scant interest in exploring its origins or in modifying it.

Things heated up. Sally returned to the attack in earnest. Now her focus was on her FEELINGS. Feelings, feelings, feelings, feelings, feelings. Like some other of my female patients, Sally apotheosized her feelings, making them, indeed demanding they be, objects of worship. I realized that she surfaced every bit of my latent misogyny. That realization made me uncomfortable. I restored my equilibrium by telling myself I was at least as much a misanthrope as a misogynist. Equal opportunity hating was more congruent with my self-image. No longer listening to Sally, my thoughts turned to Tom. Was he an adult ADD? I had my doubts. Was Tom a victim of the pathologizing of maleness in which high activity levels, physicality, high levels of aggression, and stimulus seeking are redefined as negative and pathological, setting up a secondary conflict that in turn may be self-medicated, leading to addiction? While feminists also complain about the pathologizing of femaleness, "feminine virtues" such as empathy, nurturance, and emotional sensitivity are increasingly seen as essential to "mental health." The sex role conflicts endemic to our rapidly changing culture affect men as well as women, engendering anxiety and insecurity, which predispose to addiction. It is possible that some men such as Tom find that their native endowments are now "dysfunctional," and that others, finding it beyond their capabilities to change, turn to drugs.

Tom was highly involved with AA, which takes some degree of persistence and concentration. He had worked the same difficult, dangerous, technically demanding job for twenty years. He seemed to be a limited, likable guy who was pretty content with his sobriety. Never much of a student, he described a childhood of roaming the woods and getting in minor scrapes. Like Huck Finn, he was always ready to "light out for the territories." While I found nothing pathological in his exploratory, adventurous, physically active childhood, Sally was convinced that he had ADD. She endlessly cited as evidence the fact that he didn't listen to her, particularly when she talked about her feelings. I wondered how Tom, who had worked with dangerous chemicals for years, could be alive if his attention was so deficient.

Despite my best efforts to get a dialogue going, Sally continued as an unremittingly critical monologist. Her main theme continued to be her feelings. She wasn't even talking to Tom anymore, rather she spoke to me. "He doesn't care about my feelings." I found my attention constantly wandering, exactly as Tom's was accused of doing.

Since I had come up with my pathologizing of maleness hypothesis, I felt less angry at her. It gave me a cognitive structure and some distance and objectivity. I also realized that I had been too passive in the sessions since Sally started her feelings monologue. My passivity was mostly driven by guilt because I disliked my patient. I was reluctant to be confrontational with her. I realized that I was inhibiting myself out of fear of losing control of my anger. My reaction was strikingly similar to her husband's—passive aggression. Now I was feeling less bored and angry and even feeling some empathy for Sally who must have worked those grueling hours, at least in part, to deaden the very feelings she worshiped. I said, "I doubt that the universe is much interested in your feelings, and I know that I am not." She exploded. "You call yourself a therapist? You bastard." Her attack went on for half an hour. Tom looked like he wanted to bolt the room, and I thought that he would. He didn't. When she finally stopped, red-faced, sweaty and exhausted like someone who has been exercising hard, I said, "Sally, nobody can empathize with your feelings when you use them as a club to beat them. Whatever Tom's difficulty in relating and responding, you drive him away and then you don't get the mirroring (a word she frequently used) you desperately want and demand it even harder, driving him even further away. That leaves you alone and desperate. All you can do is work to deaden your pain." Sally started sobbing, deep, body-heaving sobs. We were out of time, but I, contrary to my usual practice, let the session run ten minutes more.

The "breakthrough" didn't exactly revolutionize things, although it did allow for some renegotiation of their relationship. Sally became less demanding; Tom more responsive. I no longer heard threats of divorce. They terminated after another six sessions when Tom started a second job, which made scheduling impossible. This was partly resistance, but nothing could be done about it.

Tom, although he contributed his share to the marital difficulties, can be seen as a victim of the pathologization of maleness as he had been in his family of origin. His involvement with alcohol and drugs had given him a sense of male solidarity, acceptance, and belongingness that he had not otherwise found. His intense involvement with AA served the same emotional purpose.

Sally was paradoxically emotionally deadened. Her insistence on Tom's mirroring came from stringent emotional necessity. She needed him to confirm her aliveness. Alternately, she could be seen as having been driven by a wish/fear for symbiosis. The desperateness of the wish was evident in her demands, and the fears evident in her driving him (and me) away and in her compulsive work. That's all mother stuff, and I'm sure that she had plenty of father stuff going in her transference to husband and therapist, but we never got to that.

I came to realize that I had a powerful identification with Tom. I was a restless kid and would probably have been on Ritalin today. I'm just as glad I wasn't. I remember a grade school teacher who whacked my backside with a ruler when I was crawling on the floor, and doubtlessly some of my feelings about Sally originated in my feelings toward Miss Duncan. Each was determined to control male ADD, or what they perceived to be such. I, like Tom, liked to roam in the woods, to explore, to "light out for the territories." I still do.

Tom and Sally are still together, however happily or unhappily, and she continued to make occasional referrals until they moved to California. I'm not sure how much further progress they could have made, but I was as sorry to see them terminate as I had been to see them start.

Our next couple is illustrative of a very common paradigm, the drinking husband and the enraged or defeated or despairing wife. Most usually, the wife feels all three, consciously or unconsciously. The gender roles may be reversed, but not nearly as commonly since husbands tend to abandon alcoholic wives. Our couple is more difficult than most examples of the paradigm, yet they are not so atypical. As I have noted above, this is not a situation in which I have a high hit rate.

Sheila and Ted were referred by their internist, a man sensitized to the tragic concomitants of addiction by his brother's lifelong struggle with heroin, a struggle the brother lost a few years later. I was with Dr. C., a colleague with whom I had a fruitful collaboration, the night his brother died of an overdose. Dr. C. was in a wildly manic state, his speech pressured and almost incoherent as he tried to show off his rudimentary Japanese ordering a meal in a restaurant. Shortly thereafter, he closed his office and went into the military service. Sadly, he could not save his brother as he had saved many others from their addictions.

SHEILA AND TED: CONTROL GAMES

Sheila is a powerful woman, large, broad shouldered, assertive if not aggressive. She is take-charge. I thought she would make a respectable guard or tackle on a football team. Ted is also large; in fact, obese. He too radiates authority, but in his case, the authority is but a shadow of his former self. In the first session, it rapidly turned to truculence. He has made a lot of money in the construction business, but is no longer able to work, although he makes a show of trying. Much of the money was made working in Third World countries, so the Ns have been separated much of their married life, a state of affairs pleasing to both of them, if for disparate reasons.

Sheila is at the peak of her professional career. She is head of the science department at the high school. She runs it well and with an iron hand. She is also one of the best teachers in the school. Sheila is a supermom guiding her two teenaged children through the pitfalls of adolescence with uncanny prescience. She is an unhappy woman, however, or at least she says so all the time. Ted hasn't drawn a sober breath for years. Sheila has a few feelings about her marriage that she isn't reluctant to share.

"My sister is married to God and I am married to *him*. She sure has a better deal. I thought it was sad when she joined the convent. If I had only known, I would be there too. I am sure that God does not drink. Ted does. St. Paul said it was better to marry than to burn. Clearly it is better not to marry at all. If I did choose to marry because I mistakenly thought I needed to satisfy my natural needs, why did I have to marry Ted? Why him? He can't even keep the check-book straight. I have to write all the checks and take care of all the bills. A man should take care of money matters, but I have to do it all. If I give him too much money, he drinks. He is always complaining that his allowance is too low. Too low indeed. He drinks every cent of it. The last time he was in the hospital, I found out that Ted was taking money from the business, or what's left of it, and drinking that. If he goes off his Antabuse again, I will move to have him committed. Ted still thinks that he has rights as a father. Over my dead body. He only corrupts their innocent souls. I and I alone guide and discipline the children until he takes the pledge and lives up to it. I am God's representative in this home. I say that with all humility. If I didn't have to take charge, I wouldn't, but as long as I do things will be done as the Lord would want it. Drunkenness is ungodly. It is the sin of gluttony. Ted is a glutton. Ted is a fool. Ted is an incompetent. It is a good thing that I earn good money for I have no idea how long it—I suppose I should say he—can continue in the business. If he drinks on top of his Antabuse again, it may be the end. So be it, if that is God's will. It would be a release for all of us. Ted would have a chance for salvation if he was in purgatory. He has none here. I am being punished for marrying for sensual fulfillment. Thank God there is no more of that. Ted can't be allowed to do anything. I even have to run the business, although I know very little about it. Fortunately, I am highly intelligent. He was good at making money and I will make sure that we keep what we have. I don't believe that he will be good at making money or at anything else again. God in his wisdom has given me the penance of running this house and I will carry my cross. When Ted's liver gives out, which cannot be very much longer, the children and I will be well provided for. Thank God I had the foresight to make Ted take out more life insurance before his liver enzymes gave him away. Perhaps he will do better when he leaves the hospital this time, but I do not think so. I will do my duty and do what I must as long as the Lord gives me strength."

I said, "Hospital?" Sheila said, "Yes, I expect him to go back to rehab. That's why I brought him here. You can make the arrangements and see that he goes."

I had few doubts that a stay in rehab might be lifesaving for Ted, my friend the internist having told me of his incipient cirrhosis, but that wasn't the immediate issue. Sheila's attempt to control him and me was. As the session progressed, it became clear that her need for omnipotent control was characterological and had long preceded Ted's current collapse. Although she takes Ted to doctors and therapists and tries to put him in hospitals and rehabs, she doesn't really want him to recover. She doesn't know that and honestly believes she wants Ted to get sober. Many spouses of long-addicted mates wish for their deaths.

A classic Hero, Sheila is the daughter of an alcoholic and her death wishes for Ted are partly transferential. Ted on his part does wish to live, largely in order to spite her, but not enough to stop drinking. All in all, not a hopeful case. In a desperate attempt to hold onto some self-esteem, Ted talks obsessively about his achievements as a member of the school board—which I suppose also gives him some sort of one-upmanship over his schoolteacher wife—the meetings of which he is inevitably sober for. Sheila shouts this down with the utmost contempt. I was at a loss as to where to go or what to do. Clearly Ted is very sick, in the last stages of alcoholism, and his chances of recovery are poor. But it could happen. If it does, Ted and Sheila will almost certainly separate. Sheila exhibited the need to control, writ large. She is an extreme case, but a common one.

I have met quite a few Sheilas. In working with Sheila, a Hasidic story about a guilt-ridden rich man who goes to the Rebbe for advice, comes to mind. The rich man wants to fast and practice all sorts of austerities. He asks the Rebbe for guideposts for living an ascetic life. The Rebbe replies, "Na, na, no austerities. I want you to eat cakes and drink sweet wine." "What?" says the rich man. "Why don't you want me to fast?" "If you fast, the poor will go hungry too. You will be so certain of your piety that you will see no reason to give to charity. On the other hand, if you eat well and give yourself other pleasures, you will feel generous and contribute handsomely to charity. So the poor will get to eat also." The Rebbe was no fool. He understood the "martyr game" very well. He would have made an excellent therapist for Sheila. She plays the martyr with a vengeance. Martyrs, of course, are entitled to compensation for their suffering. Sheila's compensations are moral superiority and control.

The Ns proved to be unworkable. Ted was sicker (physically) than most of the husbands I see in similar situations. It was indeed imperative that he enter a detox and/or rehab. There is no way he would go with Sheila badgering him, and she was totally oblivious to my suggestions that she was aggravating the problem. Spouses are often forced to take control as an addict deteriorates and may come to like it, but Sheila and Ted's dynamic wasn't that. They had been playing power and control games throughout their marriage. I told them that his drinking was one long scream of "Fuck you!" to his wife (and whoever she represented), but that didn't make any impression.

Couple therapy was hopeless. I considered orchestrating an intervention, but decided not to try it. Ted hated Sheila so deeply he would reject anything associated with her. I wondered if there was any way to involve the daughters, but Sheila was determined to isolate them from their father and his problem, and I had no access to them. I asked Ted if he would be willing to continue in individual sessions; he agreed, and I terminated the couple sessions. Sheila declined help for herself and also rejected an Al-Anon referral. She literally shook her finger at Ted, saying, "You better come to the sessions if you don't want to be on the street."

I tried for some relationship with Ted over the next six sessions. Aside from talking about his work on the school board and his past successes in construction, not much happened. Sheila reported that he continued to drink. I told him that his life was in danger and that the best way he could retaliate against Sheila's various humiliations, real and imagined, of him was to live. I hoped spite would motivate him. He agreed to enter a rehab but not until after Christmas, then a week ahead. Knowing I was probably being conned, I went along with it. Sheila called to tell me that I was an incompetent. I made arrangements for him to enter the rehab. By "Christmas" he meant the holiday season, and insisted on entering January 2nd. Sheila really split a gut over that, not altogether wrongfully, but I had Ted's solemn promise, insurance clearance, and a waiting bed.

We had three more sessions in which I probed for Ted's fears of entering the rehab, pushed the disease concept, and gave him an opportunity to vent his pent up (albeit angrily acted out) rage at his wife.

Unsurprisingly, he failed to enter the hospital. I had intended to terminate if he continued his drinking after having told him that we could resume our work after, and only after, inpatient stabilization. He beat me to the punch, leaving a phone message that business prevented his entering the hospital just now and that he would call me for an appointment. Sheila did call to call me various names. I never heard from either of them again.

In a sense, I got caught up in the same control and power game that Sheila had with Ted, but with a difference—I knew that I was playing, and more or less knew what was happening. Ted was probably a dying man, and I decided to go the extra mile with him. In retrospect, I think my success with a rather similar case, that of Helen and Henry, had kept me in there. There was a difference. Helen was much less of a controller and far more capable of insight. She later did extremely well in individual therapy. Henry had fewer somatic complications, yet his dynamics were strikingly similar to Ted's. As with Sheila and Ted, we started with couple sessions; they didn't work and I continued individually with Henry who was certainly in advanced alcoholism with the goal of him going inpatient. After two months, he did, me driving him there. He never drank again. He also never forgave me for "forcing me into that fucking prison." But in Ted's case, that strategy didn't work. I considered continuing with him on a "least harm" basis with the goal of his drinking less. I didn't do that because I was too angry; I was too tired of being manipulated, and I didn't believe that it would work.

Our next two cases are illustrative of a common situation: one spouse entering therapy because of the other's drinking or drugging, and in the course of therapy, it becoming increasingly clear that both have a problem. This happens in both individual and couple work.

JASON AND KATHY: WHO'S THE ADDICT?

Kathy called to make an appointment because of Jason's pot smoking. He was willing to come for marital therapy, but she wanted to come in first because he didn't know that her purpose in arranging the sessions was to stop his pot smoking. I considered not getting involved in whatever game they were playing, but my curiosity got the better of me.

Kathy was in her early thirties, nervous, sexy, and rather scattered. She described her marriage as an unhappy one. Her husband was rich, having made a fortune young in the retail business. When she was angry at him, she would hint that his fortune was tainted by some sort of shoddy, if not outright fraudulent dealings. This made Jason indignant. Her main complaint was that her husband didn't respect her and really thought she was stupid. "He treats me like an idiot." Her other complaint was that Jason got high every afternoon and withdrew, thus ending any communication or interaction between them. They were also having fertility problems, she being anxious for a child, he consenting to please her. I was puzzled by her insistence on the preliminary individual session. I asked her, "Why couldn't you have said in front of Jason what you told me today?" She replied, "There is no reason. That's not it. It's that he overpowers me. He is so smart and so quick." That proved to be true.

In the first couple session, I got some history. Kathy had grown up in a working class Irish family lately coming up in the world. She described a happy, unexceptional childhood and a good relationship with her parents and two younger brothers. Jason agreed with her account. She had dropped out of college and had had some success in the fashion business where Jason met her. He was the only child of a Jewish businessman whose modest enterprise Jason had turned into a giant. He no longer worked at anything consistently, rather dabbling in investments and splitting his year between the beach and a ski resort. He had lost his mother young and experienced his stepmother as cold, indifferent, and sometimes cruel. Kathy described the stepmother as "crazy." I asked her why they were there.

KATHY (to me): Jason thinks I'm stupid.

JASON: Dammit, I don't think that. It's not my fault you flunked out of college.

KATHY: I didn't flunk out. I quit.

JASON: Just before they threw you out.

KATHY: I gave up a great job to marry you.

JASON: I didn't ask you to quit and it wasn't such a great job. You were making $25,000.

KATHY: He thinks his shit doesn't stink because of his money. I want to be treated with respect. You never consult me about business decisions.

JASON: You don't know anything about my business.

KATHY: I could learn. You're too damn quick. Slow down and explain things to me.

JASON (to me): That's a constant theme with Kathy. I hate it. I do respect her and I love her. She has an inferiority complex and puts it on me. I'm very smart and very quick. I finished college in three years and I was a millionaire in my twenties. I'm not bragging and I don't throw my wealth in her face like she's telling you. I enjoy my money, and so does she! Don't you, dear? I don't always discuss my business deals with her. She really doesn't get it most of the time, but she's plenty smart about other things and I *do* respect her judgment.

I thought that he was the smarter of the two and that he did rub it in when he was angry. I also thought her self-esteem fragile and the intelligence issue key to both of them. He has all the power—wealth, smarts, control. No wonder she is insecure and resentful.

KATHY: When you feel like it. You get stoned every afternoon. You know I can't stand you high.

JASON (quietly and not defensively): Kathy, that's bullshit. I don't get high every day, although I used to. I conduct my business in the mornings and then the afternoon I like to smoke to relax. I have no intention of giving it up, and you're just making an issue of it because you think I treat you like you're stupid. Unless we're at a party, I don't smoke at night, and I never let my smoking interfere with our plans.

KATHY: You're a pothead and you know it. So are all your friends.

JASON: You've been on my back since you miscarried.

KATHY: A lot you cared. You were glad we lost the baby.

JASON: You're hitting below the belt. (To me.) It's true that I don't want children in the way Kathy does, but I do want a son. I'd wait, but now is okay. I gave Kathy all kinds of support when she lost the baby. I knew how upset she was. We had an awful time conceiving. Kathy, you were inconsolable. No matter what I said or did, you said I didn't care or I was glad.

KATHY: Who would want to be comforted by a pothead?

JASON: Fuck you. What about your pills?

THERAPIST: Pills?

JASON: She takes Valium like candy, and she drinks a lot. I can't stand drunks.

KATHY: Bullshit. I hate to use 'em. I only take 'em when I'm nervous.

JASON: For Christsake, Kathy, you wound up in two rehabs because of your fucking pills. That's how you lost your last job, and they were ready to fire you from the one before.

I thought, They really know how to hurt each other. I said, "When I asked you about drugs, you said you were an infrequent potsmoker and an occasional drinker."

KATHY: But this is prescription stuff. I was in two rehabs when I was in college. I got overwhelmed and spent a few weeks in the hospital. You know college. I drank too much. When I got out, the doctor put me on Valium. I did have trouble with the pills for years. Then when I got my first good job in fashion, I was afraid I couldn't do the work. I took extra, and got in a little trouble.

JASON: A little trouble? You almost died in detox and now you're taking that shit again. The only time you really stopped was when you were pregnant.

KATHY: That's more than you did. You got stoned every time I had morning sickness.

It went on in this fashion until I called a halt. I concluded that each was right about the other's drug use and both had a problem.

The subsequent sessions were much calmer. Jason repeatedly expressed love and concern for Kathy. He insisted that the reality of the differential in their cognitive abilities had nothing to do with his regard for her and that he deeply respected her aesthetic taste and her athletic prowess. That was important to him, since he was a ski nut. Kathy conceded that her insecurity and her self-esteem made her see injury where there was none. Each vowed to change and actually did so, he being more supportive and she less prone to see rejection. He assured her over and over again that he really wanted a child and was quite willing to move up his preferred date. She seemed satisfied. I asked about his express wish for a son. He said that was true, but that he would love a daughter. He talked a great deal about how hard the loss of his mother and his stepmother's indifference had been for him. She empathized.

I didn't do much but be there, occasionally probing or asking for clarification. Some sort of holding was providing them with enough security to reinvigorate and to some extent reinvent their relationship. But there was no further mention of substance abuse by either of them. That puzzled me. Was the "fix" on in this "era of good feeling"? "I won't bring up your pill taking if you don't mention my pot smoking." Since these were two functional people in no immediate danger from their substance use, I felt no urgency to return to that topic.

Then Kathy called, raging drunk, to complain about Jason's pot smoking. The next session was like the first. I moved in on the substance use issues, confronting Kathy on her drunkenness and Jason on his pot smoking. I said, "I don't believe that you can maintain the improvement in your relationship unless you both get clean." Jason flatly refused. "I have no intention of quitting. I don't have a problem. Kathy does. I want her off those pills. I won't quit altogether, but I won't smoke in front of her and I'll stop the daily stuff. Smoking reefer is part of my social life and I'm going to do it at parties, but that's all." I said, "Why don't we try it, and if you go back to daily use, you'll know that you're deluding yourself and that it won't work."

JASON: Agreed. If I can't be just a social smoker, I won't smoke at all. But I can.

KATHY: I got drunk last night because I got my period, and I had thought I was pregnant. I couldn't handle it. Jason just doesn't care that much, and I was alone.

JASON: Not true.

THERAPIST: (to Kathy): Was there any other way to get mad?

KATHY: Yeah, kick him in the balls.

JASON: If you do it too hard, you're not going to get pregnant.

KATHY: There are other guys.

JASON: That's not funny.

KATHY: I want to get pregnant, so I'm off of everything. No booze and no pills.

I saw them for a few more months until they went to their ski condo. Kathy neither drank nor took pills, nor did she get pregnant. Jason restricted his pot smoking to Saturday night. Kathy said she didn't mind that, although I had my doubts. Mostly she talked about her wish to have a baby; he talked about his unhappy childhood. They talked much less to each other; the sessions evolved into parallel individual sessions. I commented on that, but it didn't change. Neither ever offered a dream, although I had invited them to. They had found a fragile compromise and they weren't going to rock the boat. As far as I knew, neither was abusing substances. I tried to explore the meaning of having a child, but that didn't go far. For her it was a natural wish that needed no explanation; for him, a natural expectation he was willing to fulfill, but didn't want to talk about. They didn't seem to want anything from me except my presence.

When I suggested they resume sessions when they return from their ski condo, they declined, Jason expressing resentment that I charged him for one of my books on addiction. "You're taking advantage of me because you know I'm rich." Kathy expressed similar disappointment in me for charging for the book. There was all sorts of material here. His comment partly expressed feelings he felt toward his wife, displaced onto me. That wasn't new. He had been upfront about that, but supposedly they had put it behind them as an issue. I was about to interpret the displacement and her instant support of him as being a way of diverting criticism from him when Kathy said, "You helped us. But I've had enough. The book pissed me off. I paid you plenty; you shouldn't have charged for it."

She took the book out and returned it. That was that.

My feeling was that they needed to share their anger at me to bring them closer together and to divert that anger from each other. I also thought that they needed to get angry to leave, and that to admit how dependent they had become was too threatening. I said that as they walked out the door. There was no doubt that they had made progress, but our work had been on a fairly superficial level. I had my doubts that they would maintain their respective recoveries, neither having joined a support group or committed to long-term abstinence, but for the moment, she was clean and he was controlled. They got more than they came for. A few years later, I saw Kathy pushing a baby carriage in a beach town. She didn't acknowledge me.

A GAY COUPLE

Arlene was in therapy to placate Muriel, her lover of nine years. I have never had a patient as "problem-free" as Arlene—absolutely nothing bothered her. Undoubtedly, Muriel thought Arlene had a drinking problem and "That's true in a way, but I'm not ready to deal with it. When I am, I will." I repeatedly asked Arlene why she was there. I got two answers: "I enjoy talking to you," and "It makes Muriel happy." After half a dozen widely spread sessions, there always being a "reality" reason for the cancellation, I suggested couple therapy. I was surprised that it was readily agreed upon. More often than not, I move from couple to individual, splitting off the sober spouse. In cases where the partner is there to placate the spouse and absolutely nothing is happening, at least on the manifest level, I go the other way and try and move into couple therapy. This does not always or even often work either, but sometimes it does.

Arlene and Muriel were in their late forties. Arlene dressed in rather masculine suits or in slacks, wore her hair on the short side, and had a brusque manner. She was clearly the "husband," yet none would have described her as butch. She had vitality, energy, charm, and humor. She was very bright. I found her enormously likable, albeit totally frustrating as a patient. A CPA, she was a partner in the firm she had cofounded. The firm employed over a hundred professional and support staff. Her partners were straight men with whom she had warm and close relationships that were both professional and social. A classical Hero, she had been successful all her life. An excellent athlete and top student, she had always had lots of friends. She still did—gay and straight, men and women. She reported being comfortable in virtually any social situation.

Although she dated boys and went to proms as a teenager, she reported that she was aware of her attraction to women from a very young age and had never had any conflict about it. She was contemptuous of militant feminism and political lesbianism. "Just do your thing and stay off the soapbox. I never had any trouble in school, college, my MBA program, or business. Why should I trumpet my sexuality? Straight people don't. Everyone knows Muriel and I are a couple and treat us like one. We're very social and get invited to parties all the time." When I suggested that more outspoken gay women would criticize her for getting a free ride, she replied, "Let them. It's just not my style." The one problem she conceded having, except for Muriel's objection to her drinking, she placed in the past. That was her father's alcoholism. A heavy drinking, once highly successful lawyer, the last twenty years of his life epitomized the downward mobility concomitant with an alcoholic career. He went from top jobs to mediocre jobs to no job. I suggested to Arlene that she was at risk to repeat the pattern, but I couldn't sell that one. Her only reply was, "We're different."

Arlene had had to leave a residential college to return home when her father deserted her mother for another woman. She became the "father" of her large, Polish Catholic family. Years later, her mother, described as warm, loving, spineless, and masochistic, took the father back, an act of submission that infuriated Arlene. She reported warm, close relations with her siblings, all of whom drank seriously, and with their mates, and with her mother. She was coldly civil with her father. In the course of therapy, it became clear that Arlene had always been the parentified child and had essentially raised the younger children. She hated it and directed her hatred at her father. Arlene's feelings about having raised her siblings were the basis for a conflict in her relationship. Muriel intermittently expressed a wish to adopt, while Arlene was adamant that "I've been there and I don't want to go back."

Muriel was also from a large, Polish Catholic family. It too was a drinking family. The two women reported that their shared "family orientation" was a powerful bond between them and that each was accepted by the other's family and close to them. Muriel was a biology teacher and lacked the buoyant confidence of Arlene. She often felt overwhelmed by her work, was prone to depression, and had a strong need to talk about her work and her feelings. She needed attention, affirmation, and mirroring. Arlene, content and not particularly psychologically minded, was reluctant to provide it. That elicited rage and that rage drove Arlene further away. A vicious cycle ensued, which was the subtext of the couple sessions—the manifest issue being alcohol.

Another area of relational difficulty was their different interests. They shared interest in family, church, and socializing, but not much else. Arlene's passion was sports, as both spectator and participant, particularly tennis; Muriel's interest was in poetry and theater. This difference was not a source of distress to Arlene, who was perfectly comfortable with separateness and distance; it was a source of deep distress to Muriel, who craved merger. Muriel also had the stronger sex drive, experiencing Arlene's relatively meager appetite as crushing rejection.

Both women wanted to "make it work," but there was a difference. Arlene had never been in a relationship before, and didn't want to "throw away our investment." Her fantasy was that she would be alone if they broke up and she didn't want that. Social she had been, intimate never. She valued what she had, and was willing to "settle" to keep it. Muriel had been in relationships and believed she could have a "better," meaning closer, one, if not with Arlene than with another. Her need for intimacy, perhaps for an impossible symbiosis, was deep, and she was not willing to settle.

Each had an explanation for their difficulties. In Muriel's version, the problem was Arlene's drinking; in Arlene's version, the problem was hormonal, an epiphenomenon of Muriel's incipient menopause.

So far this was a classic husband–wife conflict: "He drinks; he doesn't communicate; he's lost interest in me sexually; he has no feelings, he doesn't care about mine; he doesn't take any interest in me." "She has a bug up her ass about my drinking; she is always depressed and drives me nuts when she's on the rag (or has PMS, or is going through her changes); she's too demanding; she never leaves me alone and I can't even watch the goddamn ballgame without her bellyaching." I've heard it so many times I find it almost impossible to listen. I've often thought, John Gray (*Men Are from Mars; Women Are from Venus*) made millions on this stuff, why not me? Arlene and Muriel's style was rather different, but the stereotypic relational pattern was there and they both acknowledged it.

What I said was, "You each married your mother." Muriel repeatedly returned to her mother's preoccupation, lack of interest, and coldness when Muriel was small. They were "pals" now. I continued, "Arlene, you were attracted to Muriel because she has your mother's warmth, the part of your mother you love, and because you simultaneously hoped that she would be as worshipful and submissive to you as your mother was to your father, and that you would cure her of her 'depression,' undoing your failure to cure your mother's. It's not working. Muriel isn't submissive and you haven't cured her depression. And you, Muriel, were attracted to Arlene because it gave you a second chance to 'win over' your mother and get the kind of interest and attention you missed in your childhood. To do that, you needed Arlene to share that part of your mother's makeup and to be able to change her. That hasn't worked either."

Muriel replied, "Oh, we know that. Everyone says how much I'm like Arlene's mother and Arlene's like my mother."

I said, "You know it and you don't know it."

They each returned to their explanatory hypotheses. Muriel, "Maybe that's true, but it worked until Arlene's drinking got out of hand." Arlene, "It worked until Muriel started menopause." I pointed out that Arlene wanting to deny her drinking played a major part in their difficulties and that Muriel wanting to deny her anxiety and depression also played a major role in their difficulties. That was a theme I found it necessary to return to time and time again. I think I plain wore them down and they finally "heard" what I was saying.

Our sessions focused more and more on drinking. The extent to which alcohol permeated both their lives became increasingly apparent. Entertaining, giving and going to parties, going out for dinner, with of course cocktails and wine, consumed much of their time. Both their families drank on every possible occasion and they spent a great deal of time with those families. Arlene had told me that she had several DWI citations while in college but dismissed them as youthful foolishness. "Everyone drank in my crowd—they still do—but I learned my lesson. I leave the keys home."

Muriel had a different take on Arlene's drinking and driving, "You drive all the time when you're half in the bag." Arlene conceded this was true, "But I know what I'm doing." I asked why she believed that the college DWIs were irrelevant, ancient history. Arlene replied, "I don't drive when I'm really smashed like I did as a kid." Muriel came back, "I'm terrified when you drive after three martinis." In our individual sessions, Arlene had told me of the necessity of drinking to conduct her business, of the Friday afternoon parties in her office, of the constant business entertaining where "you have to drink" to keep business flowing into the firm. The doubtfulness of this perception became manifest when Muriel reminded Arlene that several of her partners didn't drink at all.

The degree to which Arlene's hangovers exacerbated her tendencies to withdraw also became an issue. Arlene had told me that she rarely suffered hangovers. Muriel said this was "bullshit." The same for blackouts. Arlene conceded that she was alcoholic, but counterattacked, "You don't mind drinking when *you* want to drink. 'Pick up some wine, we're having the family over tonight.' 'Get a bottle of gin, Mother's coming for dinner.' You can't have it both ways." I said, "Maybe you can't." Muriel raged back, "I don't have a drinking problem, you do."

Arlene got drunk between sessions. I said, "When you get smashed, you do it on 'fuck you martinis.'" She laughed, but denied it, maintaining that "I get drunk when I'm feeling good, never when I'm upset." After another stormy session, Arlene got very drunk once again. I spoke about drinking as a way of expressing rage. This time Arlene agreed with me. The more I heard about Muriel's drinking, the more it sounded like something other than "lifestyle drinking," either problem drinking or prodromal alcoholism.

I said, "Nothing is going to get better unless you both stop drinking. Arlene, you agree you are alcoholic. I doubt you much enjoy it anymore. It's more stubbornness [a trait of which she bragged]. No one's going to tell you what to do, and that keeps you in there. It's not so much that you want to drink as you don't want not to be able to drink. That goes against your sense and image of yourself, and it's a blow to your pride." I was here addressing the narcissistic wound that admitting that one has lost control of one's drinking inflicts. I continued, "You're a middle-aged professional woman driving drunk like a foolish college kid. It's disaster waiting to happen. And Muriel, your whole life is organized around drinking. You suffer depression and alcohol is a depressant. Yet you keep drinking it. You say that the most important thing in the world is to improve your relationship with Arlene, but that can't happen if she continues to drink and she finds it almost impossible to stop with so much drinking going on all around her. I have a suggestion. Why don't you both stop for 90 days as AA suggests [they had friends in AA and were well acquainted with the program] and see what happens. If you can't stay stopped, that will say a lot. If you can, you can see what happens to the quality of your lives. Regard it as an experiment. You can always return to drinking after the 90 days."

They agreed. I further suggested they attend some AA and Al-Anon meetings. Arlene went once and Muriel not at all, but they didn't drink for those 90 days. As one would expect, their relationship problems didn't disappear, but they were better able to cope with them. Each became more tolerant of the other. The social disruption of their abstinence was far less than they anticipated. More than one friend expressed some joy that they had stopped. They continued to be tentative about their abstinence, never making a commitment to it, neither experiencing the sense of liberation that comes from the surrender experience, but nevertheless they continued their "experiment" with sobriety. The returns remain out on this experiment. But then, as Justice Oliver Wendell Holmes (1919) said, "All of life is an experiment."

A PIECE OF CAKE

Some cases just go well. Alice and Immanuel were like that. I knew at our very first session that Immanuel would recover from his cocaine addiction. How did I know that? I'm not really sure, but it had something to do with Alice's quiet firmness when she told him, "Manny, I'm not having anymore. I didn't really know what was wrong until I went to an Al-Anon meeting and read up on it, but I know now. I'm not going to have a junkie in the house with the kids. No way. You stop or you're out." He tried several variations of "Aw, Baby," but no dice. "I mean it, Immanuel. As much as I love you, I won't have a dope fiend around my kids." "Aw, Baby, I'm not that bad." "Like hell you're not. You have to stop the pot smoking too and go to meetings and come to therapy or OUT." It had equally to do with his love for her. In those early sessions, there was lots of cursing and screaming and hollering, and Immanuel, big man that he was, could be physically intimidating to the diminutive Alice, yet under all the "Fuck you's" and "You're out," the love between them was palatable in the room. My sense of it was that he loved her more than he loved drugs, and that proved to be the case.

Full of wise saws and clever maxims, Alice was forever saying things like, "I never tell you how to work your program, but you fucking well better work it if you're going to fuck me." I found myself a little in love with her, too. She was upfront, tenacious, courageous, sensual, and sexy. One could do worse. On the other hand, her eager embrace of program language and psychobabble, particularly talking about "that piece of me" or "that part of Immanuel" as if she were selecting cuts of meat turned me off, which was just as well, since I was supposed to be listening instead of dreamily staring at her parts, so enticingly delineated by her tight jeans. Not that she was seductive; on the contrary, simply natural, but I found that all the more enticing. She had a wonderful body and she knew it and enjoyed it. Immanuel, on the other hand, looked dangerous, and professional ethics apart, prudence dictated minimizing my interest in his wife. And then there was her obvious devotion to Manny underneath her rage. She never did lose her attractiveness to me, but I thought less and less about her body as therapy progressed.

Immanuel had a long drug history. Now in his late thirties, he had smoked pot since his early teens. The child of an elderly man from Cuba and a Dominican mother, he had had a traumatic childhood. His father had treated him brutally, beating him and taunting him for his artistic interests and "femininity," calling him a "butterfly," that is, a queer. When he was in his teens, Immanuel watched as his once powerful father wasted away and died of cancer. The boy had felt triumphant as well as sorrowful, and was sure that he was "bad" because he wished his father dead. The mother had tried to protect him as best she could from the father and gave Immanuel whatever self-esteem he had. He had won a scholarship to music school, but the family had no money to buy an instrument. He had to decline. It was a narcissistic wound that would not heal. His father had been fanatically religious. Immanuel came to hate the Catholic church. The Vietnam War began, and Immanuel enlisted in the Green Berets. He loved the Berets. It affirmed his questioned masculinity and, to use Alice's language, it allowed him to enact his "male piece." He saw a good deal of combat in Vietnam and later told my therapy group, which he joined, that "war was the ultimate Super Bowl and the greatest of sports." There was much denial in that, but it was also true for him. It gave him an outlet for his aggression and a chance to prove he wasn't a *mariposa* (butterfly). Besides, he stayed stoned as frequently as possible, which was virtually every day.

He came back to a country contemptuous of those who had fought in the war. Expecting to be greeted as a hero, he was ignored or scorned, and that was another narcissistic wound. He continued to smoke grass daily. Immanuel then actualized his "feminine piece" by going to school to become a special ed teacher. He had a brief marriage to a woman Alice described as "borderline," and a son by that marriage who is a troubled high school dropout. Going to work in a school for emotionally disturbed children as a counselor, he met Alice, a counterculture, antiwar, left-leaning rebel. The sparks flew. Their sexual relationship was ecstatic. Coming out of the 1960s antiwar movement, everyone Alice knew smoked pot. She didn't think anything of Immanuel's smoking it. Alice smoked too, but she was missing the "addictive gene" or whatever. Getting high was never very important to her.

Immanuel's experience in Vietnam brought to mind an alcoholic veteran I had treated who suffered from posttraumatic stress disorder (PTSD). I wondered if Manny also had PTSD, and wondered what had happened in Vietnam that he didn't talk about or totally repressed. Gary, a test pilot, had quit drinking for six years. When the Gulf War broke out, he started to obsess about body bags. He found himself weeping for "no reason." He lived alone in a rural area. One dark night, he started seeing Gooks emerging from under his deck. The next day, driving home from work, the car "drove itself" to a beer distributor and he bought a case. Day after day, he told himself he wouldn't drink "if my ass fell off," but his car had a will of its own and inexorably went to the beer store. Gary hated himself for his "weakness." Every time he drank, his self-hatred deepened. When I suggested that he just couldn't be home alone sober because the Gooks might come back, he denied it but allowed that he saw amorphous, ominous beings in his peripheral vision as he drove home. In spite of his symptomatology, this was a functioning human being not in the least psychotic. I suggested he go on Antabuse, a drug that has no effect unless a person drinks, in which case he becomes violently ill. Antabuse works by blocking the further metabolism of alcohol after a highly toxic substance, acetelyaldehyde, is produced by the first step in that metabolic process. Breakdown of this toxin is blocked by the Antabuse and the drinker becomes desperately ill. Gary welcomed my suggestion, which was risky—might he decompensate at home sober?—and went on the medication. His depression secondary to his self-hatred over his "weakness" lessened, and he began speaking of the horrors he had seen and the atrocities he had participated in. I again wondered if Immanuel had had parallel experiences. I made a conscious effort not to assimilate Immanuel into Gary. Nevertheless, in working with substance abusing Vietnam veterans, the therapist should always be aware of the possibility of PTSD. I find Antabuse useful with people who have a sincere desire to stop drinking but poor impulse control. Gary certainly fit the bill.

Immanuel and Alice married. She was the child of a wealthy industrialist. Growing up in the suburbs of a Midwestern city, she had "never fit in." A rebel from an early age, she found her way from Haight Ashbury to college to a master's in social work. So I was working with two therapists. Expected to marry a doctor or a lawyer, Alice's marrying Immanuel was another act of rebellion. But her family liked him and her father put him in business. As the sole proprietor of a craft business, Immanuel was alone much of the time. Children came along. As much as he loved them, Immanuel had trouble handling the responsibility. Financially dependent on his father-in-law, he was ashamed and resentful. Maybe he was a *mariposa* after all. He smoked more and more. The relationship with Alice deteriorated and he became estranged from his family. Then he found coke. Within a month, he totally fell apart.

Alice, by now an analytic candidate, did her student thing and read everything on addiction she could get her hands on. A light went on. She went to Al-Anon and then confronted him. By the time Immanuel appeared in my office, he was "sick and tired of being sick and tired" and not so secretly glad the game was over. He joined Cocaine Anonymous (CA) and my recovery therapy group.

The couple sessions were very angry. It was mostly bluster on his part. He needed to pin part of the blame on her, and she wasn't receiving. After a few months, she let him back in her bed and his anger visibly subsided. Immanuel's guilt toward Alice and their children surfaced, and he started "making amends," as the ninth step of the program puts it. Alice in turn started accepting responsibility for her piece of the action. Immanuel had a "spiritual awakening." He tried going back to the Catholic church, but that didn't work for him. He started going to services at Alice's liberal church and connected. He has found solace and an outlet for his energy in his involvement with church activities. Things just kept getting better. After about a year, they terminated couple therapy, while Immanuel stayed in my group for five years. He returned to college to get a degree in management.

I largely stayed out of their way. My role was mostly that of a "translator," translating each of their subjective experiences into a language the other could understand. I occasionally interpreted the influence of the past on the present, but there wasn't much of that. I also functioned as an educator on addiction, a role these educationally minded folks greatly appreciated. But the most powerful thing I did was to give them a safe place to risk and experiment with change.

This was the holding function of therapy at work. The contextual transference gave them enough security to risk change. What about the focal transference? For Immanuel, I alternated between being the fearsome, violently punitive, mocking father, who elicited responses of fear, sullen rebellion and uncooperativeness, and rage, and being the protective mother. I was usually experienced as the protective mother, while he experienced Alice as the punitive, condemning father. There was not much negative (father) transference toward me since much more commonly he assimilated his wife into his internal father object. I commented on these transference manifestations simply and directly and in terms of the here and now, my interpretations taking the form of, "You flinched when I said you withdraw from your family when you get high as if I was your father beating you," or "When you turned red and screamed, 'Alice, you are fuckin' out to get me,' you were saying it to your father. I felt afraid of you, just as Alice does when you rage at her. You were also communicating to me a mild version of the fear you felt when your father went after—raged—against you. In becoming rageful, you become your father. If you can't beat them, join them. It feels a lot safer with him in you rather than with him out there in Alice or in me about to go after you." The genetic (historical) origin of Alice's transference to me was less clear. For her, I was always the professor—an omniscient, benign authority who would help her. I didn't interpret this.

In working with couples with an active partner, I try hard to position myself as a representation of reality rather than as a representation of the superego. Of course, I am never so perceived or experienced, yet I believe that cutting down this inexorable perception of me as a punitive projected superego through didactic interventions and interpretation of the projection of the user's usually savagely primitive superego is key.

I interpreted Immanuel's selfobject (mirror) transference to marijuana as fusion with the soothing mother and a selfobject (idealizing) transference to cocaine as fusion with and acquisition of his father's power. I am not sure how much these infrequent focal interpretations helped, since my sense of this couple is that it was a contextual transference that enabled the most change.

Families

Chapter 4 provided an extensive, multiple perspective account of therapy with a family with an addicted member. Family therapy is used in three ways in treating addiction: (1) as a means of getting the user sober, which includes all the forms we have seen with the Bakers in chapter 4, as well as network therapy and intervention; (2) as part of the treatment of early sobriety in a rehabilitation facility; and (3) as a modality for enabling growth after stable sobriety has been achieved.

In my experience, family therapy is brief. In the case of a family with an addicted member, it either succeeds within a few months or it ends. It is not uncommon for either the user or other family members to continue in some other form of therapy. Inpatient rehab centers have "family days," or sometimes "family weeks." These family sessions tend to be heavily didactic, seeking to sell the disease model partly out of conviction and partly in the service of modulating guilt and rage. They also serve to introduce the notion that every member of the family has been affected by the addiction and is in need of treatment. Sometimes that treatment takes the form of family therapy, but usually it does not. Rather the spouse or less commonly the children go into individual therapy. This use of family sessions to heighten awareness of the ubiquity of the addiction's impact is of the highest value. It breaks down denial and helps family members accept their own vulnerability and woundedness, and allows them to get help for themselves.

Although enabling is interpreted and explained in inpatient family sessions, it is almost always ascribed to ignorance rather than to unconscious motivation. That makes sense. As the old social work adage would have it, you have to "meet the client [patient] where he is at." Interpretation of unconscious dynamics is reserved until stability is attained, and either the family continues in therapy or the individual members go into therapy. This "crisis" family therapy also alerts the family that the homeostasis has been unbalanced and that there will be a period of major readjustment. Inpatient family sessions are thus limited in both duration and scope, yet they may be one of the most mutative therapeutic modalities. Longer term family therapy work in recovery is the exception rather than the rule. Few families continue in therapy once the crisis has passed. Some do, however; they return after a period of struggle with the altered homeostasis. These returning families are crisis-driven, yet not a few stay for more intensive, insight-oriented work.

In reading the family histories that follow, it is well to remember that these families love as well as hate, have their rational as well as irrational sides, although those aspects may not be much in evidence.

A POLICE FAMILY

I love cops—as patients, that is. I surprise myself in saying that. I once had a very different relationship with the police. They were "pigs" as in "Off the pigs!" and no love was lost between us. One of my most vivid memories is of John Mitchell directing his storm troopers from the balcony of the Justice Department as we protesters of Nixon's invasion of Cambodia were gassed. Given that background, one would think that my countertransference to cop patients would be problematic. I have not found it so, at least not in the way expected. Although I know I risk stereotyping, it has been my experience that the (male) cops I have treated have been angry people, obsessed with control, who enact their powerful need to control themselves, a need usually completely unconscious, by controlling others. The counter-transferential problem I have had is not the kind of hatred that led me to cheer when Mitchell was jailed in the wake of the Watergate scandal. On the contrary, it has been the surprisingly strong identification I have with that dynamic. I alternately want to dominate these archetypical superego figures or to have them vicariously externalize and enact the more sadistic sides of my superego.

There are other reasons I enjoy working with cops. It is a heavy drinking subculture and a ready source of patients. It is hard not to like a group that is so good for business. Additionally, the cops I have treated have been exceptionally bright. Working with them has given me entrée into a world I would otherwise never have experienced. Over the years, I have learned most of my Yiddish from an Irish detective, had a glimpse of the workings of the highest levels of a metropolitan force, and shared tragedy.

The Quinceys had been inexorably transformed by Larry's disfigurement. On patrol, he had noticed a car circling a shopping mall parking lot. It was late. The car pulled behind the stores. Thinking it was a couple of kids wanting to make out, Larry approached the car, flashlight in hand. He was shotgunned in the face. Left for dead, he was permanently blinded (not quite totally since he could see shadows and light), lost his senses of taste and smell, and was transformed from a strikingly handsome man who had always had his pick of women into a contorted, almost grotesque mass of facial scars. Eating was a torment, and during his treatment with me, he underwent numerous surgeries to implant teeth or to make his dental appliance more functional. None was totally successful.

An alcoholic, at the time of his tragedy Larry had been sober three years. He was an avid AA member, leading meetings, sponsoring "pigeons" (newcomers), and "working" the twelve steps. During his drinking years, he had somehow managed to finish college. He would have understood my Yiddish-speaking Irish detective, who "had to fly many fugitives to California" or at least so he told his wife, as a cover, among many, for his various liaisons. Peggy, Larry's wife, had "known and not known." She could tolerate his infidelities, but not his drinking. Although Larry tried to be a good family man, in his fashion, taking the kids to Disneyland, encouraging them to achieve educationally, and attending their sports events, his alcoholism took its toll. He became less and less functional. The fights with Peggy, who had had enough, were explosive and in mildly spoken Peggy's words, "Life was shit." After the third time he was observed swerving his patrol car, his commanding officer intervened. Given a choice of sobriety or losing his job, Larry threw in the towel. As is frequently the case, by the time things had gotten bad enough for someone to intervene, he was secretly glad. Drinking had long since ceased to be fun, yet he hadn't been able to admit he was "powerless over alcohol"; that was too narcissistically wounding to this intensely narcissistic man. But when an external force—an authority—commanded it, he readily acceded; he joined AA and immediately "found a home." Peggy had long demanded his sobriety, but acquiescence to a woman's wishes was not in his behavioral repertoire.

Things went surprisingly smoothly. Sober, he cultivated closer relationships with his two sons. Like many recovering dads, he was hurt and angry that they didn't instantly forgive and embrace him. It was only with the greatest effort that he contained, for the most part, his rage. Things also improved with Peggy. If his fidelity was less than perfect, his love for Peggy was real enough. Their sex life was resumed and Larry, who was fond of saying "There are no bad orgasms," found that the ones shared with Peggy were as good as any. He was sincerely and passionately committed to the twelve steps of personal growth of the program. Although he would not have used the term, he had insight into the problematic nature of his narcissism. I say he was narcissistic because he fulfilled a good deal of the *DSM-IV* criteria, being grandiose, having feelings of entitlement, needing omnipotent control of others, endlessly seeking approbation and becoming infuriated when it wasn't forthcoming, and being vaguely aware of the emptiness beneath his facade. Unlike many other narcissists, he knew all of this and wanted to change it. Like Anna's King in *The King and I*, he didn't always succeed, but he was a man who tried. Peggy too had grown in sobriety.

She was now less compliant, less afraid of incurring Larry's wrath, and more outgoing. She had taken an office job and was doing well at it. She had been madly in love with Larry since high school. A shy, retiring, beautiful girl lacking in confidence and thinking little of herself, she was instantly attracted to the handsome, charismatic, motorcycle-riding future cop. When it worked, it was yin and yang; when it didn't, it was hell.

I should say something about the changing police culture. Larry's style of drinking, which until his decompensation was culturally syntonic and blinked at, would no longer be tolerated, and today's better educated police are less likely to fit this old stereotype. They are more diverse, not only racially and ethnically, but also in terms of personality profile.

Unlike the majority of families with Larry and Peggy's dynamics— hard drinking, narcissistic husband, and narcissistically depleted and vulnerable wife—there was no alcoholism in either of their families of origin. Although things were now far from perfect, the Quinceys were "making it." Then the shooting occurred.

In a mad screech of sirens and whirling helicopter blades, Peggy and the boys, then in their early teens, were whisked off to a death watch. Against all odds, Larry survived. Months of hospitalization and reconstructive surgery followed. Once again, all attention was focused on Father. When Larry was finally released, he was profoundly depressed. Peggy wanted to scream each time he said, "I don't want to live." Finally, she screamed back, "So die and leave us alone." Shortly thereafter, Larry attempted suicide. He wound up in a locked ward of a mental hospital, where he stayed for two months. The Quinceys had their first experience of family therapy in the hospital. It helped. Peggy started going to Al-Anon meetings, although by the time I saw them, she had dropped out. Larry returned to AA and for the first time realized how loyal and supportive his AA buddies had been, virtually taking care of his family during his physical and mental recovery. At his sponsor's urging, he entered three-times-a-week analysis. He started speaking in schools, and later at public events and on the media, about his efforts to cope with his disability. He opened a small business and began writing a column for the local paper. The response he got was like manna to him. Once again, he was the object of adulation. This in no way lessens the social value of his activities.

In a moment of self-transcendence, he sat alone in his home listening to the sound of motorcycles on the highway. His thoughts turned to his years on his motorcycle and the feelings of freedom and power, sheer exhilaration, and participation in nature and its beauties that his cycling engendered. He then went from exultation remembered into a black hole. Like Lear's recognition that "Never, never, never, never, never" would Cordelia live, Larry "knew" as he had not known before that there would never be another motorcycle ride for him. Once again, he contemplated suicide. As he groped for a knife to slit his throat, his despair changed to rage—a rage so murderous and so powerful, his body could hardly contain it. Had he been able to reach his now long since jailed assailant, he would have dismembered him a little bit at a time. Then Larry did an extraordinary thing with his rage; he realized that he was feeling what his assailant must have been feeling when he shot him. For one instant, Larry "understood" where the man who had shattered his life had been coming from. It was a transforming moment. It did not lead to forgiveness, and like all epiphanies, it deliquesced; nevertheless, Larry was somehow less "disabled" after. I wept when I read his account of listening to the motorcycles. Though I often did not like him over the course of our work together, I always deeply respected and was awed by his courage and his persistence.

Larry's analysis had moved him away from the danger of suicide, but his relationship with Peggy would not heal. His analyst referred them for couple work. It wasn't exactly couple work because Larry's seeing-eye dog, a magnificent shepherd, was very much a part of the therapy. So it was more of a family or perhaps I should say a pack therapy. I kept a jar of dog biscuits in my office for Warrior, which in a way was a cheap shot at building rapport. Be that as it may, it certainly cemented the therapeutic alliance.

During the months I treated Larry, Peggy, and Warrior, I got many comments on those biscuits and they pulled fascinating transferential fantasies, ranging from experiencing me as a beloved childhood pet to fear that I kept a fearsome watchdog that I might loose on the patient, to speculation that I had a multispecies practice. Since Warrior was indeed a patient, I suppose the latter was in a sense true.

Couple therapy lasted several years, and mostly centered on Larry's letting go and becoming less controlling, and Peggy's becoming more assertive. Larry's necessary and intensely hated dependence on her complicated our task. We spent a great deal of time on his drinking years and their impact on Peggy. Their mutual adjustment to his disability was less center stage than their conflicting personality styles. However, I don't want to focus on the couple and canine therapy, but rather on the family therapy that evolved out of it.

Larry spent a good deal of time ranting about his older son Joe, then 20, who was flunking out of an Ivy League college. Peggy was defensive and protective of Joe, but she was also angry at him. The boy had been dishonest about money, and the parents justifiably felt ripped off. Joe was coming home, and Larry and I more or less simultaneously suggested a family session. Peggy was thrilled. She would have done anything to bring father and son together. There was resistance to the couple work in their desire to move to family work, and counterresistance to the couple work on my side; nevertheless, the boy was in trouble, the parents' emotions focused on him, and a move to family sessions seemed reasonable. Another point in favor of family therapy lay in Joe's resistance to individual therapy.

Medicine has been said to be the art of the possible; that is no less true of therapy, and I have often done family work when the patient was not available for individual, and individual work when the patient was not available for family work, in spite of the fact that the other modality may have been preferable. Joe's father, and to a lesser extent his mother, had pressured him at least as far back as his father's being shot, when he was a sophomore in high school, to go into therapy. After he started failing in college, encouragement became insistence. That insistence was met with passive resistance—appointments made and not kept; attendance at a few sessions followed by discontent with the therapist and outright refusal. Perhaps he would be less resistant to family therapy and feel less like the goat, less that he was the one who needed to be "fixed." This proved to be the case.

The first session was a revelation. Joe literally quaked in his father's presence. He was absolutely terrified of him. Larry had never hit his kids, and didn't often discipline them, but he had screamed and hollered and slammed doors and kicked walls. You could feel his rage even when he wasn't expressing it. Joe had always felt it. To make matters worse, the son was awed by the father's achievements—getting straight A's in college while working full-time, drinking like a fish and yet raising a family, recovering from his alcoholism, recovering from his disablement, addressing hundreds of people, and writing beautiful and moving prose. Joe couldn't live up to that, so why try? My attempts to tell Larry that he intimidated his son were met with denial. I countered by highlighting intimidation within the sessions—raised voice, reflexive criticism, prideful expectation mixed with scorn for failure.

Peggy was seductive and oversupportive, and I told her this. I also interpreted the family dynamic of Peggy enabling Joe's dysfunctionality just as she had Larry's, of Larry's jealous envy and subsequent ragefulness, followed by Joe's fearful dissembling, outright lying, and giving up. It was a hard interpretation to sell. All three had difficulty seeing their own part in the dynamic, although they had no difficulty in seeing the others' parts.

Having plenty of here-and-now in-session evidence, I persisted. Finally I said to Larry, "You're the kid wanting Joe to be the father and to give you the accolades of his achievements." Larry replied, "I didn't get much from my father. He was a traveling salesman. I never saw him." I said, "Joe surely sees you." And later, "You are angry at Joe because he isn't giving you what you didn't get from your father." I also said, "It's hard for you to share Peggy with Joe." I also set limits, not allowing Larry to attack Joe. Very slowly, Joe started to speak. He told Larry how afraid of him he was. Larry was disbelieving. Peggy stepped in and Larry turned on her. I told him his anger at her was a defense against looking at how his son felt about him. Joe talked a lot about not being able to live up to his father's achievements. Larry said, "But you got into Princeton." Joe replied, "I don't belong there. I only got in because of my swimming. They thought I'd be an NCAA champ, and then I dislocated my shoulder and can't swim. Nobody at Princeton cares about me now and I can't do the work." "Sure, you can," said Peggy. Larry sputtered, "If you do the work, you'll pass." Warrior got up and moved toward Joe. I said, "Larry, even your dog disagrees with you." Joe said, "I'm too stupid. I'm in over my head." He was fighting back and standing up to his father. He had never done that before. Larry came back with a lot of "You're a lazy asshole" kind of stuff. Peggy cried. Joe exploded. It was a little like having Oedipus and Laius in the room. The abused child had turned murderous rage on the father. I realized that Oedipus had come to mind because of Larry's blindness. Who was who? Was Larry Oedipus slaying Joe his father? Was Joe Oedipus slaying Larry his father to claim his mother and then destroying himself as self-punishment? I felt confused.

After the explosive session, Joe returned to being the fearful kid. But with a difference. He became confessional, telling us that he hadn't been allowed to register for the spring term, but had taken the money his parents had given him for tuition anyway. He talked about his credit card debt. Larry urged him to join the twelve-step program Debtors Anonymous (DA). Then Joe told us how much pot he had been smoking and how much he had been drinking. I suggested that with his low self-esteem and family history, he was a prime candidate for addiction. His chronic lying then became the focus of attention. Peggy said he lied because he was afraid of his father. I agreed. Larry bristled, it was all bullshit; Joe was just a liar. I said, "He's trying to be honest now, but you won't let him." Larry took that in. Then Joe dropped his bombshell. He was getting married to his high school sweetheart, a local girl from a "low-life" family. The parents finally found something to bond around. That was the end of the family therapy.

My attempts to help Joe deal with his feelings about his father's disablement and its impact on him, although much encouraged by both parents, yielded very little, as did my attempts to help Joe deal with the effects of Larry's alcoholism on him. Also conspicuously missing in this therapy was the younger son, either by allusion or by presence. He too is a heavy pot smoker and apparently keeps his distance to protect his habit. There was too much not dealt with in this therapy.

Joe married his local girl, took a low-paying clerical job, and stopped smoking pot. He did not join Narcotics Anonymous, twelve-step programs being his father's territory. The Quinceys continued in couple therapy and made further gains. Larry's narcissism, which enabled his survival, serves him poorly in personal relations. Analysis, couple work, family therapy, and the program have chipped away at his "character defect," as AA would call it, but his core pathology remains. For all their growth, his wife and son continue to tread cautiously, awaiting the next explosion of narcissistic rage.

At one point in family therapy, I said, "Joe is in an impossible position. If he fails, his mother is disappointed and his father is disappointed and enraged; but if he succeeds, his father is jealous albeit proud." Peggy immediately said, "That's not always true. Larry went to every one of his swimming meets and was really proud of him." Joe agreed, saying how close he had felt to his father when he was swimming. I said, "You have both suffered deeply but differently because of your disabilities." The profound loss Joe had suffered from his injury and subsequent inability to compete athletically surfaced, and in ensuing sessions, Joe mourned, and mourned not least the loss of the best connection he had had with his father. The immensity of Larry's disabilities made Joe ashamed of expressing his no less profound sense of loss over his shoulder injury. I spoke of his shame and reluctance to express his feelings about his loss in the family sessions, and that importantly enabled him to engage in mourning work, which was instrumental in his giving up marijuana. In this area, Larry was not competitive and was highly empathic with his son. I wondered how "motivated" Joe's injury had been.

After Joe's wife had a baby, there was a social repair. It was a kind of cure by suppression rather than working through, but a "cure" nevertheless. Joe is working, going to school, and not using. His parents are able to enjoy their grandchild. The Quinceys illustrate both working with a family in recovery, and working with a family with an actively using member.

There is a variation of the father and son dynamic, which we saw in this case, where the father is looking for mirroring from the son. In families with multigenerational substance abuse, it is not uncommon for parents struggling with adolescent substance abusers to experience them as their abusive alcoholic parents.

Alice, a substance abuse counselor, came into family therapy with her two adolescent daughters, both of whom were heavily substance involved. Alice came from an alcoholic home in which her father, frequently drunk and out of control, was both physically and verbally highly abusive. When Crystal, the more acting out of the two daughters, cursed at her mother, Alice was thrown right back into her childhood in which her father had screamed and cursed at her. The father would make such comments as, "I should have jerked off in the sink," meaning that it would have been better that his daughter had never been conceived, and frequently called Alice a fucking cunt. When Crystal used similar language, Alice effectively decompensated, alternately collapsing and becoming violent toward the teenager. It was a truly explosive situation in which mother and daughter or possibly daughters were likely to seriously injure one another. When I offered the interpretation that "you have turned your daughters into your father," Alice regained her ability to effectively parent her extraordinarily difficult children. This dynamic is frequently seen.

A final thought on the Quinceys. What was it that enabled Joe to stop his pot smoking? I think the family sessions were key sessions in which he felt sufficiently secure to confess to his parents his shameful secrets about flunking out of college, stealing from his parents, and heavy pot smoking. Having a forum in which he could experience as well as express, rather than anesthetize and act out both guilt and shame, he was able to stabilize and move into adulthood. His ambivalent identification with his father also helped him. That part of his father that was in recovery and struggling to ameliorate his "character defects" was a powerful, positive model, and once the fear that made identification with that positive side of his father impossible became manageable, that identification enabled Joe's recovery.

A STRANGE MESSAGE

The message on the tape said, "Dr. Levin, you old Jew, you're a bad boy. You have been playing with yourself. I'm going to come over and put pussy juice in your beard. Oh, oh, I'm being inappropriate.

I've gone too far. I'm a grandiose, narcissistic personality disorder, that's why I say these things. The real reason I called was I forgot my appointment time. Please call and tell me when my appointment is."

His forgotten session was to have been our third. Hank had also forgotten the time of his second appointment. He had been pushed into therapy after he had resumed drug use when he left a rehab program against medical advice. Hank was a sculptor in his early twenties; he had had years of therapy and analysis with scant results. A protean personality with many incarnations, Hank brought to mind the medieval church's reluctance to bury actors in sacred ground because they had no souls of their own. Woody Allen's Zelig also came to mind. Hank had all too many guises, yet paradoxically an all too stable pathological core.

I wondered about the message on the tape. Was it psychotic? Or was he stoned? Or both? Or was the whole thing a smoke screen, a diversion to keep the focus of therapy off his drug use? Or did it have an interpretable emotional meaning? These possibilities were by no means mutually exclusive. When I saw him, I said, "Hank I can't have long messages on my tape machine. It interferes with my keeping my schedule. Please keep your messages short." This did several things: it set some boundaries; it pointed out that I had needs too and that I intended to take care of myself; it brought him back to reality when he might have been losing contact with it; and it wasn't retaliatory. One could argue that from a strictly analytic point of view, I was closing him down through suppression and this may have been true. If it was, that strikes me as irrelevant. At the time, I would have been hard put to do more with Hank's communication because I didn't yet understand it.

Hank requested that I meet with his parents. "You can't understand me unless you meet them." Since Hank was developmentally if not chronologically an adolescent, this was appropriate.

Just as Hank had said, the session was an eye-opener. I found it fascinating that neither Hank nor his parents wanted a full family session at that point. They wanted to avoid confrontation. This was a wealthy family. Father had been a soccer star and stellar student at a top university, and subsequently led his class at Harvard Business School. Starting from a comfortable middle-class origin, he had made many millions in real estate. The family lived in a fourteen-room Lake Shore Drive apartment and owned a palatial country home. Hank described the apartment as a museum, and that was true. Old masters and contemporary art hung from the walls. Their wealth had brought little happiness. I thought of Freud's observation that wealth rarely brings happiness because money is not an infantile wish. Mother had graduated from a Seven Sisters school. There was much mental illness in her family, which was also highly creative. Her father was a successful writer. Several uncles were manic-depressive and there had been suicides in the family. As a young woman, she had had a spectacular career in fashion design, but hadn't worked for many years. Her health was poor and she suffered from depression. The family was highly cultured. Father played the violin and composed. His playing of Bach was said to be outstanding. Mother painted. Being with them was a cross between reading J. D. Salinger and the *DSM-IV*. They were extremely open, albeit rather histrionic, and offered the above history without any inquiry on my part. Halfway through the session, they started talking about what had brought them to therapy.

LEON (Father): I'm sure Hank told you I am a rageaholic. (He had.) I was. I was a real killer. I had 20 years of analysis. I don't know if it did me any good. Yes it did, my phobias lessened. I couldn't travel. I always had to pee. I was afraid to go on the expressway to O'Hare because I might have to pee. Oh yes, like I said, I'm a killer. Or was until I discovered Zolof. Since I have been on Zolof, I am transformed. (I wasn't convinced, but I was just as glad I hadn't met him before he went on Zolof.) I'm not exactly a pussycat now, but I am much calmer.

EDITH (Mother): Hank should go on Zolof. Will you send him for Zolof? I know it runs in families. (A tear or two rolls down her cheek.) If only my uncle had had Zolof. (Growing increasingly agitated.) My family is creative and so sick. (Screams.) Sick.

LEON: Edith, calm down.

EDITH: I can't take any more. My brilliant, talented son is destroying himself. We don't know what to do anymore. Please put
him on Zolof.

LEON: Edith, we have to be prepared. He's going to die! Kids like
him die! Die! We have to be prepared. He'll probably die.

EDITH: No, no, Leon. I can't take it. The doctor will save him. Just
like for you, the Zolof will work. (Weeps.) He was sexually
abused.

LEON: Hank, that is. The maid was a pervert. She used to touch
his peepee.

EDITH: Oh, God. We didn't know.

LEON: She was fired the same day we found out.

EDITH: Oh, my poor boy's peepee.

It wasn't that I doubted they felt deeply about Hank's peepee being
touched, yet somehow I had the feeling that they had been over this
ground a few times too many.

LEON: Mother, we have to be prepared. We really have to be prepared for him to die.

I wondered if this was a fear or a wish. Given Leon's self-description
as a killer, wish seemed more probable. Doubtless it was both. I thought
of the mother of a chronically addicted son who dreamt that he was
hanging. Her dream wasn't a proud mother's wish that her son was
well hung; she had had enough. She wanted him dead. It would end
the suspense and allow her to get on with her life. Leon's death wish
was less unambivalent. I vocalized, "Wish or fear?"

EDITH: No, no, no. We don't want him to die. We want him healthy.
Leon, tell us you want him to live.

LEON: Of course, I want him to live. But we have to be prepared.

Knowing that this family had had oodles of therapy, much of it
centered on their enabling Hank, I pressed my advantage.

THERAPIST: Your buying him cars and giving him money is killing him.

EDITH: (Greatly relieved.) Oh, that's what you mean. All our therapists told us that, but you don't understand. Hank living in the streets while we live in luxury—I couldn't stand it. (Sobs.) Oh, we—I—feel so guilty. Leon was a maniac when Hank was growing up and I was driven and depressed. We're Jewish culturally, not religiously, and we always had Christmas trees and exchanged presents. When Hank was 10, I decided I felt too guilty having a Christmas tree and we stopped doing it. Hank was devastated. Years later he told me, "The one good thing in my childhood, you had to take it away, you bitch." I am a bitch. I did awful things to Hank and his peepee. (Although she meant that she hadn't protected him from the maid, I wondered who had done the awful things to his peepee.)

LEON: We had to stop Christmas. You were ashamed. My parents were threatening to sit *shivah* (i.e., go into mourning), not that they ever believed in anything. . . . He *is* in danger. He might die. He walked out of the rehab after we did the intervention, and he is using again. We just have to be prepared for him to die.

Before his next session, Hank got "fucked up" on coke. There were frantic calls from his parents. His father told me that he found Hank completely paranoid, talking to a bag lady who he thought had hidden microphones to tape him. He was afraid to return to his apartment because it was staked out. He refused to go into a hospital. I told the father to call 911 if he thought Hank to be in danger, and that he should be aware that he would lose control if he called the police, and that Hank might go to prison—not necessarily a bad outcome. Father elected to do nothing. Hank was totally out of it at his next session. He was offensive with my doorman, couldn't remain seated, and started begging me to get rid of the cops. When I said, "What cops?" he pointed to the window, and said, "Don't you see them? The cars, the lights." I wasn't sure he wasn't putting me on, but I concluded that if he was that good an actor, he should go on the stage. I told him to take a cab home and to go to bed. I said this in a very authoritarian tone. He did it. He called the next day to say that he was doing better and to apologize if he had created a disturbance.

Our next session was a family one. Hank's entire interest was in convincing me that his hallucinations were real and that I had seen the cops too. This was partly razzmatazz to divert his parents and me from talking about hospitalization, but at another level, he was terrified that he was losing his mind and desperately wanted me to affirm his "sanity" by validating the reality of his experience. His parents were equally adamant that I tell Hank that in Leon's words, "I don't believe a word of that bullshit." What I said to Hank was, "It doesn't matter if the bag lady was wired or not or if the cops were outside my window. If they were, you can't use, because they have you staked out and you'll go to jail if you pick up, and if the bag lady wasn't bugged and the cops weren't there, you can't use because you go out of your mind when you snort coke. Hank, either way, you can't use coke." Hank never used coke again, although he continued for months to nag me to tell him I believed the cops were really there. His chemically induced psychosis had terrified him, and some combination of my interpretation and his fear kept him away from cocaine, if not from marijuana and alcohol.

At the next session, which was an individual one, Hank told me of masturbating to sadistic fantasies when he was high on cocaine. The cops were after him because they knew about his wish to torture women. "It's because I hate my mom, isn't? But I love her too." He obsessed about his career being ruined because the art critics and gallery owners all knew about his fantasies. He was particularly terrified that they would find out about his wish to drown a woman in feces, a wish he only had when high on coke and which greatly excited him. His working in clay was a sublimation of his anal sadism.

He told me about Susan, the girl he had smoked pot with daily before the "intervention." Her mother was dying of congestive heart failure and Hank, who was obsessed with the fear of death, "comforted" her by getting stoned with her. Neither of them could handle the proximity to death. They regressed almost literally to a womb/tomb in which they clung to each other in a dreamy marijuana-induced hazy symbiosis until Hank's parents broke it up. I interpreted his pot smoking as an attempt to return to Mother's womb, or at least to her breast, as fusion with Mother, and his cocaine use as an attempt to be sadistically powerful like Father. We also talked about death. Hank told me his favorite piece of music was Mahler's Ninth Symphony, the farewell of a dying man. This was partly pretension and partly identification with his highbrow father, for he was usually more into pop culture of which he had encyclopedic knowledge. But it wasn't only that, listening to Mahler's sensuous depiction of dying—Hank approximated dying—the music being an analogical rather than a digital symbol (see Susan Langer's [1957] *Philosophy in a New Key*); it induced a state of mournful farewell through the isomorphism of the music with the dying process, rather than pointing to that which it denoted—the experience of dying. Hank counterphobically practiced dying. I told him that, and that his drugging himself into unconsciousness was similar to a rehearsal of death. But here the counterphobic enactment went further, being a drama of death and resurrection (Mahler also composed a Resurrection Symphony). The drug stupor was the simulacrum of death and the awakening from it the resurrection.

Hank was proving his immortality as he counterphobically risked his life. I told him so. I also told him that this little drama fed his grandiosity, convincing him that he could continue on his present path with impunity, however contrary to fact that might be. This was a family obsessed with death. Hank came to his fears honestly. I wondered if he knew that many of the Bach compositions his father played had titles like "Come Sweet Death." Hank pressed me to tell him that I believed in immortality. I told him that he wanted me to guarantee his immortality. He laughed and said, "Of course, you dope." He laughed again. "You're much older. You must think about death all the time. How about it, Levin? The worms—it's terrible, terrible, terrible. It's not fair. You're going to die, Levin. Don't tell me you're not afraid."

Mother, being ill, missed the next family session. Father started out compassionately empathic, telling Hank how much he identified with him and what a hard time he had had finding himself. The effect of this on Hank was powerful. It was the first time I had seen him neither manic nor depressed. His father's loving concern was like a soothing balm to his troubled psyche. Unfortunately, Leon couldn't sustain what I took to be a very genuine attempt to reach his son. What started out as a reaching out by sharing, as a nonjudgmental way of understanding his son and communicating that understanding to his son, soon deteriorated into a monologue. Dialogue became soliloquy. It was no longer about Hank; it was entirely about Leon. The self-absorption became almost manic. When I tried to point that out, Leon spoke over me. The father's narcissistic needs were stronger than his love. Hank's face fell, and I correctly predicted that he would get high that night.

At the next family session, the topic turned to money. Hank had a trust fund from his grandfather that his father controlled. I raised the possibility of Hank receiving some regular sum from the trust so he did not have to go to his parents for every dime. All paid lip service to the wisdom of breaking a direct dependency, but the parents' need to control and the son's need to remain tied by an angry dependency on those parents was too strong, and nothing was done to make Hank "independent." In the course of therapy, I repeatedly pointed out to Hank that in spite of his ranting about his father's "cheapness," he must like things as they are since he never made a move to draw directly from his trust. Hank inevitably thanked me, "for a great idea," and did nothing.

I was now in a position to interpret the message on the tape. The family sessions, which had given me an insight into Hank I would have been hard pressed to come by if they had not occurred, dwindled, and Hank's therapy reverted to individual sessions. When the context permitted it, I said, "Do you remember the message you left on my tape, starting, 'Dr. Levin, you old Jew'"? He laughed. I continued, "The old Jew is your father. 'You're a bad boy, you're playing with yourself' is something your father either said to you, or you were afraid he would say to you. You're the bad boy, but that's so frightening you make me the bad boy. You're afraid your father will cut off your dick, so you cut it off yourself by turning yourself into a pussy. When you say, 'I'm coming over to put some pussy juice in your beard,' you turn yourself into a pussy [I thought of Leon's talking about being a pussycat]. There is no way to cut off your dick if you don't have one. Then you got scared and tried to salvage things by making a joke out of it, 'I'm a grandiose narcissistic personality disorder.' You were probably high when you called and that allowed you to be sadistic toward me, but in spite of your self-castration, you still feared retaliation, so you went further, not with words this time but with action. You got so high on cocaine that you wiped out your mind. You really castrated yourself, and then looked to your father and to me to rescue you and to reassure you that we wouldn't retaliate for your sadism and hostility toward us. But it didn't quite work, and you got your father and me mixed up with the police who really could do a job on you."

HANK: But they were there. No more coke. I told you no more coke.

This family is an excellent exemplification of Bion's (1961) theory of groups. As a task group, Leon and Edith wanted their son to recover. As a basic assumption group, they had a very different agenda. Fight/flight was all over the place in the family sessions, as was dependency, but what I found so fascinating was the pairing. I remembered this Jewish family's guilty wish to be Christian and Bion's basic assumption that the group tolerates pairing in the unconscious belief that the pair will produce the Messiah. I told Hank that there was a myth, not quite conscious in his family, that he was the Christ who would save his family from mental illness and their own destructiveness and that taking Christmas away from him was their way of repudiating that fantasy, but that the repudiation hadn't worked. And that he continued to act out his parents' unconscious fantasy, a part of which was that in order to be their savior, he, the Savior, had to die on the cross.

I went on to say that his parents' exalted expectations of him, whether for the highest artistic achievement or for salvation, were impossible to fulfill, so as great and powerful and invincible as he felt as the son of God (which said something about where his father was at), he always experienced himself as a failure. (Of course, his father's wish that "he's going to die," was part of this unconscious scenario since death was the only fate that Christ could have. This part of my interpretation I didn't articulate.) I went on to tell Hank that his drug addiction was a living out of the family fantasy with its enactment of godlike grandiosity and inexorable culmination in self-crucifixion.

Hank took it all in, I think, and said, "I guess I have ten more years" (he was then 23). This imaginative reconstruction of the unconscious fantasy life of this family may have more to say about me than about them, but it feels right and I believe at some level it is true. Hank apparently thought so too; unfortunately, true or not, it was not mutative.

Hank never achieved abstinence. He continued in therapy until he moved to Europe. His drug use had moderated, and he had become less disturbed. He had some drug-free periods in which a warmer, more related, more responsible Hank emerged. They never lasted. The commitment wasn't there, and the family's enabling, although diminished, never ceased. I regard the case as having a moderately successful least-harm outcome: pot is better than cocaine; and Hank is working more consistently at his art. I agreed with the family that antidepressant medication was worth a try, but the identified patient wasn't going that route. As controlling as his controllers, he is going to do it his way. I don't believe it, but I hope it worked for him.

The question arises, should I have terminated when Hank flatly stated that he was not interested in abstinence from pot, as he consistently did? Had I become an enabler, too? Traditional substance abuse counselors, the more dogmatic disease model people, and the Twelve-Steppers would certainly see it that way, and in some moods I would agree with them. There are certainly substance abusers whose treatment goal need not be abstinence. They are problem users rather than addicts and have a reasonable shot at becoming social users. It was not my belief that Hank is one of them, although I may be proved wrong, which would be fine with me. Rather I see this as a least-harm case.

I do terminate with patients, be they individual, couples, or families, where the treatment has become a rationalization—"We [I] am getting help, so what do you want from us [me]"—for continued use, but I don't do it often. Substance abuse is the only disorder in which the patient must be "cured," that is, abstinent, before he can receive treatment. That is irrational, yet it is the traditional wisdom in the field. As long as useful work can be done, it should be done. It is also the case that many patients benefit from previous "failed" treatments retrospectively, and it is the third or fourth therapist who is credited with the "cure." What the therapist must not do is be seduced into dealing with dynamic and behavioral issues while ignoring the substance abuse. Rather the patient must continually be brought back to the connection between present difficulties and his drug use. The decision to terminate should not be decided by fiat or dogma, but rather by a careful balancing of the benefits and detriments of continuing treatment. Generally speaking, having a therapeutic relationship is better than not having one.

INTERVENTIONS

I described how an intervention works in Chapter 2. I would like to conclude my clinical discussion with two examples of interventions, neither of which I participated in; in both instances, the intervenee became my patient.

Tom is a retired surgeon. A brilliant man with a Yale Phi Beta Kappa key, his entire life was one of academic and professional success. A deacon of his church, commander of his yacht club, his life seemed charmed. And indeed, outwardly it was. But not so inwardly or emotionally. Although it would not be accurate to say that he had been depressed all his life, something had been wrong. Although he did everything he could not to notice it, and for the most part succeeded, he was not happy. He compensated by drinking. Martinis gave him the love he neither felt for nor from his wife. There was a nagging regret that he should have married the Catholic girl with whom he was in love but whom he had relinquished when his strongly Protestant family disapproved. He had had a few brief liaisons and had enjoyed them, but had enough of his father's piety not to stay with them. He had had a bad scare with cancer as a relatively young man and that had permanently accelerated his drinking. His wife, although better controlled, was also fond of the sauce.

He came to me shortly after his daughters "intervened." He was 67 and retired. The intervention had caused difficulties in his stably unhappy marriage. His children, responding to his slurring and his not making sense if they called after 6 P.M., had excluded their heavy-drinking mother and confronted their father, insisting that he was alcoholic, that he had long been so, and that since his recent retire-ment had accelerated his "progression" to the point that they felt his life was in danger, so they were intervening. They told him that they loved him too much to sit idly by and watch him kill himself, and that either he stop drinking and enter therapy or they would stop talking to him and not let him see his grandchildren. A dutiful, lov-ing, if not overly involved parent, his children's love was important to him. Further, he "knew" that they were right. Secretly greatly relieved, he took some self-prescribed Valium for a few days and stopped drinking. He couldn't get over the fact that he didn't miss drinking. There was some denial in this, yet it was substantially true. The problem was his wife. She was furious that her daughters had bypassed her. There was a family fight and the children told her that she would never have gone along with it, which was true. If they had consulted a professional interventionalist, he or she would almost certainly not have included the mother either. Mother and daugh-ters were not speaking. Tom felt gratitude toward his daughters, and thought they had done the only possible thing.

When he walked into my office, he looked at my diplomas, and said, "You're so much younger than I." This theme of aging and his fear of death was to be a central issue. In a subsequent session, he said, "Eternity is a long time," a line that reverberates in my mind on occasion, my denial of death taking the form of a philosophical quibble that eternity does not partake of time. At the end of the first session, he told me the story of a woman who was about to be married for the third time who was still a virgin. When her friend asked her how come, she replied, "My first husband was a psychiatrist, all he wanted to do was talk about it; my second husband was a gynecologist, all he wanted to do was look at it; but this time I'm not taking any chances. I'm marrying a lawyer because I know he will screw me." I focused on the gynecologist, and sure enough the story was Tom's way of telling me that he had been impotent for ten years.

Tom was used to wielding power. He quickly positioned me as his buddy and advisor on alcoholism, asking me for reading recommendations and the like. At one point he said, "Therapy has reduced the entropy of my consciousness" in a self-mocking tone, pretentiousness not being one of his traits. Since I saw my task as reinforcing the intervention, I was perfectly happy to be expert and advisor. The focus of our work was on his drinking, with occasional forays into sex and death. The turning point occurred when he conceded that he had retired earlier than he wished because of his drinking, saying, "I decided to get out before I killed somebody." After that, I wasn't much worried about his returning to drinking, and sure enough, he was soon talking about blackouts going back twenty years and a host of other symptoms. His denial first pierced in the intervention was collapsing.

The point I want to make about Tom is that he was so perfectly intervened upon. He is indubitably alcoholic, the timing was right, his children were loving but firm, they marshaled evidence and they made it clear that they would not take no for an answer. Further, they had therapeutic leverage and were willing to use it, and a good enough sense of their mother to know that she would undermine it if included. There was no doubt in my mind that his children prolonged Tom's life.

Gwendolyn's intervention had not worked. The script was by Woody Allen in his imitation of Ingmar Bergman incarnation. The Hamptons home, the Upper West Side life, the literary people with their obsessive discussions of form and style, and their deeply felt belief in the sanctity and transcendent importance of art, especially art manifest in the written word. Working with her took me into a world and a set of values I had thought ceased to exist, one I had known as an English major at Penn lo those many years ago. Hers was a family obsessed with degrees and colleges and academic appointments, as well as literary honors. The world of high-art publishing and of the more serious kind of bohemianism was entirely within their ken.

Academics, writers, editors—theirs was a star-studded family. The noncreative fared badly in the Rostoff family. It was also a family in which pretensions didn't quite meet expectations. Money was important but only insofar as it made the "life of the mind" possible. They had barely enough for that.

Gwendolyn was a fading beauty at the end of middle age, and I often thought of her—indeed literally saw her in my mind's eye—walking across the beach to her death in the ocean like the mother in *Interiors*. She sometimes had the same vacant stare. I was fascinated with Gwendolyn and her parties with Nobel laureates in attendance, but she wasn't there to give me vicarious entry into her world. She was there because a misconceived intervention had shattered her fragile and tenuous self-esteem and had rent this family of high achievers asunder. It was a classical case of overzealous misdiagnosis. One of her daughters' therapists had convinced the daughter that her mother was alcoholic and that the family should intervene. Gwendolyn was not alcoholic, although she had become a problem drinker largely because neither she nor her husband could deal with the developmental crisis brought on by the unmistakable signs of their aging. She was a woman who had gotten drunk periodically all her adult life. That was in no way aberrant in her set, and she didn't do it very often. She had also raised four children more or less successfully, supported them after the death of her first husband, and had held responsible editorial jobs. Until the previous fall, she had been a wine-with-dinner person and an occasional drunk. Perhaps not the wisest of lifestyles, but not alcoholism.

Her first marriage had been to an academic star at an elite university. He enjoyed (and *enjoyed* is the right word) the adulation of the literati. He published "important" works. They knew "everybody," and people like Philip Roth attended their parties. They had met the Kohuts socially and Gwendolyn was one of the few in her set who had not been analyzed. When her husband fell ill, both physically and mentally, his analyst called her in and told her that her husband was a "pathological narcissist" and a "dangerous" man who had many dark secrets that she was likely to discover when he died. That proved to be true. His manuscripts were filled with tales of bizarre perversions and she later found out that he had sexually abused all four of their children—one boy and three girls. He had had many affairs with both men and women and lived for adulation. When the adulation ceased, he died. He was also dishonest about money, much of it hers, and about his work, some of which was plagiarized, and left her penniless. Whatever the ethics of the analyst's disclosure, that disclosure did help her survive the upheaval in her life.

Gwendolyn, although she was to become accomplished in her own right, had lived in the shadow of her husband, just as she had lived in the shadow of her father. After a period of bitter struggle, she prospered and moved East, took an editorial job, and embarked on an affair. She loved the man, but didn't believe that they could be happy together. After a period of independent aloneness, she met her second husband, another star, but a far more gentle and emotionally engaged man than her first husband. Once more, she was in the shadow of one of the "great" ones, but this time she was happy. He was good to her children and she was accepted by his from three previous marriages. Things went well, until they retired to their beach home. Sam, who was in his mid-sixties, was starting to have physical problems. A narcissist of another stripe than her first husband, he attempted to handle his aging by manic denial. His tennis and racquetball playing became compulsive. He insisted that Gwendolyn play with him, denying the reality that her progressing circulatory problems made this difficult, if not impossible. To face his wife's aging was to face his own and he couldn't do it. There were angry quarrels. For the first time, he became sadistic and demeaning. In her eyes, he was turning into her first husband. He would storm out, accusing her of malingering and abandonment, even as he abandoned her. She retaliated by drinking, and Sam, a virtual nondrinker in a drinking world, who had never had much tolerance for her rare episodes of drunkenness, turned on her savagely. He started complaining to her children, who called and berated her. Feeling everyone had turned against her, she drank more. It was at that point in her story that I saw her as the mother in *Interiors*.

A year earlier, she decided that she had to confront her children with their father's sexual abuse of them. The issue had festered in

her mind for two decades, and now she saw signs that their not dealing with what their father had done to them was impoverishing their
emotional and interpersonal lives. She may have been wrong about
that, for the children, with one exception, were reported to be doing
well in life, and that may have been more her issue than theirs. In
any case, she decided to confront them to force them to deal with
their past. In effect, she "intervened" with them. It was, to say the
least, not appreciated. I think that Gwendolyn's aging and health
difficulties forced her to face her own mortality, and that in turn
surfaced her guilt over not having protected her children in her en-
thrallment to her first husband. She didn't know it, but she wanted
to clear the decks before she died. The children reacted to her efforts
with fury. Without denying the facts, they minimized them, blamed
her, and maintained a defensive idealization of their father. They saw
their mother's motivation as jealousy of their love for their "amaz-
ing" father, whatever he had done. She was devastated. Here were
yet more feelings she needed to anesthetize with alcohol.

When Sam called to complain of Gwendolyn's drinking, the stage
was set for *intervention as vengeance*. Although said to be motivated
by love, this intervention was motivated by hate. The climate of the
times—the new Puritanism, which sees alcoholism in every sip of
wine—also played a role here. Uncle Toby's "Dost thou think, because thou art virtuous, there shall be no more cakes and ale?" (*Twelfth
Night*, II, iii, 117–118) comes to mind as a representation of balance
and sanity. Gwendolyn's intervention speaks strongly to the wisdom
of interventions being conducted by professional therapists—Tom's
case being the exception that proves the rule. Families are simply too
emotionally involved to have the objectivity necessary to assess the
need for and implement an intervention.

The family demanded that Gwendolyn enter a rehab program.
Having nowhere to turn, she reluctantly agreed. The experience was
a profound narcissistic wound. She was shamed and humiliated. Her
always fragile self-esteem, which was never too high as the pygmy
living in the world of (alleged) giants, was shattered and she arrived
in my office with the blank stare previously described.

There is no question that Gwendolyn had developed a drinking problem that fall, but she was far from addicted. There is also no question that her drinking had become a danger to her, and that she was at a risk for late-onset alcoholism. She needed help, but not the help that she got. Her intervention, no matter what its manifest purpose, was at the latent level an acting out of complex intergenerational family dynamics that needed therapeutic exploration, clarification, and interpretation, not enactment. Enormous harm was done.

The repair work went slowly, and the therapy gave Gwendolyn an opportunity to work through long-standing conflicts. Sam eventually apologized, and by then Gwendolyn had vented enough hurt and rage in therapy to accept his apology. They were prime candidates for couple therapy, but he was not available. There was a sort of couple therapy by proxy however, as she took her insights home from therapy, and they are now once again a reasonably happy couple. Sam has become more realistic about their physical limitations and spends more time with Gwendolyn. And she has become more assertive of her need for some of the limelight. She no longer has a blank look on her face; on the contrary, she is quite animated. The break with her children has also healed. They never admitted that the intervention had been wrong-headed, but when Gwendolyn invited all to Christmas dinner, they came and acted warmly. Gwendolyn has decided to believe that they were motivated by misguided concern, which is partly true, and to make Sam the villain of the piece. It is a strategy that works for her. The scars inflicted by the intervention will never heal, but Gwendolyn has decided to put the experience behind her. She has succeeded in this, and her bitterness has faded. She has returned to drinking a glass of wine with dinner and one drink on social occasions. She has had no difficulties with this and her husband and family have accepted it.

As is clear from my account of Tom's intervention, I am in no way against them. On the contrary. They are lifesaving tools when used properly. However, they need to be very carefully considered and planned with an experienced therapist in the role of "director."

SUMMING UP

Quotations from two of my favorite authors come to mind as expressing the essence of what I have to say about the treatment of substance
abuse. One is the transcendental poet and philosopher, Henry David
Thoreau (1854, p. 97). "In eternity, there is indeed something true
and sublime. But all these times and places and occasions are here
and now. God Himself culminates in the present moment, and will
never be more divine in the lapse of all the ages." Leston Havens
(1986) must have had something similar in mind when he said that
if there is one single moment without transference, the patient is
cured. None of us can be fully here and now, but few of us are as
much there and then as substance abusers and all who are caught in
the net of addiction. You can't be maximally here-now until you fully
work through then-there, and that working through, that release from
the demons of the past, is of the essence of what we do whether it is
structural or systemic or intrapsychic dynamic.

The other quotation is from a political scientist searching for a guide
to a nonmessianic, noneschatological path to human liberation and
finding it in a great text. Michael Walzer's ideal of a circumscribed,
realistic—not reaching for too much—political process to effectuate
improvement in the human condition, resonates with Learned Hand's,
"The spirit of liberty is the spirit which is not too sure that it is right,"
which is the epigraph of this book. So we have come full circle.

In his conclusion to his great *Midrash* (commentary) on the book
of Exodus and the interpretive uses to which it has been put by men
and women struggling for liberation in sundry times and places,
Walzer (1985) tells us that we are always in Egypt, that there is always a Canaan which is simply a better place and not an ideal one,
and that "there is no way to get from here to there except by joining
hands and marching" (p. 149). Substance abusers are always and most
certainly in bondage in Egypt; sobriety is assuredly a better place,
albeit and significantly not a perfect one, and just as assuredly, the
only way to get there is to join together and march, join together in
transference and alliance with therapist, group, spouse, family, and
twelve-step meeting, and to march through, work through, the wil-

derness of denial, conflict, and emotional arrest. And we therapists are privileged to go on our patients' march from slavery to freedom, from Egypt to Canaan, from the darkness of addiction to the light of the better place of sobriety. But we too are in our Egypts and we too need to join together and march to a better place. And if we do it right, it is not only that we march with them; they march with us, and both patient and therapist arrive at a better place.

Manorville, NY, February 11, 1997

❖ REFERENCES ❖

Abraham, K. (1908). The psychological relations between sexuality and alcoholism. In *Selected Papers on Psychoanalysis*, pp. 80–90. New York: Brunner/Mazel, 1979.

Ackerman, N. (1994). *The Psychodynamics of Family Life: Diagnosis and Treatment of Family Relationships*. Northvale, NJ: Jason Aronson.

Aeschylus (458 B.C.). *The Orestes Plays of Aeschylus*, trans. P. Roche. New York: Mentor, 1962.

Alcoholics Anonymous World Services (1953). *Twelve Steps and Twelve Traditions*. New York: Author.

Alexopoulos, G. S., Lieberman, K. W., and Frances, R. J. (1983). Platelet MAO activity in alcoholic patients and their first degree relatives. *American Journal of Psychiatry* 140(II):1501–1503.

Amark, C. (1951). A study in alcoholism: clinical, social, psychiatric, and genetic investigations. *Acta Psychiatrica Neurologica Scandinavica* 70:1–283.

Balint, M. (1969). *The Basic Fault: Therapeutic Aspects of Regression*. New York: Brunner/Mazel.

Bateson, G. (1971). The cybernetics of "self: a theory of alcoholism." *Psychiatry* 34:1–18.

Bateson, G., Jackson, D. D., Haley, J., and Weakland, J. (1956). Towards a theory of schizophrenia. *Behavioral Science* I:251–264.

Bateson, G., and Ruesch, J. (1951). *Communication: The Social Matrix of Psychiatry*. New York: Norton.

Beckett, S. (1954). *Waiting for Godot*. New York: Grove.

Begleiter, H., Porjesz, B., Bihari, B., and Kissen, B. (1984). Event-related brain potentials in boys at risk for alcoholism. *Science* 225:1493–1495.

Bem, J. D. (1967). Self-perception: an alternate interpretation of cognitive dissonance phenomena. *Psychological Review* 74:183–200.

Bertalanffy, L. von (1968). *General Systems Theory: Foundation, Development and Applications*. New York: Braziller.

Binswanger, L. (1958). The case of Ellen West. In *Existence*, ed. R. May, E. Angel, and H. F. Ellenberger, trans. W. M. Mendel and J. Lyons, pp. 237–364. New York: Basic Books.

Bion, W. R. (1961). *Experience in Groups*. New York: Basic Books.

Bleuler, D. M. (1955). Familial and personal background of chronic alcoholics. In *Etiology of Chronic Alcoholism*, ed. O. Dretheim, pp. 110–166. Springfield, IL: Charles C Thomas.

Bohman, M. (1978). Some genetic aspects of alcoholism and criminality: a population of adoptees. *Archives of General Psychiatry* 35:269–276.

Boszormenyi-Nagy, I. (1987). *Foundations of Contextual Therapy: Collected Papers of Ivan Boszormenyi-Nagy*. New York: Brunner/Mazel.

Bowen, M. (1974). Alcoholism as viewed through family systems theory and family psychotherapy. *Annals of the New York Academy of Sciences* 233:115–122.

——— (1978a). *Family Therapy in Clinical Practice*. New York: Jason Aronson.

——— (1978b). On the differentiation of self. In *Family Therapy in Clinical Practice*, pp. 467–528. Northvale, NJ: Jason Aronson.

Bradshaw, J. (1988a). *The Family: A Revolutionary Way of Self-Discovery*. Deerfield Beach, FL: Health Communications.

———— (1988b). *Healing the Shame That Binds You*. Deerfield Beach, FL: Health Communications.

Buber, M. (1937). *I and Thou*, trans. R. G. Smith. New York: Charles Scribner's Sons.

Cadoret, R. J., O'Gorman, T. W., Throughten, E., and Heywood, L. (1984). Alcoholism and anti-social personality: interrelationships, genetic and environmental factors. *Archives of General Psychiatry* 42:161–167.

Cannon, W. (1932). *The Wisdom of the Body*. New York: Norton.

Child, I., Bacon, M., and Barry, H. (1965). A cross cultural study of drinking. *Quarterly Journal of Studies on Alcohol* (Suppl. 3), pp. 5–96.

Chomsky, N. (1957). *Syntactic Structures*. The Hague: Mouton.

Cloninger, C. R. (1983). Genetic and environmental factors in the development of alcoholism. *Journal of Psychiatric Treatment and Evaluation* 5:487–496.

Cloninger, C. R., Bohman, M., and Sigrardson, S. (1981). Cross-fostering analysis of adopted men. *Archives of General Psychiatry* 36:861–868.

Cox, W. M. (1987). Personality theory and research. In *Psychological Theories of Drinking and Alcoholism*, ed. H. Blane and K. Leonard, pp. 55–98. New York: Guilford.

Cruz-Coke, R., and Varela, A. (1966). Inheritance of alcoholism: its association with color blindness. *Lancet* ii:1282–1284.

Descartes, R. (1642). *Meditations on First Philosophy*, trans. L. J. Lafleur. New York: Library of Liberal Arts, 1951.

Deutsch, H. (1965). Some forms of emotional disturbances and their relationship to schizophrenia. In *Neuroses and Character Types*, pp. 267–281. New York: International Universities Press.

Dewey, J. (1934). *Art as Experience*. New York: Putnam.

Dicks, H. (1967). *Marital Tensions*. New York: Basic Books.

Erikson, E. (1950). *Childhood and Society*, 2nd ed. New York: Norton, 1963.

———— (1968). *Identity, Youth and Crisis*. New York: Norton.

Eysenck, H. (1957). *The Dynamics of Anxiety and Hysteria*. London: Routledge & Kegan Paul.

Fairbairn, W. R. D. (1952). *Psychoanalytic Studies in Psychiatry*. London: Routledge & Kegan Paul.

Fenichel, O. (1945). *The Psychoanalytic Theory of Neurosis*. New York: Norton.

Field, P. (1962). A new cross-cultural study of drunkenness. In *Society, Culture and Drinking Patterns*, ed. D. Pittman and C. Snyder, pp. 48–74. Carbondale, IL: Southern Illinois University Press.

Framo, J. L. (1982). *Explorations in Marital and Family Therapy: Selected Papers of James L. Framo*. New York: Springer.

Freud, S. (1897). *The Complete Letters of Sigmund Freud to Wilhelm Fliess*, trans. and ed. J. M. Masson. Cambridge, MA: Harvard University Press, 1985.

———— (1905). Jokes and their relation to the unconscious. *Standard Edition* 8:1–236.

———— (1909). Analysis of a phobia in a five-year-old boy. *Standard Edition* 10:3–152.

———— (1910). "Wild" psychoanalysis. *Standard Edition* 11:219–230.

———— (1912a). Recommendations to physicians practicing psychoanalysis. *Standard Edition* 12:111–120.

———— (1912b). The dynamics of transference. *Standard Edition* 12:97–108.

———— (1913a). On beginning the treatment. *Standard Edition* 12:121–144.

———— (1913b). Totem and Taboo. *Standard Edition* 13:1–161.

———— (1914). On narcissism: an introduction. *Standard Edition* 14:67–104.

———— (1916). On transience. *Standard Edition* 14:303–309.

———— (1917). Mourning and melancholia. *Standard Edition* 14:237–258.

———— (1920). Beyond the pleasure principle. *Standard Edition* 18:1–64.

———— (1921). Group psychology and the analysis of the ego. *Standard Edition* 18:65–144.

———— (1923). The ego and the id. *Standard Edition* 19:1–66.

———— (1928). Dostoevsky and parricide. *Standard Edition* 21:173–194.

————— (1939). Moses and monotheism. *Standard Edition* 23: 7–140.

Fromm, E. (1941). *Escape from Freedom.* New York: Rinehart.

Fromm-Reichmann, F. (1948). Notes on the development of treatment of schizophrenics by psychoanalytic psychotherapy. *Psychiatry* II:253–273.

Gabbard, G. O. (1996). *Love and Hate in the Analytic Setting.* Northvale, NJ: Jason Aronson.

Galanter, M. (1993). *Network Therapy for Alcohol and Drug Abuse: A New Approach in Practice.* New York: Basic Books.

Gergen, M. (1989). "Doing theory" in psychiatry: feminist re-actions. In *Recent Trends in Theoretical Psychology II*, ed. W. J. Balker, M. E. Hyland, R. Van Hezewijh, and S. Terrel. International Society for Theoretical Psychology Conference, 1989. Arnhem, The Netherlands. New York: Springer-Verlag.

Glover, E. (1928). The aetiology of alcoholism. *Proceedings of the Royal Society of Medicine* 21:1351–1355.

Goodwin, D. W. (1988). *Is Alcoholism Hereditary?* New York: Ballantine.

Goodwin, D. W., Schulsinger, F., Hermansen, L., et al. (1973). Alcohol problems in adoptees raised apart from alcoholic biological parents. *Archives of General Psychiatry* 28:283–343.

Greenson, R. (1965). The working alliance and the transference neurosis. *Psychoanalytic Quarterly* 34:155–181.

Guntrip, H. (1968). *Schizoid Problems, Object-Relations, and the Self.* New York: International Universities Press.

————— (1971). *Psychoanalytic Theory, Therapy and the Self.* New York: Basic Books.

Haley, J. (1973). *Uncommon Therapy: The Psychiatric Techniques of Milton H. Erickson, M.D.* New York: Norton.

————— (1976). *Problem-Solving Therapy.* San Francisco: Jossey-Bass.

————— (1984). *Ordeal Therapy: Unusual Ways to Change Behavior.* San Francisco: Jossey-Bass.

————— (1990). *Strategies of Psychotherapy*, 2nd ed. Rockville, MD: Triangle Press.

Hand, L. (1944). What is the spirit of liberty? *Life*, July, p. 3.

Hartocollis, P. (1968). A dynamic view of alcoholism: drinking in the service of denial. *Dynamic Psychiatry* 6:309–325.

Hartocollis, P., and Hartocollis, P. (1980). Alcoholism, borderline, and narcissistic disorders: a psychoanalytic overview. In *Phenomenology and Treatment of Alcoholism*, ed. E. E. Farr, I. Haracan, A. D. Pokorny, and R. L. Williams, pp. 893–1110. New York: S P Medical and Scientific.

Havens, L. (1986). *Making Contact: Uses of Language in Psychotherapy*. Cambridge, MA: Harvard University Press.

——— (1989). *A Safe Place*. New York: Ballantine.

Hegel, G. W. F. (1807). *The Phenomenology of Mind*, trans. J. B. Baille. New York: Macmillan, 1931.

Heidegger, M. (1927). *Being and Time*, trans. J. Macquarrie and E. Robinson. London: SCM Press, 1962.

Hoffman, L. (1981). *Foundations of Family Therapy*. New York: Basic Books.

Holmes, O. W. (1919). *Dissent in Abrams v. United States*.

Husserl, E. (1929). *Cartesian Meditations: An Introduction to Phenomenology*, trans. D. Cairns. The Hague: Martinus Wijhoff, 1960.

Jellinek, E. M. (1994). Heredity and premature weaning: a discussion of the work of Thomas Trotter, British Naval Physician. In *The Dynamics and Treatment of Alcoholism: Essential Papers*, ed. J. Levin and R. Weiss, pp. 28–34. Northvale, NJ: Jason Aronson.

Jorgenson, J. (1989). Where is the "family" in family communications: exploring families' self-definitions. *Journal of Applied Communication Research* 17:27–41.

Joyce, J. (1916). *Portrait of the Artist as a Young Man*. In *The Portable James Joyce*, ed. H. Levin, pp. 245–528. New York: Viking, 1949.

Jung, C. G. (1961). *C. G. Jung: Letters, vol. II, 1951–1961*, ed. G. Adler, pp. 623–625. Princeton, NJ: Princeton University Press, 1973.

Kaij, L. (1960). *Alcoholism in Twins: Studies on the Etiology and Sequels of Abuse of Alcohol*. Stockholm: Almquist & Wiskell.

Kaminer, W. (1993). *I'm Dysfunctional; You're Dysfunctional*. New York: Vintage Books.

Kant, I. (1787). *The Critique of Pure Reason*, 2nd ed., trans. M. K. Smith. London: Macmillan, 1929.

Kaufman, E. (1974). The psychodynamics of opiate dependence: a new look. *American Journal of Drug and Alcohol Abuse* I:349–370.

———— (1976). The abuse of multiple drugs: psychological hypothesis, treatment considerations. *American Journal of Drug and Alcohol Abuse* 3:293–304.

Kaufman, E., and Kaufmann, P. (1992). *Family Therapy of Drug and Alcohol Abuse*, 2nd ed. Boston, MA: Allyn & Bacon.

Kempler, W. (1981). *Experiential Psychotherapy with Families*. New York: Brunner/Mazel.

Kernberg, O. (1975). *Borderline Conditions and Pathological Narcissism*. New York: Jason Aronson.

Kerr, M. E., and Bowen, M. (1988). *Family Evaluation: An Approach Based on Bowen Theory*. New York: Norton.

Khantzian, E. J. (1981). Some treatment implications of ego and self-disturbances in alcoholism. In *Dynamic Approaches to the Understanding and Treatment of Alcoholism*, ed. M. H. Bean and N. E. Zimberg, pp. 163–188. New York: The Free Press.

Kierkegaard, S. (1849). *The Concept of Dread*, trans. W. Lowrie. Princeton, NJ: Princeton University Press, 1944.

Klein, M. (1921–1945). *Love, Guilt, and Reparation and Other Works 1921–1945*. New York: Dell, 1975.

———— (1946–1963). *Envy and Gratitude and Other Works 1946–1963*. New York: Dell, 1975.

Knight, R. P. (1937). The dynamics and treatment of chronic alcohol addiction. *Bulletin of the Menninger Clinic* 1:233–250.

Kohut, H. (1971). *The Analysis of the Self: A Systematic Approach to the Psychoanalytic Treatment of Narcissistic Personality Disorders*. New York: International Universities Press.

———— (1977a). *The Restoration of the Self*. New York: International Universities Press.

———— (1977b). Preface. *Psychodynamics of Drug Dependence*, ed. J. D. Blaine and D. A. Julius, pp. vii–ix. Northvale, NJ: Jason Aronson, 1993.

Kramer, P. D. (1993). *Listening to Prozac*. New York: Viking Penguin.

Krystal, H., and Raskin, H. (1970). *Drug Dependence: Aspects of Ego Function*. Northvale, NJ: Jason Aronson, 1993.

Laing, R. D., and Esterson, H. (1964). *Sanity, Madness and the Family, vol. 1: Families of Schizophrenics*. London: Tavistock.

Langer, S. (1957). *Philosophy in a New Key*, 3rd ed. Cambridge, MA: Harvard University Press.

LeBon, G. (1895). *Psychologie des Foules*. Paris: Alcan. [*The Crowd: A Study of the Popular Mind*. London: Unwin, trans. R. Meton, 1920.]

Levin, J. D. (1987). *Treatment of Alcoholism and Other Addictions: A Self-Psychology Approach*. Northvale, NJ: Jason Aronson.

——— (1991). *Recovery From Alcoholism: Beyond Your Wildest Dreams*. Northvale, NJ: Jason Aronson.

——— (1992). *Theories of the Self*. Washington, DC: Taylor & Francis.

——— (1993). *Slings and Arrows: Narcissistic Injury and Its Treatment*. Northvale, NJ: Jason Aronson.

——— (1995). *Introduction to Alcoholism Counseling: A Bio-Psycho-Social Approach*, 2nd ed. Washington, DC: Taylor & Francis.

Litz, T., Cornelison, A., Fleck, S., and Terry, D. (1957). The intrafamilial environment of schizophrenic patients. *American Journal of Psychiatry* 114:241–248.

Locke, J. (1690). *An Essay Concerning Human Understanding*. New York: Dover, 1959.

Loper, R. G., Kammeier, M. L., and Hoffman, H. (1973). MMPI characteristics of college freshmen males who later became alcoholic. *Journal of Abnormal Psychology* 82:159–162.

Low, A. (1950). *Mental Health Through Will-Training*. Boston, MA: Christopher.

Madanes, C. (1984). *Behind the One Way Mirror: Advances in the Practice of Strategic Therapy*. San Francisco: Jossey-Bass.

Mahler, M., Pine, F., and Bergman, A. (1975). *The Psychological Birth of the Human Infant: Symbiosis and Individuation*. San Francisco: Jossey-Bass.

Maslow, A. (1968). *Toward a Psychology of Being*, 2nd ed. Princeton, NJ: Van Nostrand.

Masters, W. H., and Johnson, V. S. (1970). *Human Sexual Inadequacy*. Boston: Little, Brown.

Masterson, J. F. (1976). *Psychotherapy of the Borderline Adult: A Developmental Approach*. New York: Brunner/Mazel.

May, R. (1969). *Love and Will*. New York: Norton.

McClelland, D. C., Davis, K., Kalin, R., and Wanner, E. (1972). *The Drinking Man: Alcohol and Human Motivation*. New York: The Free Press.

McCord, W., and McCord, J., with Gudeman, J. (1960). *Origins of Alcoholism*. Stanford, CA: Stanford University Press.

McCrady, B. (1992). Behavioral treatment of the alcoholic marriage. In *Family Therapy of Drug and Alcohol Abuse*, ed. E. Kaufman and P. Kaufmann, 2nd ed., pp. 190–211. Boston, MA: Allyn & Bacon.

McDougall, W. (1920). *The Group Mind*. Cambridge, England: Cambridge University Press.

Mello, N. K., and Mendelson, J. H. (1970). Experimentally induced intoxification in alcoholics: a comparison between programmed and spontaneous drinking. *Journal of Pharmacology and Experimental Therapeutics* 173:101–116.

Menninger, K. (1938). *Man Against Himself*. New York: Harcourt, Brace.

Miller, A. C. (1981). *Drama of the Gifted Child*. New York: Basic Books.

Minuchin, S. (1992). Constructing a therapeutic reality. In *Family Therapy of Drug and Alcohol Abuse*, 2nd ed., ed. E. Kaufman and P. Kaufmann, pp. 1–14. Boston: Allyn & Bacon.

Minuchin, S., and Fishman, C. H. (1981). *Family Therapy Techniques*. Cambridge, MA: Harvard University Press.

Minuchin, S., Montalvo, B., Guerney, B. G., Jr., et al. (1967). *Families of the Slums: An Exploration of Their Structure and Treatment*. New York: Basic Books.

Minuchin, S., Rosman, B. L., and Baker, L. (1978). *Psychosomatic Families: Anorexia Nervosa in Context*. Cambridge, MA: Harvard University Press.

National Institute on Alcohol Abuse and Alcoholism (1988). *Fifth Special Report to the U.S. Congress on Alcohol and Health from the Secretary of Health and Human Services* (DHHS Publication No. 85–0009). Rockville, MD: Author.

O'Farrell, T. J. (1993). A behavioral marital therapy couples group program for alcoholics and their spouses. In *Treating Alcohol Problems: Marital and Family Interventions*, pp. 170–209. New York: Guilford.

Ogden, T. H. (1982). *Projective Identification and Psychotherapeutic Technique.* Northvale, NJ: Jason Aronson.

———— (1986). *The Matrix of the Mind.* Northvale, NJ: Jason Aronson.

O'Neill, E. (1929). *The Great God Brown.* In *The Plays of Eugene O'Neill.* New York: Random House, 1967.

Perls, F. S. (1969). *Ego, Hunger and Aggression.* New York: Vintage.

Pitts, F. N., and Winokur, G. (1966). Affective disorder—VII: alcoholism and affective disorder. *Journal of Psychiatric Research* 4:37–50.

Plato (375 B.C.). *Symposium.* In *Plato: Collected Dialogues*, ed. E. Hamilton and H. Cairns, trans. M. Joyce, pp. 526–574. Princeton, NJ: Princeton University Press, 1961.

———— (368 B.C.). *Theaetetus.* In *Plato: Collected Dialogues*, ed. E. Hamilton and H. Cairns, trans. F. M. Cornford, pp. 845–919. Princeton, NJ: Princeton University Press, 1961.

Pollack, V. E., Volavka, J., Goodwin, D. W., et al. (1983). The EEG after alcohol administration in men at risk of alcoholism. *Archives of General Psychiatry* 40:857–861.

Porjesz, B., and Begleiter, H. (1983). The pathogenesis of alcoholism, biological factors. In *The Biology of Alcoholism*, vol. VII, pp. 415–483. New York: Plenum.

Propping, P., Kruger, J., and Mark, M. (1981). Genetic disposition to alcoholism: an EEG study in alcoholics and their relatives. *Human Genetics* 35:51–59.

Rado, S. (1933). The psychoanalysis of pharmacothymia. *Psychoanalytic Quarterly* 2:2–23.

Riesman, D., in collaboration with R. Denny and N. Glazer (1950). *The Lonely Crowd.* New Haven, CT: Yale University Press.

Robins, L. N., Bates, W. N., and O'Neil, P. (1962). Adult drinking patterns of former problem children. In *Society, Culture and Drinking Patterns*, ed. D. J. Pittman and C. R. Snyder, pp. 395–412. Carbondale, IL: Southern Illinois University Press.

Roe, A. (1945). The adult adjustment of children of alcoholic parents raised in foster homes. *Quarterly Journal of Studies on Alcohol* 5:378–393.

Rogers, C. (1961). *On Becoming a Person: A Therapist's View of Psychotherapy*. Boston, MA: Houghton Mifflin.

Russell, B., and Whitehead, A. N. (1910–1913). *Principia Mathematica* (3 vols.) Cambridge, England: Cambridge University Press.

Saint Augustine (397). *The Confessions of Saint Augustine*. New York: Collier, 1961.

Salinger, J. D. (1951). *The Catcher in the Rye*. New York: Bantam.

Sartre, J.-P. (1956). *Being and Nothingness: An Essay on Phenomenological Ontology*, trans. H. Barnes. New York: Philosophical Library.

Satir, V. (1964). *Conjoint Family Therapy*. Palo Alto, CA: Science and Behavior Books.

——— (1972). *People Making*. Palo Alto, CA: Science and Behavior Books.

——— (1982). The therapist and the family: a process model. In *Family Counseling and Therapy*, ed. A. M. Horne and M. M. Olsen, pp. 12–42. Itasca, IL: F. F. Peacock.

Schafer, R. (1976). *A New Language for Psychoanalysis*. New Haven, CT: Yale University Press.

Scharff, D. E. (1992). *Refinding the Object and Reclaiming the Self*. Northvale, NJ: Jason Aronson.

Scharff, D. E., and Scharff, J. S. (1991). *Object Relations Family Therapy*. Northvale, NJ: Jason Aronson.

——— (1994). *Object Relations Couple Therapy*. Northvale, NJ: Jason Aronson.

Scharff, J. S. (1992). *Projective and Introjective Identification and the Use of the Therapist's Self*. Northvale, NJ: Jason Aronson.

Schuckit, M. A., and Gold, F. O. (1988). A simultaneous evaluation of multiple markers of ethanol/placebo challenges in sons of alcoholics and controls. *Archives of General Psychiatry* 45:211–216.

Searles, J. S., and Windle, M. (1990). Introduction and overview: salient issues in the children of alcoholics literature. In *Children of Alcoholics: Critical Perspectives*, pp. 1–8. New York: Guilford.

Segal, H. (1973). *Introduction to the Work of Melanie Klein*. New York: Basic Books.

Seilhamer, R. N., and Jacob, T. (1990). Family factors and adjustment of children of alcoholics. In *Children of Alcoholics: Critical Perspectives*, ed. M. Windle and J. S. Searles, pp. 168–186. New York: Guilford.

Selvini Palazzoli, M., Boscolo, L., Cecchin, G. F., and Prata, G. (1978). *Paradox and Counter Paradox: A New Model in the Therapy of the Family in Schizophrenic Transaction*. New York: Jason Aronson.

Shakespeare, W. (1608). *King Lear*. New York: Folger Library General Readers Shakespeare, Pocket Books, 1960.

Shotter, J. (1993). *Language and the construction of the self*. Paper presented at the Constructed Realities: Therapy, Theory and Research Conference, Lofoten, Norway, June 22–25.

Silford, D. (1989). A psychiatrist discusses creative writers and alcohol. *The Philadelphia Inquirer*, January 2, p. 5-C.

Slipp, S. (1988). *The Technique and Practice of Object Relations Family Therapy*. Northvale, NJ: Jason Aronson.

Sperry, R. (1993). The impact and promise of the cognitive revolution. *American Psychologist* 48(8):873–885.

——— (1995). The future of psychology. *American Psychologist* 50(7):505–506.

Spitz, R. (1965). *The First Year of Life*. New York: International Universities Press.

Stanton, M. D., and Todd, T. C., and Associates. (1982). *The Family Therapy of Drug Abuse and Addiction*. New York: Guilford.

Steinglass, P., with Bennett, L., Wolin, S., and Reiss, D. (1987). *The Alcoholic Family*. New York: Basic Books.

Szasz, T. (1958). The role of the counterphobic mechanism in addiction. *Journal of the American Psychoanalytic Association* 6:309–325.

Tabakoff, B., Hoffman, P. L., Lee, J. M., et al. (1988). Differences in platelet enzyme activity between alcoholics and non-alcoholics. *New England Journal of Medicine* 318:134–139.

Tarter, R. E. (1981). Minimal brain dysfunction as an etiological disposition to alcoholism. In *Evaluation of the Alcoholic: Implications for Research, Theory and Treatment*, ed. R. E. Meyer. Washington, DC: National Institute on Alcohol Abuse and Alcoholism.

Tarter, R. G., and Alterman, A. I. (1988). Neurobehavioral theory of alcoholism etiology. In *Theories of Alcoholism*, ed. C. D. Choudren and D. A. Wilkinson, pp. 29–102. Toronto: Addiction Research Foundation.

Thoreau, H. D. (1854). *Walden*. Princeton, NJ: Princeton University Press, 1971.

Trotter, W. (1916). *Instincts of the Herd in Peace and War*. London: T. Fisher Unwin.

Vaillant, G. E. (1983). *The Natural History of Alcoholism*. Cambridge, MA: Harvard University Press.

Varela, A., Rivera, L., Mardones, J., and Cruz-Coke, R. (1969). Color vision defects in non-alcoholic relatives of alcoholic patients. *British Journal of Addictions* 64:67–71.

Walzer, M. (1985). *Exodus and Revolution*. New York: Basic Books.

Watzlawick, P. (1978). *The Language of Change*. New York: Basic Books.

Wegschieder-Cruse, S. (1985). *Choice Making*. Deerfield Beach, FL: Health Communications.

Whitaker, C. A., and Bumberry, W. M. (1988). *Dancing with the Family: A Symbolic-Experiential Approach*. New York: Brunner/Mazel.

Whitehead, A. N. (1929). *Process and Reality: An Essay in Cosmology*. New York: Macmillan.

Wiener, N. (1948). Cybernetics. *Scientific American* 179(5):14–18.

Winnicott, D. W. (1956). Primary maternal preoccupation. In *Through Paediatrics to Psycho-analysis*, pp. 300–305. London: Hogarth, 1958.

———— (1958). The capacity to be alone. In *The Maturational Processes and the Facilitating Environment*, pp. 29–36. New York: International Universities Press, 1965.

———— (1960). Ego distortion in terms of true and false self. In *The Maturational Processes and the Facilitating Environment*, pp. 140–152. New York: International Universities Press, 1965.

———— (1965). *The Maturational Processes and the Facilitating Environment.* New York: International Universities Press.

Winokur, G. (1974). The division of depressive illness into depressive-spectrum disease and pure depressive disease. *International Pharmacopsychiatry* 9:5–13.

Wittgenstein, L. (1953). *Philosophical Investigations,* ed. G. E. M. Anscombe and R. Rhees. London: Blackwell.

Wolin, S. J., and Bennett, L. A. (1984). Family rituals. *Family Process* 23:401–420.

Wolin, S. J., Bennett, L. A., and Noonan, D. L. (1979). Family rituals and the reoccurrence of alcoholism over generations. *American Journal of Psychiatry* 136:589–593.

Wordsworth, W. (1805). *The Prelude.* In *The Poetical Works of Wordsworth,* pp. 632–752. New York: Oxford University Press, 1910.

Wurmser, L. (1978). *The Hidden Dimension: Psychodynamics in Compulsive Drug Use.* New York: Jason Aronson.

Zetzel, E. (1956). Current concepts of transference. *International Journal of Psycho-Analysis* 37:369–376.

❖ INDEX ❖